T0116347

Made in America

Made in America

The Most Dominant
Champion in UFC History

MATT HUGHES

with Michael Malice

SIMON SPOTLIGHT ENTERTAINMENT
New York London Toronto Sydney

S|S|E

SIMON SPOTLIGHT ENTERTAINMENT
An imprint of Simon & Schuster
1230 Avenue of the Americas
New York, New York 10020

Copyright © 2008 by Hughes & Moore, Inc.

All rights reserved, including the right to reproduce this book or portions thereof in any form whatsoever. For information address Pocket Books Subsidiary Rights Department, 1230 Avenue of the Americas, New York, NY 10020

First Simon Spotlight Entertainment trade paperback edition January 2009

SIMON SPOTLIGHT ENTERTAINMENT and colophon are trademarks of Simon & Schuster, Inc.

For information about special discounts for bulk purchases, please contact Simon & Schuster Special Sales at 1-800-456-6798 or business@simonandschuster.com.

Designed by Gabe Levine

Manufactured in the United States of America

10   9   8   7   6   5   4   3   2   1

Library of Congress Cataloging-in-Publication Data
Hughes, Matt, 1973–
Made in America / by Matt Hughes with Michael Malice.–1st ed.
p. cm.

ISBN-13: 978-1-4169-4883-4
ISBN-10:   1-4169-4883-X
ISBN-13: 978-1-4165-8995-2 (pbk)
ISBN-10:   1-4165-8995-3 (pbk)

1. Hughes, Matt, 1973– 2. Mixed martial arts–Biography.
I. Malice, Michael. II. Title.
GV1100.A2H84 2008
796.8092–dc22
[B]
2007036318

Contents

CHAPTER 1

This Is Farm Life

"You can go see your family now," the man told my dad. He had long white hair and cowboy boots, a flannel shirt, and some blue jeans on. My dad looked him up and down. *Why is the janitor telling me that I can go see my wife?* he wondered. It was 1973, and even in rural Hillsboro things were a little kooky. "Who was that?" he asked my mom when he entered her hospital room.

"He's the on-call doctor," she told him. "Dr. Draper is away at a football game."

Dad shrugged. He was more interested in seeing his newborn twin sons.

They say there's a lot you can do in five minutes. You can change a tire, eat a sandwich, or choke out Frank Trigg (again). But that October 13, I wasn't doing anything but a whole lot of crying in the five minutes between my birth and that of my twin brother, Mark. "The doctor says they're fraternal," Mom said, "but I think they're exactly alike." But just because we were alike didn't mean that we weren't going to be rivals. I say that everybody with any sense knows that being born is a race, which means that I won because I was first. But Mark tries to argue that it's a test of stamina to see who can hold out the longest, so *he* won.

The next day our parents took us back to our farm on the outskirts of Hillsboro. Hillsboro is a small farming town in central Illinois, an hour or so away from St. Louis and home to about five thousand people. The town square is just a spot where four streets intersect in front of an old courthouse, and the sign above the video store reads VIDEO STORE. There's an Orpheum movie theater, one bookstore, one hotel, and a Subway restaurant that has both Mr. Pibb and Mello Yello. The tallest structures are silos and water towers. More people chew tobacco than smoke in Hillsboro, and just about everybody wears blue jeans, white sneakers, and white socks. When the radio announcer mentions how the girl's high school basketball team is doing that year, we pay attention.

We own guns and hunt. We don't worry about someone breaking in through a window, because they can just open the front door. The people in Hillsboro who don't believe in evolution aren't jerks about it. Most everyone is friendly, both in the sense of being amiable and in the sense of knowing things about you. There's an idea city folk have that everyone in a small town has a secret. It's true that there are things that people don't talk about openly, but those things aren't hardly secret.

The Hughes farm was around fifteen hundred acres when Mark and I were born. Our older sister Beth was still living at home, but Dad's daughters from his first marriage, Annette and Evelyne, were older and had moved on. Our house sat on a hill, so if you stood next to it and looked around in a full circle, everything within eyesight was our property. We had fields of corn, beans, and wheat, and we raised chickens, turkeys, horses, and cows.

One day Dad asked Mom, "Why are we burning our money when there are two perfectly healthy milk cows up there?" Baby formula was expensive, and Mark and I went through two cases a week. "I'll just milk them, pasteurize it, and give the boys whole milk." From then on, the Hughes twins were raised like cattle in a lot of ways.

Quickly, my parents realized that bringing up Mark and me wasn't going to be like bringing up Beth. One day when we were two years old, Mom and Dad did the farm work, got done late, and came in tired. They had recently remodeled the house, which was a lot of work on top of their usual load. They sleepily ate their supper, fed us, and then put us to bed. At two in the morning, Mom heard a sound and went to the kitchen to investigate. She returned to the bedroom and woke up our dad. "You're not going to believe what they've done," she told him. The kitchen had a refrigerator with a freezer on the bottom. Mark and I had gotten into it, pulled out the butter, and smeared it everywhere. All the new paneling and drywall they'd put in now looked like the inside of a baked potato.

Dad decided to build us a cattle fence to keep us out of trouble. He spent all of one morning getting that fence halfway done. When he stepped back to admire his work, he saw Mark and me climbing over it, back and forth, just for fun.

As soon as we could walk we could run, and as soon as we could run we could climb. When you're a little boy, a farm is the best playground you could possibly imagine. There are mudslides, woods to run through, trees to climb, and old footpaths to explore. We could scream our heads off, and no one would ever be bothered by it. And when you're a twin, you constantly have your best friend around you. He likes the same things you like, and he has the same energy level as you do. Even after we got our own bedrooms, we didn't like to be separated, and we'd just get up and go to the other brother's room after Mom left.

When we were only about two or three years old, barely able to talk, Mom took us to another family's house. Mark and I were outside playing with their son, who was older than we were. Suddenly Mom heard a scream. She ran outside and saw that Mark was crying: That boy had bit him. She took Mark inside and was looking after him, trying to calm him down and make him feel better.

Then they heard an awful yell, much louder than Mark's. Mom ran outside again and that boy was shrieking as I pinned him, punching him with my little fists as hard as I could. "He bite Marky!" I yelled, as she tried to pry me off. "He bite Marky!" She separated me from him, and I never did get in trouble for it. Mom thought that was just fine.

My brother and I didn't care about material possessions as long as we could have fun. We had a lot of toy trucks and tractors. We had our own little piece of ground where we played outside, making little roads and plowing imaginary fields. Mom once told us to pick our toys up and put them away, but Mark and I just dug a hole out there, put the toys in it, and covered it up. And that was the end of it.

Once, Dad and the crew put up an entire harvester in one day. They came into the house to have some iced tea. "Hey, where are the boys?" Dad asked the men. They shrugged, looking around. "Shoot, I forgot to take that stepladder down," Dad said. "They couldn't have . . ." It took an eight-foot stepladder to get to the ladder that climbed the harvester, and that's all that Mark and I needed. Dad looked up to the top of his new harvester and there we were, sixty feet in the air.

By the time the day came when Beth ran into the house, yelling, "Dad, you better get out there quick! One of the boys filled a wagon full of gas and the other one's got a lighter!" no one was even shocked—it was already par for the course.

Our nearest neighbor was over a mile away. As kids, our only real friend was our cousin Mikey. Three years older, he was cool no matter what he did. He liked the outdoors, so we would go shooting with him. He was always messing with motors and automotive stuff. He was the big brother we never really had.

We always liked to be around when there was work to be done. It was fall and Mark and I watched them shelling corn. The corn went out the bottom of the wagon into a hopper, and then the auger shot it up into the bin. I climbed the ladder up the side of the wagon and jumped into the corn, with Mark right by my side. We could see the corn flowing out the door in the bottom of the wagon; it was like we were standing inside an hourglass.

Mark's legs got buried in the corn as it slid out from under us. I could see from his happy expression that it was as fun as it looked. It was like we were on some sort of slide. Then my legs got caught in the corn too. We couldn't get our legs out; we were in a kind of corn quicksand that was pulling us under. Then I saw the chains that went across the wagon and tightened up to keep it from busting. I grabbed a chain with my right hand and with my left arm kept Mark's head, now barely above the corn, from getting sucked under. Beth heard us and climbed up the ladder to see what was happening. "Oh my gosh!" she yelled. She ran down and shut off the wagon so we wouldn't get sucked down any farther. She came back and grabbed my hand and tugged as hard as she could. When we didn't budge, she said, "Hold on, let me go get Dad."

Dad came up and he started pulling on my arm. Nothing. He cleared away the corn from Mark a bit and tried to pull him out. Still nothing. "I'm going to rip them in half before I get them loose," he told Beth, shaking his head. "I guarantee it." Dad stood there for a moment, thinking about what to do. He pulled the wagon up away from the auger and opened the door wide. All the corn shot out the door, taking us with it like we were on rockets. "Look at them," Dad said to Beth. "They think that was some amusement park ride or something."

Mark and I were still grinning. "Can we go again?" I asked.

"You know what?" Dad told us the following summer. "If you like being around farm equipment so much and you've got so much energy, maybe you should actually be doing something instead of just messing around. I'm going to put you boys to work. Now, we have to bale twenty-five acres of hay off of Uncle Jack. It's going to take all day. I've got a crew coming, but they won't be here until the afternoon. Do you want to help me out tomorrow?"

To Mark and me, this felt like Christmas.

The next day, the hay had already been cut and raked and was waiting for us to bring our baler along. We got on the wagon with Dad. "We can put it on here so then the crew can unload it in the barn," he explained. "When the bale comes onto the wagon, you stack it as best you can."

As the bales kept coming, Mark and I made it into a competition. We waited for that hay, and then each of us grabbed for it. Instead of taking turns, we were knocking each other off the wagon to get to the bales. Finally, we were in a fight over every single bale. We felt a jerking motion; Dad had stopped the tractor. "We're going to be here until dark!" he yelled. And this was summertime, so that meant eight or nine o'clock. "Just absolutely stop it!" he shouted, exasperated.

The 1970s were real good years for the farm community, and grain prices were extremely high. My parents were even able to expand their acreage. Then came 1981 and the government embargo. Farmers couldn't ship grain overseas anymore, which made the price of grain collapse. It went from $9 a bushel to $4 a bushel. It was like getting your salary cut by more than half, practically overnight.

At the time, the Federal Land Bank Association, backed by the federal government, was basically setting the price of farm ground. They were the ones who lent the money to farmers who

wanted to buy new land. It wasn't some sort of welfare or a program to assist farmers; they were out to make a profit. If someone
needed $100,000, then they'd have to borrow $105,000 worth of
stock. That $5,000 worth of stock was what the association made
their money on.

Because they were setting the prices of ground themselves,
they could run it up. The higher the price of ground, the higher
their percentage, and the more money they made. If they could
set the price at $200,000, then they made $10,000 on their own—
while borrowing the money that they lent from the federal government. No risk, all reward.

While my parents were sitting on fifteen hundred acres of
ground, the interest rate at Federal Land Bank went up. They had
borrowed the money to buy the land at 8 percent, and it went up
to 16 percent on a six-month payment plan. There were many,
many people who were crushed by the interest alone. Add to that
the collapse in grain prices, and a lot of farmers had the same
fate my family did: bankruptcy. From '83 to '85 the farms started
falling like dominos. Mom and Dad tried really hard to keep us
from having to declare bankruptcy. Somebody told them that they
could get a Small Business Administration loan. Mom was a very
good bookkeeper, and they worked for a month on the paper-
work. They sent it off to the SBA and hoped for the best.

A letter came back: Denied.

Mom and Dad never talked to us kids about money troubles,
but we were smart enough to know something was up. In 1979
my dad had bought a brand-new truck. I remember plain as day
the first time I saw that '79 Ford F-250 with the white rims on

it. One day I noticed it wasn't at the farm anymore. "What happened to the truck?" I asked Beth.

"Dad sold it," she said. "He's selling some of the land, too." We went from farming about fifteen hundred acres to about seven hundred, basically down to the homestead.

"Really?"

"Yeah, and Mom's getting a job at Hucks, so I'm going to have to keep my eye on you little jerks when she's not around."

"What about Dad?"

"He's going to drive a truck for a bean mill plant in Grand City."

Mark and I looked at each other. We were more confused than worried. We knew our parents would take care of everything, because they always had before. Dad drove for the plant ten hours a day, five days a week. Plus he had to spend an hour getting there and an hour getting home. He would kind of let the farm run down for a while, then he would stop trucking and get the farm caught back up. Then he went back to trucking again, putting in really crazy hours. He went from setting his own schedule and doing what he loved to doing something he hated, around the clock.

We had a big picture window in front of our house. Mark and I stood there, watching our sister do her aerobics from one of those exercise shows on TV. She'd stretch her body into weird angles. Mark gestured to me and, trying hard not to giggle, I followed him inside. We waited until she started doing squats, working out her quads.

"Hey, Beth!" I yelled out. "Do you need to go to the bathroom?"

Her head spun around real quick. "Get out! Both of you, get out! Go outside and do something and leave me alone!"

"She pooped her pants," Mark said. "She pooped them so bad she has to take a shower."

"Beth, did you poop so bad you have to take a shower?" I asked.

"Leave!" she screamed.

"We're not getting out," Mark told her.

She grabbed us both by the back of the arm and yelled again, *"Get out!"*

"No!" I yelled back at her. She dragged us away from the TV and out of the living room, and then Mark and I started putting up a fight. I pulled back and hit her as hard as I could right in the stomach. The wind went right out of her. She bent over, gasping for air like a fish on the floor.

Mark and I just looked at each other and walked outside. *You need to know that you don't push me out of my house,* I thought. *I don't care what you've got going on. It's my house too. She's not the big dog around here anymore.*

Something had clicked when Mark and I stood up to Beth. Not that long after this incident, a boy named David got on the school bus coming home and saw us sitting there. He was four years older than we were, and tall. He started shoving Mark around, which was the kind of thing he did for fun. I was watching him, my eyes flashing red with anger.

As we got off the bus, I told my brother, "I know how we can take care of this guy."

"How?" Mark asked. "He's a lot bigger than us."

"I have a plan," I said. It wasn't one of those sit-down-and-talk-with-him plans, either. The next day we got on the bus and sat on either side of the aisle. My hands were in tight fists. Mark and I had been waiting all through the school day, and now the moment was finally here.

David walked on the bus and stood in front of my seat, but turned for a second to face the front of the bus. I didn't need to look at Mark; he was on a hair trigger too. I jumped up, grabbed David from behind, and locked my hands so that his arms were trapped. I fell backward onto the floor with David on top of me, wedged between the seats. I felt him struggling to break free, but I squeezed him as hard as I could. Mark quickly got on top and started punching him, over and over. Once Mark thought David had gotten the message, he got up. I let go and rolled away underneath the seats. Nobody on the bus said a word—least of all David.

When we hit junior high, Mark and I started having a bit of a change in our relationship. It's like wearing your favorite shirt every day, or listening to your favorite song over and over, for years at a time. Suddenly the shirt starts to chafe or the music gets cheesy; the sound annoys you. We still made a great team when we wanted to, but we didn't want to that much of the time. We each found our own friends in school.

One time I went down the hill behind our house over to the field, passing the thin creek that ran under the trees. There was Mark, smoking a cigarette with Brian Cameron. *He thought he could get away with it,* I realized. *You can't see the house from down here and the house can't see you.* "What, are you smoking now?" I asked. Mark shrugged and took another drag. "I think I'm going to talk to Mom and Dad about what you're doing here."

"Just leave me alone," Mark muttered. "Come on, don't go tell them."

"I'll tell you what," I said. "I like that Simmons knife you got. You're going to have to give me that."

"I got that for my birthday!"

"I know it was for your birthday. Mine's the same day," I told him, laughing. Mark just stared at me.

"That's a real nice knife," Mark pointed out. "I don't think that's fair."

"I don't care what you think is fair or what isn't fair. Mark, you need to give me that knife," I insisted.

"You need to just give him the knife," Brian said.

"Fine," Mark said. "Just go take it and get the heck out of here."

I went up the hill and found the knife in his room. I took it and claimed it as my own, never thinking anything of it.

Another day Mark told me, "Hey, I've got a great idea."

"What is it?"

"You'll see," he said, running down a path that led away from the house. A minute later we were at the seven-and-a-half-acre pond on our property. It was practically a lake, so big that a nearsighted person couldn't make out the other shore. Where we stood, on that narrow path, we could see the plants growing in the water and the bugs skimming around on the surface. It was straight out of a Mark Twain story. "See that over there on the far side?" Mark asked me, pointing.

"You mean that big oak tree?"

"Look how it's leaning halfway over the water. Let's take a bunch of planks and nail them up the tree to make a ladder. Then we can tie a rope to it so that we can swing and jump into the pond."

"That's perfect," I agreed. "The bank's really steep on that side of the pond."

"Exactly!"

We quickly rounded up our hammers, some nails, a bunch of wood, and a rope. We took some of the nails and ran them through boards so they'd be ready. Arms full, we lugged all those materials into our boat. We paddled fast to get to that tree and make our vision a reality.

"You climb up and get started," I said to Mark as we jumped out of the boat. "I'll start the rest of the planks down here and pass them to you." Mark grabbed a few planks and carefully made his way up the tree. Using the trunk as a workbench, I began pounding nails through boards.

Suddenly, *wham!* Mark's hammer slipped out of his hand and hit me right on the top of the head. I leaned over and grabbed the hammer. "Get down here!" I yelled at him. *I want vengeance,* I fumed. "I said, get down here!"

My twin looked down from his branch, saw a crazy person waving a hammer in a threatening manner, and decided he didn't want to move toward me one inch.

I took that hammer, cocked back my arm, and threw it directly at him. He watched it go by, not even close, as it flew past him into its new permanent home at the bottom of our pond. Mark moved out over the water on a branch. *Oh, he's not getting away from me*, I thought. I jumped in the boat and watched as Mark kept climbing out, farther and farther, until he got so far on that branch that he couldn't go back to the tree. I put the boat right underneath him and waited for him to hit from thirty feet. *He can only hold on for so long.*

"Matt, move the boat!" he yelled.

"Why are you firing hammers down at me?" I screamed back. "Did you think that was funny or something?"

"It was an accident! Could you just move the boat?"

"Usually when people do something by accident they apologize for it! That's what I've always thought!"

"Okay! I'm sorry! Now can you move the boat?" he pleaded.

"Okay, okay," I said. I sat down and rowed the boat a bit away. Mark saw that I was clear and dropped down into the water. I seized my oar and starting swatting him with it as best I could.

With all of our aggressive energy, it's no surprise that Mark and I took to sports. There weren't really any official wrestling programs for the junior high kids, but after the high school wrestling season was over, they brought the mats to the junior high and taught us what they could during the week. Then we had a wrestling tournament at the end.

I wrestled a guy named GP Grabbe and beat him pretty bad in the first round. Mark did well also, and it ended up being me and him in the finals. The battle lines had been drawn. We weren't twins or even brothers anymore. Now we were rivals. He got a reversal on me for two points and ended up taking me by a point. I was so bad at athletics in junior high that my brother beat me.

CHAPTER 2

Things Drift Apart

Mark and I dabbled a bit in football during high school. Because we were so similar, we would play the same spot on opposite ends of the field. I would be the running back, and Mark would be the inside linebacker.

Then our cousin Mikey got into wrestling and he showed us a thing or two. In terms of wrestling, Mark and I were what's called "true freshmen," because our freshman year in high school was our first year wrestling in a real program. It's the sport where we really hit our stride and, given what was going on at home, it was one of the few sports we could do.

Wrestling happened in the wintertime, where there's nothing to do on a farm. If it had been in the spring and the summer, our parents would have had to come off the tractor, take us into town for practice, and then come back and pick us up two hours later. That wouldn't have worked.

And, importantly, wrestling was free. It didn't matter that

Mark and I had three pairs of pants between us, or that our note-
books were old and tattered. It didn't matter how poor we were,
because there's really no equipment to buy. They give you the
headgear and the singlet. To be a wrestler, all you need is a pair
of wrestling shoes. The strength and the knowledge you need are
costly, but not financially.

One day at practice I looked at the bleachers and found Dad
sitting there. Mark and I walked up to him. "You're early yet,"
I said.

"I'm here to watch," he said. "I want to know what it is you
both are so excited about."

"Suit yourself," Mark said, shrugging. We went back to the
mat and continued our drills.

After the workout Dad came over and shook Coach Ball's
hand. "You sure look like you know what you're doing out
there," Dad said, chuckling. "I hadn't realized just how technical all this stuff is, with all these moves and whatnot. You think
of wrestling and you think of guys just throwing each other
around, but I tell you, there's a heck of a lot more to it than
that."

"You're absolutely right," Coach said, proud. "And for every
move, there's a counter, and for every counter, there's a counter."

"And what is your background?" Dad asked. "I know that
Hillsboro is known for its wrestling program."

"I've never wrestled a match in my life," Coach admitted.
"Everything I know I got from books and videos."

"Is that right? Well, I think that's very interesting. It was great
meeting you," Dad said. Mark and I got showered up and then

we all hopped into the truck. "I've got a surprise for you," Dad said, looking at us through the rearview mirror.

"What do you mean?" I asked him.

"You'll see," he said, grinning.

"You know, I think I can make varsity this year," Mark chimed in.

Dad looked over at him. "You're a freshman in high school. Now how in the world do you plan on making varsity?"

"Two nights before every competition, there's a challenge match," my brother explained. "You can challenge a guy on the team, and if you beat him, you wrestle varsity in his position."

"Yeah, right. Varsity," Dad muttered. "If you want to make it as a wrestler, it's going to take a heck of a lot of work. I've got something to help you out. You'll see." When we got home, Dad walked over to a stationary bike and pulled it into the center of the living room. "Surprise! Now which one of you is going to go first?"

"What's this?" I asked.

"It's important to keep fit and be able to go the distance in these matches," Dad said. "After practice, I want you on the bike for fifteen minutes. If you're going to be serious about it, let's be serious. In this sport, there's no team and no excuses. It's just you against the other guy. If you put the work in like I've always taught you, like on the farm, I guarantee it'll go well for both of you."

Only a couple of nights later, Mark announced that he did actually make varsity. Mark was a pinner; it's two points a pin. Now his goal became to letter, which required forty-two points

in a season. By Christmas our freshman year, Mark had both
made varsity and lettered.

I can't let Mark beat me, I kept thinking. *There's no way. He can't
be the number one wrestler in this family.* Jason Milonas was the
varsity starter for my weight class, so I challenged him. It was
close, but I won the match. Jason, in turn, went down two weight
classes and challenged Mark at 125—and beat him, knocking my
brother off of the varsity team.

My jaw dropped when I saw it happen. *I beat somebody who
was able to beat Mark. Maybe I'm good at this wrestling thing.*

In terms of our actual wrestling styles, Mark and I were very
different. Mark was in your face and strong. He let his foes know
that he was going to beat them, and he was going to push them
back, and they had better try to do something besides match him
muscle-to-muscle. He was like a bull about to charge through
somebody. Strength wise, Mark and I were very similar, with
him probably getting the nod. But on the technical side of the
sport, I was a lot more well versed than he was. He just didn't
care about that at all.

I didn't want to use my strength. I wanted to use technique and
put my strength on reserve. If an opponent came at me with muscle, I cut that and came at them with some technique that would
make them feel bad. I'd let them up, take them down; let them up,
take them down; turn them on their back, take them down. I liked
to ride, to get on top of somebody and not let them up.

We both always had real good balance and real good endurance. We were also gifted with stamina and what you might call

farm strength. And if you have those two things, you can really wear on people and beat them in the end.

One Friday night Mark and I were playing basketball. The main sounds were the crickets and, far off, some vehicles on the road. Hummingbirds buzzed like gigantic mosquitoes. Mark took the ball for a layup. I tried to block, but he got the shot anyway. It hit the rim and bounced off. I leaped for the ball and caught it. Then Mark and I saw a pair of headlights.

I tucked the ball under my arm and the two of us hustled back into the house. We heard the piano being played, and we heard Beth singing. When Mom and Beth noticed the door opening, the music stopped. They saw the car lights through the door. Mom shut the piano and shoved the bench under it. We all looked around to make sure nothing was out of place and everything was ready.

Dad was home for the weekend. "Why hasn't anyone mowed the pasture?" he said, first thing. We all looked at him, not saying a word. He glanced over at me. "Oh, I see. You have time to play basketball, but you don't have time to do what I ask you. Not once, but twice. What did you do all week? Nothing, that's what." I felt my chest tightening. "Why is there always something that needs to be done around here when I come home?" he demanded. The thing is, there's *always* something to be done on the farm, on any farm, which meant that there was always something for him to get upset about.

"Can you get me the checkbook?" he asked Mom.

"I haven't gotten around to balancing it yet," she confessed.

He paused so we could all realize what an idiot Mom must be. Then he said, "It has been two weeks, and you still haven't balanced it? How am I supposed to know how much money we've got? I suppose I'll just guess, huh? Is that what I should be doing? I just can't believe how lazy you are sometimes."

I turned around and went to my room. Beth came up the stairs right after me. "You can't let him get to you," she said. "You know how Dad gets."

"Well, I was hoping tonight might be a fun time for everyone. I just made regionals and all," I told her.

"I know. That's great!" I smiled at the fact that Beth was always so supportive.

"Well, maybe, maybe not. Do you remember Ken Clayton?" I asked her.

"Yeah, you guys talk about him like he's Paul Bunyan or something."

"Ken is probably the best wrestler Hillsboro has ever seen. Last year, when he was a senior, he placed fourth in state for the second time. Well, this guy Barry Brown from Shelbyville beat Ken when he was a junior and Ken was a senior. And he's who I have to face at the Litchfield tournament."

"Matt, I'm sure you'll do great. You've beaten some guys already that you said were considered to be pretty good."

"Uh-huh," I said.

A few weeks passed, and then the day of the Litchfield tournament arrived. First thing, my teammate Jimmy came up to me and said, "Ha, ha, ha! You're gonna wrestle Barry!"

"What makes you think this Barry guy is so different from anyone else I've wrestled?" I snapped.

"Good luck is all I can say to you!"

As the match was about to begin, I felt weirdly calm as I stared down Barry. Sure, he was three years older, a lot bigger than me, and pretty developed; but this wasn't weightlifting. This was wrestling. I was going to counter his muscle with my technique.

The two of us locked up. The whistle blew.

Less than two minutes later the match was called for Barry.

If there's ever a fifteen-point difference between the two wrestlers in a match, it's all over. It's called a technical fall, but it's known as the skunk rule. Barry had skunked me in the first round. I had never heard of that happening to anyone before.

I hung my head low walking off that mat. *How did that happen? It was all over so fast! Man, I can see now why everyone was laughing.*

A week later was Regionals. I blew through them and won, but since I wasn't as good a pinner as Mark was, I still hadn't gotten my forty-two points. As Regionals ended, I stood there brooding until Coach Ball asked me, "Did you hurt yourself or something?"

"Nuh-uh."

"Then why are you so ticked?"

"Because I still haven't gotten my forty-two points!" I told him.

"Matt, when you go on to Sectionals, you automatically letter."

"Wait, then I've caught up with Mark!" I whispered to myself.

"What about Mark?"

"Nothing, nothing," I said, finally starting to smile.

A week after Regionals was Sectionals, and I made it to the finals. *I am not really wanting to go out there,* I thought, as I stood by the mat. Barry Brown faced me again, calm and ready. *He probably doesn't even remember me. We didn't even wrestle for but two minutes. He thinks I'm a fish. Calm down. Try and remember his moves and remember what the counters are. For every move, there's a counter.*

Three rounds later, and two weeks after the time he skunked me, Barry beat me by thirteen points. But he didn't skunk me—I had gone the distance. When I left the mat I was disappointed, but at least I wasn't humiliated. I would go on to State and lose both my matches, but those two tough losses did much more for me than two easy wins would have.

Months later Beth got married and we had a wedding reception for her. There was a keg and an open bar, but Mom didn't allow underage drinking—no exceptions. Our buddy Jason Robie was there, and he knew what Mom was like. He definitely knew he shouldn't walk around with a beer in his hand in front of her.

"Jason, where are you going with that beer in your hand?" she demanded.

"I'm just going to have one."

"No, you're not," she said. "Jason, give me the beer. You're not old enough to drink. You're not drinking. I'm not going to allow it. And Jason, if you give me any trouble, you're going to have to go home."

Forty-five minutes later, she caught him sitting at a table with a beer next to him. "Jason, whose beer is that?"

"Oh, it's this guy's here."

"'That guy there' is my brother. And he doesn't drink. I'm sorry, but you're out of here."

"Don't kick me out," he pleaded.

"I warned you. I told you exactly what was going to happen, and now it's happening."

Jason came over to us, defeated. "I guess I have to go," he said. "Can you believe your mother is going to kick me out?"

"Mom's tough," Mark shrugged.

I looked at Mom and thought, *In her own way, Mom's a fighter as much as the rest of us; she just knows when to pick her battles.*

A few weeks later we came home from school and found Mom in the kitchen. She was trimming some steak, and she was practically humming to herself. "Hey, Mom," Mark said. "What's going on?"

I looked at this woman who gave life to me and my brother, but it was like I was looking at a person I didn't know. "Boys, I had an idea and I talked to your father about it and he agreed. It's obvious to everybody that things are tough in the house and everyone is kind of miserable. So I thought about it and realized, 'You know what? If there's a problem on the farm, in general, and we can't do it ourselves, we get help. Well, this situation is also a problem on the farm. And we need help for this, too.'"

"Mom, I don't really know what you're talking about," I said, laughing.

"I think we need to go see a counselor, as a family. Maybe if we sat down and talked to a professional, he might make things a bit easier here for *everybody*. For your father, too."

"And Dad agreed to this?" Mark asked. "How in the heck did you get him to agree to this?"

"I don't know if it was a full moon, or if he didn't realize what he was getting himself into. But I wasn't about to argue or ask any questions."

A few days later we were in the counselor's office. There were certificates in Latin framed on the wall. The seating was comfortable, and the room was quiet. It had been designed that way, I figured. "Now, we're all here to discuss the difficulties you seem to be having at home," the counselor began. "To keep things organized and fair, everybody has to wait their turn and nobody is allowed to interrupt. This is a place where you can discuss your feelings openly. We're not here to attack anyone. We're here to figure out a way for everyone to move forward in a better direction. Why don't you start?" he said to my mother.

She let out a deep breath and paused. "I don't know if you are aware of the effect you have on the household," she said, turning to Dad. "You always come home in a bad mood. Always."

Dad rolled his eyes. "Have you ever worked an eighty-hour week?" he said.

"Please don't interrupt her," the counselor jumped in. "You'll have your turn."

Dad looked at the guy. He wasn't used to being told what to do, but at the same time, he had agreed to the rules.

"I know you work very, very hard. I know you work long hours," Mom said. "You've told me this, you've told *all* of us this.

Repeatedly. But I would think that after you work such a long time, you would want to come home and relax, and not to get upset at us. Not yell or worry about what is wrong. That's what we can do, as a family. That's what we *already* do, until you come home. You never spend any time with the family, even when you are home."

Dad stared at her like she was a lunatic. "Are you some sort of a crazy person? When do you want me to spend time with the family? Do you think I'm working all day every day on the road because it gives me pleasure? Do you think that when I come home exhausted I want to go into the living room and turn cartwheels and do jumping jacks? I mean, listen to what you're saying, and then ask me why I call you stupid."

"Please . . . ," the counselor said.

"I wasn't interrupting her!" Dad said, folding his arms. "She was finished! Now one of the boys can go on telling me how I'm a terrible father. I'll be quiet and let them speak. Go ahead. What's wrong with me now?"

"I don't think it's right the way you talk to Mom, calling her lazy or stupid and this and that," Mark said. "What are we supposed to do, hearing our mom being talked about that way? That's not right. You can point something out without being insulting about it." Dad started to turn red and was on the verge of mumbling to himself. Mark and I looked at each other, because he had actually stopped interrupting.

Wow, this is all right! I thought. *At home, it's his way or the highway, always butting into people and cutting everyone off before they can criticize him in any way. Now we can really speak our minds!*

"I just wish that you would try as hard as we are to make things pleasant around the house," I told him. "I know sometimes things don't get done when you're gone, and that's wrong. I'm not making excuses, because there is no excuse. But all I'm saying is that you don't have to make it so that everyone is on eggshells around you all the time."

After our session, we all got up and got into the truck. I felt like this was the start of something new, like Dad would calm down and hear what we were all so desperately trying to tell him. As soon as the car doors were shut, Dad declared, "That was a total waste of money."

It didn't take very many days for my mind to wander away from the therapy session and back to wrestling. *If I had been stronger at State, I might have won one or both of my matches,* I thought. *I need to find ways of making myself stronger. You know what? When Mark and I load and unload all that wood, and then split it, that's a heck of a workout. And Dad's got that knotty hard-splitting stuff in the shed. That'll be even more of a good exercise.*

Mark and I went in the shed and beat on that wood for hours at a time, for weeks. We had a couple of Monster Mauls, sixteen-pound splitting mauls. One day Mark said to me, "Hey, you know what? I'm not feeling this as much as I used to. Before when we did this, I could barely feel my arms when we were done. Now I could go for another hour, easy, and it wouldn't be that big of a deal."

"Let's talk to Dad and see what he thinks." We found him in the living room, watching his nature show. "Hey, Mark and

I were out in the shed splitting the wood and it's gotten kind of easy."

"Oh, yeah?" He smiled. "Well, I think we can make it harder on you boys again." Dad went to the machine shop and welded a ten-pound piece of metal on top of each of our mauls. Now we were tossing over twenty-five pounds with each swing. We were developing the strength, but we still didn't have the knowledge we needed. So Dad entered us in tournaments all around.

The first year Dad only put us in the freshman tournaments. After that we realized that we could learn more if we lost than if we won. So then sophomore year we wrestled in the senior tournament, and as juniors and seniors we competed in college-level tournaments. Then we went to wrestling school at Southern Illinois University, where Coach Larry Kristoff taught us a lot.

But the one person neither of us learned from was each other.

One time Mark and I were at practice at Hillsboro High. I was trying to figure out the best technical move, and he was trying to throw me around the mat like a rag doll. I tried to go for a takedown, and instead he pushed me back as hard as he could. I fell on my butt. I got up, walked up to him, and shoved him. He shoved me back.

All the other wrestlers stopped. We were a second away from punches being thrown when Coach Ball shoved his way in between us. "What is wrong with you two?" he demanded. We kept looking at each other in silence. The only thing keeping me from taking Mark's head off was Coach's arm across my chest. "I want you two to work out together, so I am going to stand right over you," Coach said. "Now go."

Not five seconds later, he had to tear us apart again.

Mark wrestled right before me at meets because of our weight classes. At first, when Mark would be coming off the mat and I would be coming to the mat, we'd slap each other's hands or say some encouraging words or something. Now we wouldn't look at each other anymore. Wherever I went he was there, like some sort of living mirror. I was competing against myself not only as a person, but also as a twin.

Because we were wrestlers, Mark and I knew how to get control of a fight. That first punch—always to the face—is a big deal, because you're setting the stage. I'd hit a guy and knock him down. He'd look up, and his face would be saying what was on his mind: *If I get up, he's going to hit me and knock me down again.*

One day there was a knock on our door. "I need to talk to your sons," the cop told Mom. We went over to see what he wanted. "I hear you boys have been getting into a lot of fights," he told us.

"We haven't been in that many," Mark told him. "And the ones we've been in haven't been our fault, really."

"It doesn't matter," the cop went on. "You both know that fighting is wrong. Someone could get hurt. I mean, obviously in a fight that's the point. But I'm not talking about like bruises or black eyes or things like that. I mean really, really hurt badly. What if someone cracks their head open on the concrete or something like that? I mean, come on. You're young men. You should act like it."

"Is this about something specific?" Mark wanted to know.

"No, not really."

"Are we in trouble?"

"Not yet. But keep it up and you will be. I don't want to come back here ever again and tell you this stuff. You know what I'm saying. None of this is news to you. Now I want you to promise me you'll try to take it easy, okay?"

"That's fine," Mark said.

"What about you, Mark?" he asked me.

"I'm Matt. But yeah, that's okay with me."

"Well, good. Consider this a warning, then."

You can say whatever you want, I thought, smiling and nodding at the cop. *But there's nothing you can do about it.*

CHAPTER 3

Fighting Solves Everything

We were sitting at the kitchen table, our fingers and faces messy from the ribs we were eating. "You know, my dad's a bit lonely now that his wife passed away," Mom said to everyone. "He's thinking about moving to Hillsboro." Her dad, Chet, had been a linotype operator in St. Louis, an hour away from Hillsboro. With the advent of the computer age, the demand for linotype operators went away to nothing and he had lost his job. Then he got himself a paper route out in Collinsville delivering the *St. Louis Post-Dispatch.*

Dad looked up from his food. "Well, what about his paper route?"

"He said he'd sell it."

Dad shrugged. "There's a spare house on the property. If Chet wants to live there, he's welcome to it."

"Really?"

He stared at her for a minute so we'd all know he thought she was thick in the head. "Well, of course. You've got to take care of the family, and he's your dad, isn't he?"

Soon, Chet sold his house and his paper route and moved in. He came down every night and ate supper with us. After supper he played cards with the family. But Dad would never play cards with him. He claimed it's because Chet stopped speaking to his own son for years over a card game.

Months later Chet waited until Mark and I were alone and said, "Boys, I've got some big news for you. I've been living the retired lifestyle here for a while, and it's pretty boring. So you know what I did? I went over to Litchfield and bought a paper route there."

"That's great," Mark said.

"What I want you boys to do is help me throw the papers in the morning."

"What do you mean?" I asked.

"Well, you'd have to wake up real early, like three o'clock in the morning, so that everyone would get their papers by the time they wake up at six."

Mark and I just looked at each other. *He can't be serious.*

"Did I mention that I'll buy each of you a car? You can pay me out of the money you make delivering papers. What do you think?"

Weeks went by before I wasn't shocked by the alarm going off. I looked at the clock. 3:00. I reached over, turned off the alarm, put on some pants, and went out to my sharp '84 Camaro. The streets looked like they were haunted: dark and creepy. There was no movement in anybody's home. The traffic lights flashed red even though I was the only car around. When I was finished, I came back home and collapsed on my bed. The alarm went off again for school an hour later, as if it were some recurring nightmare. I reached over and turned off the clock. *I'll just have to get twice as much learning in tomorrow,* I thought, falling back asleep.

One night Chet went back home after we were done playing cards. "You know what?" Dad said, staring at the news on TV. "I can't believe that guy, buying you boys cars. I let him move here on my property, and then he took that away from me. I will never be able to buy my sons their first vehicles." He started shaking his head. "I tell you what, that is some nerve he has."

Mom just sat there and let him vent his anger, but Mark and I got up and left the living room. In my room my brother and I sat down on the bed. "That is totally stupid," I said. "He should be happy for us that we got cars and it didn't cost him a dime. He's always going on about how he has to work these long hours and having to sell land and this and that, and we just all saved him a bunch of money *and* we're working for it. He should be writing Chet a thank-you note."

"I can't take much of this anymore," Mark said. "I mean, this is nuts."

"I'm going to talk to Mom about this." I went back downstairs. Dad was still ranting and Mom was still listening. From the look on her face I could tell that she wished he would stop, but telling him so would make it much worse; then he'd be ranting about her, too. "Mom, can I talk to you for a minute?"

"Of course," she said, following me to my room.

"Mom, this is absolutely crazy," Mark told her right away. "I mean, what is the big deal about us have a pair of freaking cars? Dad should be glad."

She stood there in the doorway, thinking, and finally she said, "I'll tell you what. Let's all sit down with your dad and talk with him."

I folded my hands across my chest, and Mark and I just looked at each other. "Mom, do you really think it's going to make much of a difference? This will just be like at the counselor's office."

Mom stared at the floor for a second. "I'll tell you something, Matt. Do I really think it's going to make much of a difference? Well, no, I can't say that I do. But do I hope that it will? Am I going to try to do everything I can to make life better, not just for me, but for my kids? And for your dad, too? Well, yeah, you had better believe it."

Mark shrugged. "That's fine with me, then."

"All right," I said. "Let's try it."

"Now you know how defensive your dad gets. We can't go in there and attack him," Mom advised us. "That's what happened at the counselor's office; he felt like he was being ganged up on in front of some stranger. We just have to tell him that, *as a family*, we need things to be different so we can continue on *as a family*."

We all went to the living room. I grabbed the remote and turned off the television as casually as I could. "We need to talk to you," Mom said, easing into the couch. "It's important that you hear us out, so please do listen to what we have to say." I didn't know it then, but it was like we were having an intervention.

Dad glanced at me from his recliner, then at Mark, and then back to Mom. "Well, I'm listening, aren't I? Go ahead!"

"Dad, it's really not right the way you treat everyone in this house," Mark said. "We can't live like this anymore. Whenever you're here, we're all uncomfortable because something's always pissing you off and this and that. I mean, if one of us does something, you can just talk to us about it, you know? We're not stupid. We're old enough to understand. You don't have to throw a fit and get ticked and make everyone in the house tense. I, uh, guess that's the main point." Mark turned to me, a little confused. He couldn't believe Dad let him talk as long as he had.

"There's other stuff too," I said. "It's also not right the way you talk to Mom. We know you work very hard. No one denies that and no one is pretending that doesn't happen. But Mom works hard, and me and Mark work pretty hard for the farm, too. Maybe we don't work as hard as you or as hard as you would like. But it's not like we're sitting around watching TV and drinking pop all day."

"You make it so that none of us feel at ease in our own home," Mom said. "You're constantly in a bad mood and that makes it so that everyone else is constantly trying to do things to keep you from getting in a worse mood. That's not a way for a group of people to live, especially a family. This is not acceptable to us and we're not going to live like this anymore."

Dad leaned forward, got his cup, and spit some of his tobacco juice into it. The bulge in his cheek from the chew and his blank expression made it seem like we had just been talking to a cow. He waited a few seconds until it was clear that none of us had anything else to say to him. "Pass me that remote," he said, gesturing to me. I handed him the remote control. Dad turned the TV on and went back to watching his show. The three of us sat there for a little bit before we stood up and left.

The summers in Hillsboro are hot and humid, but there had been rain that summer of '91. The corn was coming up, the beans were coming in, and I was going to begin my senior year in high school.

Mom was in the kitchen, cutting some steaks for dinner. I was with my buddy Jason, and we were doing what we could to help. Jason was kind of a hard-luck case from a broken family. He was from the neighboring town of Litchfield. We made it a point to make him feel welcome over at the farm. Dad came in from work. "Hello," he said to Jason. Jason nodded back to him. Then Dad looked around. "Where's Mark at?"

"He took Jason's bike down to Central Park Pool," I explained. "He'll be back in a couple of hours."

"His bike? Do you mean that motorcycle of yours?" Dad said.

"Oh, it was all right with me," Jason told him.

Dad stared at him. "I don't care if you did give him permission or not. Those motorcycles are dangerous and they're *stupid.* I'm not going to have my son taking his head off because he wanted to be a tough guy and look cool for some of his buddies!" No one knew what to say. Dad really didn't either, but that never stopped him—not once he got started. "I bet he doesn't even have a helmet on. What's he going to do if it rains? The roads are going to be real slippery and then that's it. That is *it*."

The phone rang. *Saved by the bell,* I thought. I walked over and picked it up. "Hey, it's me," Mark said. "Is Jason still over at the house?" My brother never called to check in any other time. It was just the worse kind of fate.

"Yeah, he's here." I stretched out the cord and walked as far away from Dad as I could. "Hey, uh, Dad's got a problem with you having that motorcycle," I told him in a low voice.

"How bad is it?"

"It's bad."

"I'll be right there," Mark said. Not loud, not strangely quiet, but decisive.

I hung up. *Mark's pissed,* I thought. *He's going to be getting more and more pissed all the way home.*

When Mark pulled up and walked into the house, we were all sitting in the living room. Dad probably had some rant ready to give Mark, but Dad didn't have a chance to say anything. Mark came into the room and grabbed Dad in a headlock. Mark flipped him over and threw him on the ground. He hit him once or twice in the face, before anyone could even react, and then I jumped up to help Mark. We didn't beat Dad so much as we restrained him. We were going to force him to listen, and make him feel firsthand how tight it felt for us whenever he walked into the house.

"Look what you've done to this family!" I yelled at him. Mom started screaming and trying to get in the middle, but Jason stepped in and held her back. No one in the room could believe what was happening, including Mark and me. "Look what you've made us do!" I went on. "We're not tolerating this anymore. We told you! This is it. This is *bullshit*."

As I mentioned before, you can do a lot in five minutes. Breaking a family up for good is one of them. Mark and I released Dad, and his lip was bleeding. All of us waited there for a moment. Then Dad turned to our friend and said, "Jason, you're never welcome back on the farm again." Jason got up and left, awkwardly.

"We're out of here," Mark said. "We're not going to listen to your mouth anymore or listen to your bullshit. We're leaving. C'mon, Mom. Let's go." He said it without even knowing where we were going. Mom simply went upstairs, threw some clothes into some plastic bags, and we left right then. We walked out that door and went as far away from him as we could afford to could go: the other house on the property.

We moved in with Chet. A day or two later we returned home when Dad wasn't there; he was back out on the road. But it wasn't even our home anymore. It was now his house. We gathered up the rest of our things into garbage bags and left.

A few weeks went by, and things seemed a lot more peaceful. But some of the tension of the old house had followed us into the new one. One day, out of the blue, Mark screamed at me, "You have my tape!"

"No, I don't!" I screamed back. "I don't have your tape!"

"Where did you put it? I know you have it!"

"Well, what tape is it?" I said, kind of smirking.

He walked right up to me. "My Def Leppard cassette."

"I've never seen it."

Mom came into my room. "What are you yelling about now?" she wanted to know.

"Matt has my tape," Mark repeated. He started turning so red that I laughed right in his face. Then he came up and shoved me.

Mom got in between us before I could do anything. "Quit it!" she told Mark. "I'm sure your tape is around here somewhere. Calm down!" But it was too late. Mark had reached that point. The cuss words that came out of his mouth would have made the *Exorcist* girl blush. "Don't talk to me like that!" Mom snapped. "Quit it!"

"I'm gonna get you, Mom! I'm gonna get you!" he barked.

"No, you're not. I'm telling you to quit."

Mark punched the wall, putting a big hole in it. Mom looked at the two of us, turned her back, and went downstairs. We could both hear her crying.

A few weeks later Mark and I were in the weight room for zero period before school started. I came back to my locker and opened it up. My pants weren't there. I took everything out of the locker and then got down on the ground to see if they had fallen under the bench. Nothing. I went around the aisle and found my brother. "Hey Mark, where're my pants?" I demanded.

"I don't know what you're talking about," he said.

That's what any crook says when they're caught, I thought to myself. *What a bad liar.* I grabbed a pair of his pants, threw them in the shower, and turned on the water. I sat on the bench, waiting until he was ready to get changed. Mark came back, saw me, and right from the look on my face he knew what I had done. "Where are my pants?" he wanted to know.

"I think someone threw them in the shower over there," I told him.

He shoved me, and I hit the lockers and fell down on the floor. I was trapped between the bench and the lockers, helpless. Just then I knew how David must have felt on that bus. Mark got on top of me and started firing punches at my face. I finally got out from under him and stood up. Right then and there, we both left school, got into our cars, and went home.

I went into my room and saw that all three pairs of my pants were still in the dresser. *He didn't hide them after all,* I realized. I didn't apologize, though. The two of us had a ways to go yet.

Weeks later I knocked on my buddy Tommy Moore's door to announce I was there, and then let myself in. "Hey, Matt!" Tommy said, greeting me in the entrance hall. He was a small guy, a pretty boy who had never gotten dirt under his fingernails. His family had somehow become almost surrogates to Mark and me. I walked with him into the living room, an open area with the kitchen attached. It had huge windows opening out to a wooded backyard. Tommy sat down on the sofa. "What's going on?"

"Not much . . ." I opened the fridge door and found some orange juice. I grabbed a glass out of the cabinet and poured myself some. "Is there any chicken?"

"Yeah, there should be some on the middle shelf." I found it and popped some into the microwave. "You seem quiet," Tommy said. "Is something the matter?"

I grabbed my food and drink and sat down next to Tommy. "Yeah, kinda. My uncle Stan called."

"Who's your uncle Stan again?"

"He's my dad's brother. He called us at the house and said that he needed to come over and talk to us with his wife. So we just said okay, we'd be there and wait around for them. I didn't have any idea what was going on. It could have been about my dad, or it could have been that they wanted to go deer hunting. They didn't let on much over the phone." I heard a light bouncing down the stairs from the other room. "Is that Audra?"

"Yeah," Tommy said.

Tommy's little sister ran into the room. "Well, hi there, Auggie Doggie," I said to her. "Why don't you come sit down next to me and your brother?" She came over and squeezed in between us. "Do you want to rub my back?" I asked her.

"No!" she said, mortified.

Tommy and I laughed. She probably thought we didn't know she had a crush on both me and Mark. "You've got to learn how to rub your boyfriend's back, Dog. That's part of being a good girlfriend."

"You're *not* my boyfriend!"

"Where was I again?" I asked Tommy.

"Uncle Stan was coming over."

"Right, Uncle Stan was coming over. Anyway, he and his wife came to the house—the new house. They walked up a couple of the steps and they didn't even get in the door. 'Evelyne's been killed in an accident,' they said." Then I just shrugged, because I didn't know what else to say. I still wasn't done hearing it myself.

"Oh my gosh, Matt. I'm so sorry. Who's Evelyne?"

"She's one of my two half sisters from my Dad's previous wife. She's eleven or twelve years older than me and Mark. I was never really all that close to her. She wasn't around a lot when I was growing up; she never lived with us or anything." I sat there shaking my head. "I just can't believe it. I can't believe it." I looked out the window at the still trees.

"Well, what happened?" Tommy asked. "We don't have to talk about this if you don't want to."

"No, that's all right," I said, finishing the food and wiping my face. "She was the type of person who was absolutely gorgeous and was going to have a better life dating an older man because she could do that. Her boyfriend owned a bunch of restaurants, hotels—stuff like that. He was commissioned in St. Louis; he wasn't a sheriff or deputy, but it was something along those lines. Anyway, he flew them out on a helicopter to eat at this fancy restaurant. They got a call that a swimmer had been run over by a boat and cut by a prop. He wanted to see if they could help. You know how right by St. Louis there's a part of the Mississippi that runs east and west?"

"Uh-huh," Tommy said, nodding.

"Well, they were flying by that part with the sun in their eyes, and he flew them into unmarked power lines. And, um, that was that."

Tommy sat there the same as me, sad and baffled. "Is your dad okay?" he said in a quiet voice.

"Uncle Stan hadn't been able to get a hold of Dad, so Mom was the one who had to go find him and tell him. She said he was completely emotionless, that it was as if he didn't hear her.

She told me that he sat there for a while, and then he got up and went home. I don't know what went through his head. It must be the most horrible thing in the world."

A few weeks later I went by the house. Right outside his bedroom door, Dad had hung a huge framed photograph of Evelyne. Over the years the guests who come down to the farm look at it and wonder who this beautiful woman is.

Shortly after we moved I ran into Dad at the old house and he told me that I'd never win State without him. I was determined to proved him wrong, and my senior year I went undefeated in wrestling. I didn't even have a close match. State wrestling competitions were usually held at a college. The bleachers were filled with as many people as for a basketball game. When I got a reversal, the crowd cheered. I took down my opponent and won State for the second year in a row, seven to three. I stayed on the floor and watched Mark take the mat for his match, the next weight class.

Mark made a mistake right off the bat. His opponent got him in a headlock in the first round and put him down, for five points. By the time the buzzer rang for the third round, Mark was still behind five to nothing. Then Mark tied it up. "Mark!" I yelled. "You've got to let him up and have a point for escape! Then you can take him down and win 7-6!" I didn't know if he heard me or if we just thought alike, but he tried to do just that. But he couldn't get the takedown. The buzzer rang for the end of the match. Mark lost the finals six to five.

They called me up and awarded me my plaque. Then I went

up to the very top of the bleachers where Dad was sitting by himself, watching us from a distance like always. I felt really sad. *Mark should have won too,* I thought, tearing up. *That's who I root for, right before and right after I punch him in the face.* "I'm going to go grab a shower, Dad." He nodded and I jogged down to the locker room. There was Mark, laughing and joking around with his buddies, not looking upset by his loss in the slightest. *Well, shoot, if Mark's not upset and he's in such a good mood, there's no reason for me to be upset either,* I thought.

There were 140 of us graduating that year from Hillsboro High. As I stood there in my cap and gown, I thought about what every graduate thinks about: I reflected on what high school had meant to me. I reflected on my wrestling career: As a freshman I went to State; as a sophomore I was undefeated until I went to the State tournament and I lost twice. Both as a junior and a senior I was undefeated the whole season and won State. I didn't even know how many wins in a row that was, but it was enough to get me into college in the fall.

Then I saw my cousin Mikey standing there among all the people, in his army outfit. "Hey, Mark! Look!" Mark called out. We ran right up to him. "What are you doing here?" I blurted out. I grabbed him in a hug so tight he grunted a bit.

"I've come home to watch you graduate," Mikey told us. "I'm proud of you. You've been doing great with the wrestling."

"I haven't seen you in forever, man!" Mark said. "I don't think I've seen you since *you* graduated. Hey, how's army life treating you?"

"I *love* it. I am learning so much, it's unreal."

"Will the graduates please take their seats?" the principal said into the mike.

I hugged Mikey again and started crying a bit as I went to my seat. *I can't believe he came all this way just to see us graduate,* I thought.

That night after graduation there was a big outdoor party, with practically as many kids as there were graduates that day. Tommy came up to me with a beer in his hand. "This is great and all," he said, "but where's the music? I thought your car had a loud stereo in it. Let's crank it up!"

"I know, I know! Mark was going to pull it up so that everyone could listen," I told him. "But the dickhead ran over a stump and messed up the front end."

"How bad's the damage?"

"It'll be fine. We just had to send it to a place to get it fixed."

Suddenly, something caught my attention. Just like a shark can smell a drop of blood in the swimming pool, Mark and I were attuned to the sounds of fighting anywhere in our surroundings. As Tommy kept talking, I tuned him out and listened to the sounds. *That's a fight,* I realized.

We saw some people beating up on this guy Chris by the cars, and I ran over at the same time as Mark. Chris was older than we were, so we didn't really know him, but his sister was our year at school. He was in the driver's seat of his car and one of the guys was holding his leg out of the car door. "Holy shit!" I said to Mark. "He's wanting to slam that door on Chris's leg!"

By the time we ran over and got in the middle to break it up,

the fight had been cooling down already. We shoved Chris's leg
into the car and slammed the door shut. "Just get out of here!"
Mark yelled at him. Chris drove off as fast as he could.

The next day Mark and I drove to the auto shop to pick up
my black '84 Camaro. There was glass all over the floor and
inside the vehicle. "What the hell happened?" Mark asked me.

We walked a circuit around the car, trying to figure it out.
I opened the passenger door. There on the seat was a tire rim.
"Look at this," I said to Mark. "Someone threw this through the
window."

"Chris did this."

"What? How do you know that?"

Mark bent over and pulled something out from among the
glass. "This is his key chain." He walked over and gave it to me.
It said his name as plain as day.

"What kind of an idiot drops their keys when they're breaking a stinking window?" I said, shaking my head. "Why would
he do this?"

Mark shrugged. "He must have thought we had something
to do with the fight."

Later that summer we were at the Butler Truck Pulls, sitting in
the back of a truck with the other spectators. We could hear the
engines roaring as they were tested to their limits. "Hey, look
who's over there." I pointed.

Mark scanned the people in their pickups. "Isn't that Chris's
buddy?" We jumped off the truck and casually walked over to
the guy. "I need to talk to you," Mark said. The guy slid out and

looked my brother up and down. We led him away from the crowd so no one would see us. "You were with Chris when he broke Matt's window, weren't you?"

He shrugged, half-smiling, not even bothering to deny it.

Mark took him straight down to the ground and started pounding away at the guy's face with his left fist. When my brother got done and got up, the guy's face looked deformed. Soon after, an ambulance took him to Springfield.

That was the end of our fighting career in Hillsboro. That was the end of our wrestling career in Hillsboro, too. It was time for Mark and me to fight and wrestle elsewhere.

The Hughes boys were going to college.

CHAPTER 4

Big Man on Campus

Mark and I both went to a junior college called Belleville Area College (BAC). Wrestling was the only reason I went to college, and it was the only reason I stayed. I'd rather be out on the farm working with my hands than sitting in a classroom, studying something on a chalkboard.

I was a good athlete, and the school knew it. They rewarded me for it. Teachers let me slip by because I was on the team. I got an A in a class that I never went to; I needed another credit, so they tacked it on halfway through the semester.

One Sunday I was sitting in my mom's new house, over in Litchfield. The house itself looked just like our house in Hillsboro, with the sort of kitchen you'd find on a package of potpourri. But Mom didn't look the same; she looked like she'd had a facelift after the marriage ended. Her calmness took years off her expression. "What time was Mark supposed to get here?" she asked. He was going to drive us back to school.

"Seven o'clock," I said.

Mom looked up at the clock. "It's already seven thirty," she said.

"He'll be here."

"Do you want to give him a call?"

I shook my head. "No, he's at his girlfriend's house. He's too busy to pick up."

I started looking around for something to do. Finally, an hour later, Mark came strolling in. I was sitting there, fuming red, while he had a dopey smile on his face, radiating afterglow. "Sorry I'm late," he said casually.

I didn't say anything and followed Mark out to his maroon Dodge Daytona. I got into the car and slammed the door shut. "Where were you?" I demanded as soon as we got on the road.

"I was with my girlfriend," he said. "You knew that."

"Just like you knew that we were supposed to meet up at seven to go back to school."

"Jeez, will you just relax?"

"You're freaking an hour and a half late! I could have been back at school already, or at the very least I could have been spending an hour and a half with Liz."

Mark shrugged. "We're going *now*, ain't we?"

I stared at him for a minute, then I cocked my fist back and punched him right in the face. I connected square on the nose, the best place for that first punch. Blood started pouring down his face. "What the fuck are you doing?" he yelled. He kept trying to drive, but I was ready if he was going to try anything. "Screw this," he muttered. He turned the steering wheel and did a U-turn. "I'm going home. You can just freaking drive to school by yourself."

I ended up having to take one of my mom's cars out to campus.

Mark dropped out and never went to BAC again, but I stayed, and that year I ended up as a Junior College All-American for BAC. Unfortunately, the school was going to drop their wrestling program the following year, so I transferred to Lincoln Junior College. Barely any of my credits were carried over, and they told me it would take another two years to complete my associate's degree. Mark ended up going there too.

One of our first days at Lincoln, Mark and I were sitting on the steps outside of our dorms when we saw a guy pull up. Most wrestlers can recognize one another on sight. Wrestlers have the thickest necks, because you're either standing, pushing and pulling on people's heads, or you're on the ground trying to bridge off your back. But the dead giveaway sign is the cauliflower ears. The cartilage eventually detaches from constantly getting bumped and ground along the floor. Then the space fills up with fluid, and the ear gets real tender. Finally the fluid hardens, and a wrestler's ear is permanently gnarled and twisted like a cauliflower. It's a sign of pride that you've done your time.

"Hey, you see this?" I said, elbowing my brother.

"Oh, I see it. I'm just not sure what it is."

Thick neck? Check. Cauliflower ears? Check. He was wearing a wife-beater, blue jeans, and some cowboy boots. The tattoos were showing. He was one half-empty beer can away from being on *Cops*. He walked right up to us. "Hey, I'm Marc Fiore," he said, shaking our hands, acting like he knew us. "You guys are on the team?"

"Yeah," I said, knowing which team he meant. "I'm Matt and this is my brother Mark."

"Nice to meet you," he said.

"You want us to help you get some stuff out of your truck?" my brother asked.

"Could you?" Fiore said. We walked over to his truck and started unloading.

"So where are you from?" I asked him.

"I'm from right outside of Chicago."

"You guys herd a lot of cattle right outside of Chicago?" Mark wanted to know.

"Huh? No . . ."

"Then what's them boots for?" I said.

Fiore started smiling, because we were talking to him like his old buddies must have talked to him. "Hey, I'm not some city pud. I got out to the farm. My high school coach, Coach Hahn, he's got horses in this country area and I go there and help him bale hay sometimes."

Mark and I started cracking up, almost dropping the boxes we were carrying. "Oh, wow! You're a regular farm boy, ain't ya?" I said. "Hey, do you have any tips about walking beans?"

"Wait a minute," Mark said, pretending to think. "I've heard of you. Marc Fiore. I knew that name sounded familiar."

"You have?" Fiore said, looking at me to see if Mark was putting him on.

Mark snapped his fingers. "I know how I know you. You're the guy that heard the fields had a lot of problems with bare spots, so you went out and shot a grizzly."

After we helped him move in, we all went straight to the wrestling room to feel each other out. We took him down and he took us down, so we all knew that we were on the same page, that we'd all be on the starting team together. Then we just began hanging out all the time, telling stories. After that, Mark and I weren't twins anymore; we were now triplets.

A couple of weeks later Fiore walked into my room. Mark and I looked up at our friend. He seemed reserved, shuffling his feet and staring at the floor. "I just wanted you guys to know that I'm heading home," he announced. "Like, for good. I wanted to say goodbye before I left and see if you could help me load my stuff back into my truck."

I sat up on the bed. "Slow down, slow down. What the hell are you talking about?"

"What happened?" Mark said. "Is everything all right?"

Fiore walked in and shut the door behind him. He leaned against the wall and kept shaking his head. "I thought I could handle it here but I just can't. I'm not going to be able to pass any of my classes."

"Fiore, we haven't been in school but four weeks," I pointed out. "What makes you so sure you're going to fail?"

"Because I went to English class today, you know, and the teacher assigned us all an essay about what we did over the summer. And I can't do it."

"You don't know what you did over the summer?" Mark asked.

Fiore rolled his eyes. "I can't write, man," he eventually said.

"How'd you get through high school, then?"

He shrugged. "People helped me. You know those stories about kids from the inner city who make it to the NFL and they can't really read or write. Well, even though I'm a suburban white kid, it's pretty much the same thing. I got by because of my athletic ability."

"Don't forget your stunning good looks," I added.

"Come on, don't make this any harder than it has to be," Fiore said.

"Well, I don't think we should make it easy for you either," Mark argued. "I mean, there's got to be something you can do. You can't just quit. Let's sit down and try and figure something out."

"There's nothing to figure out," Fiore said quickly. "It's done, okay? So can you help me pack? Please?"

Mark and I looked at each other, not knowing what to say. We followed Fiore to his room and loaded his truck as best we could. "Well, what are you going to do with the rest of your stuff?" I asked after we were finished.

Fiore looked over what couldn't fit into his vehicle. "I was going to throw it out. You guys want it?"

"What I want is for you to unpack your truck," I said.

"Well, that's not going to happen," he answered.

"In that case, dibs on the microwave," I said before Mark could get a word out.

As soon as Fiore was gone we went to the wrestling room and found Coach Klemm. "He just left," I explained. "He can't read or write but I know he's not lazy and I know he'll work really hard, whatever it takes."

Coach let out a deep breath. "I'm glad you boys came and found me. I'm going to see what I can do. I don't want to lose a wrestler, but I also don't want Marc to lose an opportunity for an education."

Within a week Mark and I heard another knock at the door. Our buddy was standing there with that goofy grin of his. "I'm back!"

We got up and gave Fiore a big hug. "What happened?" Mark asked him.

"I talked to Coach Klemm and he told me that we'll make it work," Fiore said. "Somehow, we'll make it work. He promised me that he'll put the word out himself that I can't read or spell but that I was a good person, that I meant well, and I'd try my best to do what I could."

"Even that English class?" I asked.

"Oh, I dropped that. First thing. I went to drop it before I even came back to see you guys." The three of us were smiling like we were on laughing gas. Then Fiore looked over my shoulder at my newest home furnishing. "Oh, so you bought a stand for the microwave that I gave you?" he asked me.

"I sure did," I told him.

He looked at me, waiting for me to say something, but I wouldn't. He knew better than to ask, because it would be pointless. We stood there staring each other down. "It still works, right?"

"Yep. And I thank you for giving it to me."

The team was back, and everybody at Lincoln knew it. They had no choice. We'd clog the shower with toilet paper and someone would wake up in the morning to ankle-deep water. We'd trap people in their rooms by squeezing pennies between their door and its jamb. The hall fire extinguisher was filled with water, and we'd spray it at each other almost every other day.

Then we got creative.

One night at ten or eleven the three of us crept to where our wrestling buddy Wade had parked his car. It was quiet and dark. "Look at this pile of junk," I said, pointing to Wade's car. The paint was peeling off and it was worn down all over. The Indiana license plates were weathered. "Mark, doesn't this remind you of that sedan we got?"

"Yeah!" Mark said, laughing quietly.

"What are you talking about?" Fiore whispered. "This isn't a sedan. This is a Datsun."

"What he means is that the first car Matt and I ever got, we didn't buy it to drive it; we bought it to wreck it," Mark explained. "We got ourselves this yellow sedan for around $150 and we made it a convertible."

"Huh? How can you make a sedan into a convertible?"

"When we brought it back to the farm the first thing we did was to take a chainsaw to it and cut the top off," I told him, whispering. "Now it's a convertible. We took that car all over the burms. Do you remember, Mark?"

"Yeah, I'm surprised it lasted as long as it did, given all the punishment it took."

"Wait," Fiore said, laughing a bit because we were. "What's a burm?"

"A burm is like a rise in the land along the edge of a creek, to keep it from overflowing into the fields," I said. "Down behind our house there's a big hill and at the bottom is where those burms are. We would take this car down there, rain or shine, and hit those burms *fast*. That car would fly and then it would hit the ground—usually in mud."

"Like *Dukes of Hazzard*."

"Yes, exactly like *Dukes of Hazzard*. We just kind of had our way with that car. If we wanted to run it into a tree or something, that's what we did with it."

Mark, Fiore, and I all got behind Wade's trunk, pushed with all of our strength, and slowly the wheels of the car began to turn. We eased it very gently toward the baseball diamond about one hundred yards away. We left it parked right on the pitcher's mound. I stood up and dusted my hands off. "Good work, guys!"

The next morning Wade found us in the wrestling room. "Ha, ha. Very funny," he said. "They called me in about my car. Everyone knows it was you. Don't even try to deny it."

"I don't know what you're talking about," Mark said. "We were in our rooms catching up on our schoolwork last night between ten and eleven. Matt, do you know what he's going on about?"

I shook my head. "I don't understand. Do you know what he's talking about, Fiore?"

"I haven't a clue," Fiore said, smiling. "Not the foggiest idea."

"You know, it was bad enough the first time. Now I had to

try and explain to them why I *keep* parking on the baseball diamond!"

Mark got up and slapped Wade on his shoulder. "That's not a proper parking space here, Wade. I don't know how things are done in Indiana. Maybe things are different there. But you should know that here in Illinois, it is not correct procedure to park your vehicle in the center of a ball field."

"Don't they have driver's ed over there in Indiana?" I asked. "Don't you have to take some kind of a test to get your license? Mark, I guess they must not have had that question on the exam: 'Are you allowed to park on a baseball diamond? Yes or no.'"

"Laugh all you want," Wade said. "They know you all did it and it doesn't matter anyway because this will never happen again."

"Well, I'm glad you learned your lesson about where you're allowed to park," Mark told him. Wade stormed out of the room and the three of us were laughing so hard it was a wonder we didn't turn blue.

A few weeks passed. We waited until it was very dark out, and we brought along our buddy Rob just in case Wade had gotten crafty. We all got behind the car and pushed as hard as we could. It only moved a few inches. "I bet you that knucklehead didn't think to lock the door," I said. I walked around to the driver's side and pulled on the handle. Nothing. I tried all four doors. "Well, I guess Wade thinks he thought of everything."

"Well, that leaves Plan B!" Mark said, rubbing his hands together.

"What, do you want to make it a convertible?" Fiore asked.

"No, I don't have a chainsaw," my brother answered. "We've just got to tip her over."

"How are we going to do that?" I wondered.

"We all four go to one side, lift it up, and then we gently tip it over."

"Oh man, he's going to be pissed," I said.

"So you don't think it's a good idea?" Rob said.

"Oh, we're tipping her over," I assured him. "I'm just pointing out that Wade is going to be *pissed.*"

The four of us easily lifted the car up on its side. Then Fiore and I got on the far side and lowered the car down slowly so that the roof wouldn't collapse. Then we ran away as fast as we could. Mark and Rob bumped heads as they ran, and Rob's tooth cut Mark's head.

The school administration had seen enough. They decided to bring in a detective to solve the crime, even though everyone on campus knew all the particulars. The detective took me into an office and sat me down across from him. *Maybe I'd break if he put me under some hot lights, but this is quite comfortable,* I thought. *Scratch that. Hot lights wouldn't do a thing, given how often I sweat to make weight. I'd just pretend I'm in the sauna wearing my plastics.*

"Are you even listening to me, Mr. Hughes?" he yelled. His hair was receding, and the aggressive voice probably used to work on people back in the day. But not this day.

"What was the question?" *This guy's decided that he's going to bust us. He honestly thinks he's going to get us,* I realized. *He's bringing us in*

*one by one to see if he can make us crack or whether we'll have discrepancies
in our stories.*

"We took fingerprints from the top of the car," he told me,
"and we think that we're going to know if they're yours or not."

"Well, you probably will," I admitted. "I jumped all over that
car when we pushed it over to the baseball diamond before. So,
yeah, I'm gonna bet you that my fingerprints are all over that car."

"Those fingerprints stay on there for up to six months," he
went on.

"I guarantee you there's a lot of my fingerprints on top of
that car if they stay up there for six months," I said. "If I'm sitting in the car and I lean my hand out the window or something,
that's going to leave fingerprints, right? I don't know about these
things. I'm no detective."

He brought Fiore in, and he brought Mark in, and he couldn't
get us to crack. No matter what he did, we stood firm. The school
president finally said, "We know you did it. Wade's car's not running right. Change the oil for him, get it running right, and we're
going to act like this never happened."

Fair was fair. We got Wade's oil changed and got the sedan
running for him all right. Wade was mad but he got over it. The
school got over it too. Everyone got over it but that poor detective. He had brought us all in several times, and he was going
crazy because he couldn't get us to slip. It's been over ten years,
but this is for you, Detective: I hereby make a full confession
in writing. (I've been told to make it clear that Mark and Fiore
continue to maintain their innocence.)

Right after Christmas break my brother was wrestling in

a tournament for Lincoln in Colby, Kansas. There's a certain type of wrestler who is all about looks, the kind of guy who is strangely tan at Christmastime. To win the tournament Mark had to get through such a person, a guy by the name of Frank Trigg. No question but that Trigg was full of power; top of his game. But he also had an air of cockiness about him. When he thinks he is going to win, he is very positive that he is going to win.

Mark was not in shape after Christmas. He was doing well the first round. Then in the second round Trigg rallied, and the third round was all Trigg. Trigg won the match and ended up winning Nationals that year. It's just too bad he never really made anything of himself.

A few months later Mark, Fiore, and I pulled up to Uncle Jack's farm. The old house on the property was in ruins. On the right was a wooden barn; it too had seen better days. Right up against the road was a fence with hogs inside. The grass was eaten away by the pigs. "Hey, Uncle Jack!" I yelled from the driver's seat.

"Hi, boys!" he waved back. He was in denim overalls like always, with a straw hat and some boots. He looked his advanced age and then some.

We all hopped out of the truck. The weather was mild, so the mud wasn't bad. "Uncle Jack, I want you to meet our buddy, Marc Fiore."

Fiore shook my uncle's hand. "Nice to meet you, sir."

"Fiore thinks that because he bales hay sometimes that makes him a farm boy," my brother said. "We wanted to bring him here to show him what it's really like."

"Jeez, will you shut up?" Fiore said. "I don't think I'm a farm boy."

"You don't listen to these two," Uncle Jack said. "Baling hay is a lot more than most folks do. And this is a farm, and you're a man, so that makes you a farmer even if it's only for today."

"How you been?" I asked him.

A little dark spot appeared on the front of Uncle Jack's pants. I acted like I didn't notice Fiore staring at it as the spot grew and grew as Uncle Jack pissed himself. "The grass in the pasture just isn't growing. I wish it would grow a bit."

"Well, if you pen your cows up in one area for a little while, the grass will grow," I told him.

Uncle Jack shrugged. "I guess maybe you're right. I can move the fence." By now the spot had become a trickle down his overalls. Fiore kept shooting Mark and me glances, but we were blind to him in perfect twin tandem.

"We can grow some bluegrass in there," Mark told him. "We can get some seed down over there at Rural King. We'll help you with that."

"I think that's what I'll do," Uncle Jack said. "I don't like that look of just empty ground."

"Well, we're here to cut hogs for you, and that's what we're going to do."

"Okay. You boys have fun."

"Nice to meet you," Fiore said. We turned and went to get our scalpel from the truck. "Did you guys not see that?" Fiore said as soon as Uncle Jack was out of earshot.

"See what?" I asked. We got the knife and headed to the pen.

"You did not see your uncle?"

"Yeah, I saw my uncle."

"No. Did you not see that he was just standing there peeing in his pants? You could see it in his pants! He was peeing. He was *obviously* peeing."

"Yeah, he's old, he does that," Mark said. "And now we're going to show you how to cut a hog. If you see a pink animal with a corkscrew tail, that is what we call a 'pig' around here."

"I know what a pig is!"

"I just didn't want you getting scared of it or nothing," my brother went on. "Maybe you think that pigs are like unicorns or leprechauns up in Chicago." Mark and I started laughing at the guy, and all Fiore could do was roll his eyes.

"You're going to kill a pig right here?"

"Cut it," I interjected. "That's when you take off its balls."

"You brought your own knife?" he asked.

"I don't trust Uncle Jack's knives for such delicate surgery." Mark and I got into the pen and managed to each catch one baby pig. They were about a foot to a foot-and-a-half long, no more than twenty to thirty pounds. "It's a lot easier to catch them when there's a lot of them so they can't run around," I explained. "First, you've got to get a grip on the pig. Then you slice open the skin, squeeze it a bit so that the balls flop out, and then cut the cord that holds the nuts to the body. Do you want to do one?"

"Maybe later," Fiore said, turning all kinds of colors.

I held the pig and slit it open. It screamed hysterically. I pulled the testicles out, snipped them with the knife, and tossed the nuts on the ground. Then I let the pig go into the next pen to keep them separate. Mark and I got through about two before Fiore started looking around for something to distract him.

"Hey, you guys," Fiore called out. "I think this one here's dead. He's not moving."

We didn't bother looking over. "When a sow makes her nest, she usually rolls over and crushes some baby pigs," Mark explained. "If you look around down there you'll probably see a few more that she's killed."

Fiore bent over to examine the nest and try to figure out which of the piglets were dead and which were just sleeping. I put the scalpel on top of a shelf, leaned over, and threw something at Fiore. He ran his fingers along the back of his head and looked at his hand. "Very funny," he said, turning around. "What, did you just throw pig shit at me?"

Right on cue, Mark lobbed a pair of pig testicles at Fiore's face. My brother and I leaned over and grabbed as many testicles and dead baby pigs as we could. Fiore took off running, and we ran right after him chucking pig parts at our buddy. It was a wonder we didn't slip, because Mark and I were laughing so hard we were almost crying, and our ammunition was literally all over the ground.

"Quit it! What are you guys doing?" Fiore kept yelling through his laughter. His fun trip to the farm had become *Green Acres* on crack. Finally we cornered him in the barn. We stood there for another minute pelting him with testicles and dead baby pigs, while he tried his best to block the carnage. Mark and I were All-American wrestlers, so quitting was not an option.

A few weeks later Mark and I were cleaning the mats in the wrestling room. "Fiore, you got the keys?" I said.

"Yeah, I'll lock up here after I grab a shower and you guys are done mopping."

He headed to the bathrooms next door. I waited until I could hear Fiore start his shower and then I held my finger to my lips so that Mark wouldn't say anything. We put down our mops and tiptoed into the shower area. I went into Fiore's bag and took his pants; the keys jingled in the pocket a little. I walked toward the shower to throw his clothes in there, but Mark grabbed me by the shoulder and gestured. I looked to where he was pointing.

Next to the showers was the school pool. It was a full-size Olympic pool, high dive and all. We walked over and I turned the handle to the pool room so I could toss Fiore's clothes in. Locked. I looked down at the pants and went through the pockets. I pulled out the key and tried it. The door unlocked. We looked at the key and then at each other.

The key that opened up the wrestling room also opened the door that went to the pool. That meant that whoever got the keys so they could mop up after the team also got to go swimming whenever they wanted to. The key practically started glowing in Mark's hand. It was like a choir started singing behind us.

"Pool party," I said.

Mark nodded very slowly, his mind reeling at the potential.

We'd wait until the security guard did his circuit of the

building. But once he went by, at around eleven o'clock, he didn't come back. Night after night, Mark, Fiore, and I would take six of our favorite girls and go down to the pool. Then we'd proceed to get wet.

The following month, I got back from the post office and found Mark waiting for me outside the dorm. He hadn't noticed me walking up and he kept moving about like there were bugs on him, just restless and unable to stand still. The look on Mark's face was one of shock and confusion and sadness. It was a look I had never seen before on him. "I need to tell you something," he said.

"Sure." We went upstairs to my room. I put down the stuff that I'd bought and sat on my bed. Mark stood there and sighed.

"I'm going to tell you exactly what Mom just told me," he said. "Just listen."

"Go ahead."

"You know that Mikey was head over heels for that girl, right?"

"Yeah . . ."

"Well, their breakup got him real upset. He went to her house yesterday with a high-powered rifle."

My eyes popped open wide. "What?"

"I don't think he was going to hurt anyone. He told her he wanted to talk. He said that if she didn't come talk to him he was going to kill himself. That's how he got her outside. The police got called and there was a huge scene."

"Is everyone okay?"

"No."

"No?"

"He, uh, he did it, Matt. He did it right there in front of her house, in front of the police and everybody."

Can Mikey really be gone? Why would he do something like this, over a girl who wasn't even his wife, who he hadn't known for a year? Why didn't he try to call? I felt like I was being physically shaken. I just couldn't calm down. "When's the funeral?" I said. It even hurt to talk. I didn't want to talk, or sit, or be comfortable in my room. I didn't want it to be like there was anything normal going on.

"Mom says they're having an early showing for him on Wednesday, and the funeral is Thursday."

"Mark, Thursday's the start of Nationals."

"I talked to Mom, and she and I both think he would want us to go. Uncle Stan said that. I mean, he was a wrestler and he taught me a lot, he taught both of us a lot. He'd want us to go and he'd want us to win. And he'd want us to have fun doing it, too."

And that's exactly what we ended up doing.

Later that week at Nationals, I was in the weight room. I stripped naked and got on the scale. I was 161.25, trying to get to 159. I stepped off and waited until Mark checked his weight out. "I'm about a pound over, too," he said. "Let's go out for a run."

"Good idea," I told him. We put our sweats back on and then we slipped on our plastics over them.

"Hey, Ryan?" Mark called out to one of our Colby, Kansas, wrestler buddies. "Matt and I are heading out for a run to make weight. You want to come with us?"

"Sure."

"I bet you do!" Mark yelled. All the guys burst out laughing at Ryan.

I walked out of the weight room into the hall. Out of nowhere Jeremiah, a real bruiser from Garden City, came up and popped me in the mouth. Then he turned around and sat back down against the wall with his girlfriend. *Did he just hit me?* I ran my hand against my face and shook my jaw back and forth. *He just freaking hit me!* I looked down at Jeremiah sitting there acting perfectly natural in his singlet, sweating. If I hadn't felt it I would never have guessed what had just happened. I clenched my jaw and went back into the weight room. Everyone was still laughing.

"Hey, I need you out here *now*," I told my brother.

Mark saw the look on my face and walked out right behind me, with a few other guys. "What's going on?" he wanted to know.

"I'm about ready to take this idiot's head off. I just got sucker punched, basically." I went up to Jeremiah. He and his girlfriend stood and faced me and my friends. "What is your freaking problem?" I asked.

"You think it's funny that I lost my match?" he said. He had won Nationals the year before and was a key player for Garden City.

"Relax," his girlfriend said to him.

"How the hell am I supposed to know that you lost your match? Are you stupid or something? I was in the weight room with my buddies, you freaking idiot!"

"Then why were you laughing at me?" he said.

"I *wasn't* laughing at you. I was laughing because someone

said something funny. I *should* have been laughing at you because you're obviously too damn stupid to tell the difference between someone joking around and someone making fun of you! You're an idiot. You are just a moron. There's no better way to put it." I could feel Mark over my shoulder turning red. He was wanting to pop, but I didn't want it to escalate there.

We turned around and left him there, standing with his girlfriend and feeling anxious.

When I got back from my run, Coach Klemm found me. "Matt, did you get into a fight with one of the Garden City guys?" he said, concerned.

"He hit me out of nowhere because he thought I was making fun of him. Maybe it's because he was in front of his girl."

"And *were* you making fun of him?"

"No, a bunch of us were joking around. I didn't even know he was there until he jumped up and popped me one."

"So you didn't lay a hand on him?"

"Of course not. I'm not stupid."

"I'm not going to let this go by," Coach Klemm assured me in that authoritative way that any good coach has.

After wrestling was done for that day, I was in the lounge at the hotel, hanging out with my brother. One of the guys from Lassen came up to me. "Hey, are you the guy that got into a fight with Jeremiah?"

"Yeah. I mean, he hit me, if that's what you want to call it."

"I was wondering if I could take a picture with you?"

"What?" *This is the weirdest tournament I have ever been to,* I thought.

"After your coach complained, they disqualified him, took away his points, and now we're co–national champions with Garden City. He cost them the championship."

My jaw dropped. "You're yanking my chain."

"I am totally serious."

"Well, yeah, you can take a picture!" Me and the guy put our arms around each other and he handed the camera off to his friend. I patted him on the back. "I bet I probably scored as many points for you by taking that guy out as some of your own wrestlers did."

"You won the title for us, man."

"You can just mail me my trophy."

Months later I was driving to Indiana to have a guy work on my transmission for me. The highway was straight and empty, and sitting in the passenger seat was Tommy Moore's little sister, Audra. She was the one who went on road trips with me, listening to country music and just being young. It was like she was my kid sister also. "So what are you going to do now?" she asked me. She turned around and laid down against me, using my leg as her pillow.

"I'm going to go to Eastern Illinois University in the fall," I told her.

"Don't you want to be a professional wrestler?"

I laughed. "Well, there's being a professional wrestler and that's like those guys on TV in the WWF. Then there's wrestling professionally, and I can't do that either."

"Why not?"

"Do you remember when Mark and I went to that tournament up in Austria?" She nodded. "I ended up placing fourth at the big tournament we competed in there, right, and that put me on the Olympic ladder. I also got offers from the Army, for both the freestyle and the Greco sides."

"What're those?"

"Freestyle and Greco are the styles," I explained. "Greco is all upper body; you can't shoot on legs, you can't attack legs, and freestyle is anything. Anyway, no matter which one of those I pick, there's just no money in wrestling. You can coach, and that's what our buddy Fiore is going to do at Lincoln. But I'm going to go to school, compete some more, and figure out what I want to do."

"Is Mark going with you?"

"No, he's going to stay at home and do construction, so you'll get to see him all you want. You'll forget all about your big brother Matt, just you wait." I couldn't see her face that well but I could tell she was blushing. "You're going to spend all your time with him."

"Ew, no! Mark's gross!"

I did a bit of a doubletake. "Why is he gross?"

"Because of his gross face and his gross hair and his gross everything."

I laughed at her and she crossed her arms. But she didn't sit up as I drove along the highway. "We're twins, Auggie Doggie. If you think his face is gross, than you think my face is gross. And if you think his hair is gross, you think my hair is gross. We have the same hair."

"I like yours better."

"You like my mullet better? Aw, that's sweet." I rubbed her head. She didn't react, but I knew she liked that. "So do you have a boyfriend yet?"

"No . . ."

"I told you, you need to work on learning how to give a guy a good backrub like I showed you. Then, a pretty girl like you, you'll have any guy you want." Audra didn't say anything. "So have you kissed a boy yet?"

"Yes . . ."

"I know *who.*"

"Huh?"

"Did you and Mark not kiss?"

Now she sat up from leaning on my lap. Audra scooted on the passenger seat toward the window and looked at the trees blurring into green. "Yeah," she admitted.

"So was it like a kiss on the cheek?"

She blushed, hard. "No, like a real kiss," Audra said, in an older-than-high-school voice.

"How did this end up happening?"

"I thought he told you."

"I want to hear it from you."

She sighed. "I was sleeping in the basement. Mark was out with Tommy and he came over to stay the night, like he always does. He laid down next to me on the pullout coach and then he started kissing me. I was freaking out that my mom was going to come downstairs and see it."

"Is that it?"

"Yes, that's it! He must have realized that I was in eighth grade or something and he stopped."

I could hear the AC blowing in the car, and the vibration of the wheels against the road as we thundered to the auto shop. Audra was still staring out the window but she was waiting for my reaction. "I guess I'm glad that my brother has good taste," I said.

That June, my first year at Eastern was done. I had ended up as a Division I All-American in wrestling, one of the top eight wrestlers in the country. Me and my six roommates, all wrestlers, had started the year as strangers but ended it as the best of friends. There were twenty college kids in our house that day, a bunch of guys with thick necks and cauliflower ears. And girls. It was like the end of every college film ever made, because the school year had let out and everyone was ready to let loose. Our house on Polk Street was like a manufacturing plant producing waste. The process was simple. People would come in, put some beer in the fridge, take out two, hand one to their buddy, drink their own, and then go upstairs to pee.

"Let's go swimming!" our housemate Tim screamed out. "Come on, let's go to the spillway and go swimming, everybody! Everybody, we're going swimming!"

We looked around and shrugged our shoulders, trying to think of a reason why we wouldn't. But there weren't reasons not to do things anymore. Hangovers are fine if you don't have class. We could stay up all night with no meets to go to. The girls didn't have to study for finals.

It was time to get wet.

We all piled into vehicles and drove over there. The grass was still damp when we walked across it, barefoot, and the air smelled of earth. The moss on the ground was so vibrant that I wondered if the rain had come down too fast at the farm, running off instead of soaking into the soil.

"What's that?" one of the girls asked me. "Is that the spillway?" We were on the hill between the lake and the river down beneath us. A concrete slide connected the flow between the two at a forty-five degree angle.

I nodded and then pointed with my beer. "Yeah, there's usually a wall at the bottom there so the water coming down off the lake doesn't erode the riverbank. I guess it's submerged from all the rain we've had. That water looks like it's about ten feet taller than usual." *I'm not that drunk,* I thought. *The water really is that out of control.*

"Ooh, are those *whirlpools?*" she giggled.

Over by us and also on the far side, the water was frothing in circles. "Yeah, that wall must be messing things around underwater."

My roommate Joe came over and put his arms around the two of us. He leaned forward because the alcohol was making his arms heavy. "We can't swim in there," he told us. "It's just too dangerous."

"I don't think it's that bad," Tim interrupted. He tore off his shirt, ran past us, and jumped into the water. We started to applaud; he even got a few cheers. Then the whirlpool grabbed him, spun him in a circle, and brought him right back to shore. It was like he was on the teacups ride at the fair. It looked kind of funny.

"We don't need to be out here," Joe told him.

Tim rolled his eyes and hopped back in. He flew past the whirlpool by us this time, into the middle of the water. But instead of gently bouncing around in a circle in the flow, I saw him slip like he had stepped on a banana peel. The water pulled him under like there was a pit bull on his ankle. Where the current hit the submerged wall, it shot him back up again. And again.

And again.

Holy shit, he's not joking around, I realized. I set my beer on top of a truck and jumped in after Tim. I felt the water surround me. It was like the water was magic, because it gave me amnesia—as soon as I was in the spillway, I forgot all about Tim.

For almost ten years I had been throwing people around on mats; I had been lifting weights to build up my strength; I had been swimming my entire life. But all these things were a joke compared to the power of that rushing water. My body flew all around that spillway. I couldn't control where I was going. I didn't have a choice as to where I was going to end up. It was a feeling that I had never experienced before or since: complete helplessness.

The water took me down at first, and then it took me back a little ways. I pushed off the concrete floor. It was good and sturdy when everything else around me was both pure liquid and pure force. I shot up off the bottom, and then the current took me back to the center of the spillway, and then it sucked me down again. I didn't know when I was going to pop up; I didn't know when I was going to get pulled under.

After three cycles of this, I thought, *There's nothing you can do. This is it. You're going to die.* Though I didn't know it at the time, someone up above was looking out for me, because an idea came into my head. *If you curl up in a ball, you might get shot past that submerged concrete wall. Then you'll be far enough along that you'd surface downstream instead of back where you started.*

I grabbed my feet with my hands and tightened myself up underwater. The current shot me like a cannonball, past the wall and beyond the whirlpools. I struggled to stand in the water. When I walked to shore it was like I was dragging a sack of rocks. I could barely stand. I could barely get my wind.

But I *could* stand. And I *could* get my wind.

It all had taken less than a minute. I stepped onto the ground and slogged my way back uphill, where two truckloads of kids looked into the water. They were holding their beers, and their breath. "Joe jumped in when he saw you couldn't save Tim," our roommate Juan told me. "We haven't seen either of them for a couple of minutes."

I turned and watched the water with everyone else. The ground still felt damp beneath our feet. The afternoon sun still warmed us. The water down the spillway still sloshed around. One by one, the kids changed their expressions. One by one, we realized there was no point in looking at the water anymore. You would never know from looking at that water that it had just claimed the lives of two of our friends. It was just some water. You see it every day.

My eyes welled up as my shoulders began to shake.

*   *   *   *

When I got back home I picked up the phone and called Mark. "Hey, it's me," I said.

"What's wrong?" my twin asked right away.

"We all went out to the spillway, just to have some fun or whatever, and there was an accident–"

"What do you mean?" Mark interrupted. "What sort of an accident? Are you all right? Is anybody hurt?"

"Tim went swimming and then the current got him. I jumped in after him and it got me, too. I got out but Joe jumped in after Tim when he saw I couldn't help him. They both drowned, Mark. Joe and Tim."

"Do you want me to come up there?" he asked.

The idea that he would do that never even crossed my mind. "Well, yeah!" I told him. "Yeah, come up here! I'll be working at the bar tonight."

The music was blasting that night. People tried to elbow past one another to get the bartender's attention. When the manager saw me come in, he tried not to act surprised. "Matt?"

"I want to stay occupied and try to get my mind somewhere else. I just want to be busy doing something."

"I hear you," he said.

It seemed to me that the heat in the bar was making everyone uncomfortable, like you just couldn't sit right. For a couple of hours I hauled ice for the bartenders and brought beers out. I went up and down stairs and lifted things until I sweat through my work T-shirt. *This isn't as good as farm work, but it'll do,* I thought.

"Matt Hughes, come to the DJ booth," echoed over the PA.

If I have to break up a fight tonight–tonight of all nights–*then there's going to be hell to pay.* But when I walked up to the booth, I saw Mark. I sprinted over to him and wrapped my arms around my brother and hugged him as hard as I could. "Let's go up to the walk-in cooler," I suggested.

"You lead the way," he said, squeezing my shoulder. We went up a half level into the cooler. There was an ice machine inside and frost everywhere. We each popped open a beer and sat down on some kegs. "I've got to tell you, I am pretty freaking ticked off at you," Mark told me.

I thought I had misheard him. "What? You're pissed off?"

"Don't you ever fucking do anything like that again. Ever. You do not risk your own life to save somebody else's life."

"Mark, Mark," I said, stammering. "It wasn't like that."

He held up his hand to shut me up. "Don't give me that. That's exactly what it was. That could have been you instead of Joe. What was I going to do, if you had died? You're my brother, my *twin* brother. You cannot do this to me, Matt. Never again." His arms were practically shaking.

I took a long swig out of that beer. I felt like he had punched me in the stomach. "I don't know what to tell you."

"You don't have to tell me anything. You know how I feel and I know how you feel. But when I was driving up here I couldn't help thinking about what could have been, and I didn't know what to do with myself. I still don't." He let out a deep breath and started welling up, and that got me to start crying too.

"I'm sorry," I said. "I didn't think, really."

"You are so stupid," he said, smiling through his tears. "Stupid."

I chuckled a little. "Mark, I'm sorry. Maybe you're right. I don't want to have my brother not have his brother, because I can't imagine not having my own brother around. I'm sorry."

"Promise me," he said.

"I promise, I promise." I wiped sweat from face with my shirt and chugged down my beer.

I went home after the bar closed and laid in bed all night. I waited and waited and waited, but I don't know what for. I thought about what had happened that day, and I realized something. I had been as close to my own death as I could have possibly gotten, but I hadn't found it to be such a horrible thing. It wouldn't have been a peaceful death, but it wouldn't have been an unspeakable tragedy. It wasn't something for me to be afraid of.

The next morning a bunch of us went back to the spillway to watch the rescue crew get to work, even though there was no one left to rescue. The rain was coming down and we all sat down at a picnic table under a pavilion top that they had put up. The drops hit against the fabric with soft thuds. My mom was there and she saw me looking at where I'd jumped in, where I had almost died. "What's going through your mind?" she asked me.

I exhaled. "A million things. Stupid stuff. I don't know."

"Like what?"

"Like I think I'm going to get a motorcycle," I blurted out.

"Excuse me?" she said.

"I don't know why that popped into my head. Maybe because you always said it was too dangerous and now I'm thinking that

that doesn't matter. First Evelyne, and then Mikey, and now the boys. My time could come tomorrow; my time might have even been yesterday, you know? I'm going to do what I want on this earth while I'm walking around."

I saw one of the rescue men gesture to the others. They brought a bag into the water and moved it downstream. A few minutes later I saw them take it back out of the river. It took more than one man to lift that bag up.

The following fall Mark enrolled at Eastern for a while, but he got there late and had some problems with his classes. It was too much for him, so he dropped out. But he stayed with me in that house on Polk Street for the entire year, and he went out with me all the time.

One night we were at a fraternity party. We didn't know anybody there. It wasn't a jock fraternity or a stoner fraternity; the house wasn't as dirty as it could have been. After some time, I caught a glimpse of my brother standing against the wall, holding the same beer he'd been nursing for an hour. We never got drunk because if the girls weren't friendly, then that left Plan B: a good fight.

We were fishing, but the girls weren't biting. I had talked to a few but I couldn't even get a nibble, let alone reel one in. Mark shrugged—he was in the same situation as I was—and went over to the kitchen cupboards. He opened them up and did an inventory of what was there, looking for something to eat. He slammed them shut and turned to the fridge. Then I saw three smaller guys, fraternity brothers, come up to him. "Hey, you can't do that," one of them said.

"Okay," Mark agreed. He shut the fridge for their benefit and they turned around and left. Seconds later, a dude walked in without his shirt on. *Here we go,* I thought. *The three fraternity brothers went and got their stud. If I can't get a girl tonight, at least I can get a fight.* He was bigger framed than Mark and me, but as I watched him saunter over to me I wasn't afraid at all. I was practically licking my chops.

"Hey, why are you going through the cupboards?" Captain Shirtless demanded, confusing me with my brother.

Now, if you're in a fight, you don't want your buddy next to you. The main fighters are within two or three feet. You want your guy in the background so he can move in if he needs to. I sensed my brother a few feet away. Mark was that guy on the outside. "Huh?" I said, in my best drunk voice. "Wass goin' on?"

The Captain pushed me onto the couch, and I kept looking around like I had no idea what was going on. He started to think I would roll over easy. He was going to be the big man for his buddies. Then I hefted the guy up and charged with him, hitting a light switch in the process. The lights shut off as I ran this kid into a window and ended up smashing his butt right through it, literally.

There in the dark, Mark and I looked at each other and then looked around. There were a heck of a lot more of them than there were of us. We put our hands over each other's shoulders and ran to the door. Then I turned around to see how many of them were giving chase.

But there was nobody there.

The lights were still off, and the frat brothers were all trying to get outside at once. Mark and I stood there side by side in the doorway and readied our fists. We took turns punching faces—one guy would fall back and just as quickly another one would take his place. We did this over and over. It was like those clown toys that keep bouncing right back up. A few minutes later we heard sirens. We ran. The party was officially over.

Although I was done at Eastern, I stayed around to coach. One day I got a phone call. "Hey, Matt, it's Chris Dwyer. We met at the tournament. I said I'd give you a call?"

I paused for a second. "Oh, right. Hey, Chris."

"How you been? Still coaching?"

"Yep, they let me stay on as assistant coach here."

"You sound pretty happy."

"Uh-huh! I've got the coaching job; Janelle and I are living together now. Plus, one of the other coaches has an electrical company, so I'm making some money helping him out, too."

"Well, I know someone else who can use your help."

"And am I talking to that person?" I said, laughing.

"You might be! I'm getting into this competitive fighting thing. You've heard of it, right?"

"Yeah, Mark and I rented a tape of one of them."

"So I was wondering if you could show me a few wrestling moves or something that could help me out in the ring. You saw how that Gracie guy did stuff?"

"I've been in a lot of fights, and truthfully? He didn't look too tough. Now Mark Severn, he's too big for me. But Royce didn't seem too tough. He's small, and he didn't look that aggressive," I said, having no clue that Royce would have absolutely destroyed me. "I'll be glad to teach you some things."

We met at Eastern's wrestling room. Chris was shorter than I was but clearly was a guy who had a GNC card. We were in T-shirts and some workout shorts. "Okay, first thing I'm going to explain is that there's pretty much two types of moves in wrestling. First and most important, you got your basic moves. Basics are just singles or doubles, like a single leg takedown. That's this." I faked left and dove at Chris's lower body. By grabbing his leg, I dropped him hard on his back on the mat. It stunned him for a second. I stood and helped him up. "Basics are what's going to win matches, from high school kids on up. Even if you look at the national championships, people that do basics very well go pretty far just by that."

"What's the other type of move?" Chris asked.

"The other type is a clinic move. Clinic moves are moves that look good in front of a group of people but aren't 100 percent reliable. A clinic move is something like this." I shot for his ankle, held it, and pushed him over. Again Chris was dropped on the ground, and I helped him right back up.

"What was that called?"

"That's an ankle pick, where you reach down and you grab your opponent's ankle and, hopefully, you can push him over."

"Let me show you a move and maybe you can tell me how effective it would be." Chris laid down on the mat with me. He held my shoulder in between his legs and used both his hands to leverage my arm. I could feel the pressure in my elbow and in my shoulder. I leveraged my way out of it pretty quickly. "That's a keylock," he explained.

"You know what? That's a good hold," I told him. "Why don't we spend some time with me trying to get you into one and you trying to get out of it, and then we can reverse."

Three times a week for about a month, Chris and I tried to figure our way through the world of fighting. "Hey, are you interested in fighting?" he eventually asked me. "We could get you a fight. I mean, you're a lot more aggressive than I am at this and I think you'd be good at it."

"That's fine."

"Oh, come off it. I know you miss the competition."

"Yeah, I do. Is it that obvious?"

Just a few weeks after talking to Chris I drove up to Madonna High in Chicago. Even though I had never seen a mixed martial arts (MMA) fight in person before—much less fought in one—I wasn't particularly excited. I knew I'd be good and it still wouldn't be anywhere nearly as big of a deal as wrestling Nationals or being an All-American. The all-girls Catholic high school had a cage set up in the center of the gymnasium, with bleachers for parents, friends, and the weirdos who wanted to see live violence.

There were twenty-eight of us, fourteen fights. I got on the scale, made weight, and looked at the competition. I scanned for the thick necks; the wrestlers would be trouble.

They announced my name and the people hollered a little. In the stands were my family, including my brother and sister. I could feel their support just like I had in countless wrestling tournaments in the past. I looked at my opponent, Craig Quick. He called himself the Terminator, and he liked to strike. But if you're close enough to punch a wrestler, he's close enough to take you down.

Before anyone knew it I had him on his back on the mat. My hand was on his throat and I began blasting him in the face with punches. "Is this legal?" he yelled out to the ref. "Is this legal?"

"Yep, yep," the ref said.

My opponent tapped. I finished Craig quick, ninety seconds into the fight. The ref raised my hand. "I think I can make a champion out of you," he told me.

Whatever you say, I thought. *I don't believe you, but you're entitled to your own opinion.*

Chris got me another fight months later, and I took out Eric Schmidt faster than Quick. *Man, this is a pretty easy sport,* I thought. The third fight was some months after that. I was grappling with Daniel Vianna and we accidentally bumped heads with each other. He walked over to his corner as his forehead trickled blood all over his face. They called it a no contest; he couldn't continue.

I went and collected my pay, $300 in cash from the promoter. A man who looked kind of like Santa Claus without the beard came over to me. "Hi, I'm Monte Cox."

"Matt Hughes," I said, shaking his hand.

"That wasn't right, what just happened to you," he told me. He didn't speak like he was a fan telling you what he would have done in the cage. Monte spoke almost like a coach, someone who had been around and knew the mistakes you were about to make.

"Yeah, he should have been more careful," I agreed.

"No, I mean, that shouldn't have been a no contest. He couldn't continue, so that should have been a victory for you."

I shrugged. It wasn't like this was on television in front of an Olympic committee. "Well, there's really nothing I can do about it now."

"Who's your manager?" he asked.

I frowned. "My manager? I don't have a manager."

"So who gets you fights?"

"Oh, that's what you mean. My buddy Chris Dwyer does." I gestured with my head to where Chris was standing. Monte didn't bother to look.

"If you let me be your manager, I'll be there to make sure that never happens to you again. Plus, I can get you more fights and more money each time you fight. I get a percentage, so I only make money if you make money."

"Let me think about it," I told him.

"What gym do you train out of?" Monte asked.

"I'm an assistant wrestling coach at Eastern Illinois."

"Well, you should really join a gym where you can learn this stuff. Pat's got a good one that's not too far away."

I gave him a blank stare. "Who's Pat?"

"The ref. Pat."

I looked over at the guy. He was a bit hunched over, with dark hair cropped close and his eyes kind of beady. "Yeah, he told me I should come train with him."

"The ref is Pat Miletich. He's the welterweight champion of the world."

CHAPTER 5

Committing

The top eight football players to graduate college every year are instant millionaires. This top eight wrestler who graduated college in 1997 got to stay on as assistant wrestling coach at Eastern, as well as do electrical work on the side for $14 an hour—$28.88 if it was a state job, time and a half for overtime. But it was work, and I was using my hands, so it didn't bother me. Twelve-hour days were fine, but nine to five was not.

There is no venue for wrestlers after we graduate, except for the low-paying, constantly traveling world of the Unites States Army team. Professional wrestlers are talkers first, bodybuilders second, and stuntmen third. Even if I could figure out how to run my mouth like the men on television, I would still never be one for waxing, tanning, and developing the perfect male body just because I had to look the part. I couldn't yell at my buddies in front of the camera, even if everyone knew I was really just putting on a show.

And it wasn't competition.

So I waited for the calls every so often from Monte, letting me know who I was going to fight next. A name, a hometown, and some background about who they were. There were wrestlers, and jiu jitsu experts, and boxers. They walked into the cage not caring or knowing that they were fighting Matt "Who?" Hughes. At best they were told that I was a Division I wrestling All-American, but no one trained very differently in the few weeks notice—if that—that they got. The Big Show is when you train to defeat your opponent. When it's the little show, you just want your check and the experience.

It was the fall of 1998, and Monte was promoting what was for him a big tournament; practically every folding chair in the audience was filled. The tournament would be eight men. On all four sides of the cage, a crowd of people five rows deep applauded as each of the eight names was announced. The audience was dressed in their Wal-Mart best; this was Wisconsin. Then they cheered, less this time, when the first fighter walked into the cage and his name was announced for the second time in ten seconds.

I waited backstage, maybe one hundred feet away, as Victor Hunsaker walked down the aisle into the cage. "In the blue corner, Matt Hughes," the announcer said, speaking into a mike even though everyone could have heard him without one. I pulled back the curtain and stepped out, Mark directly behind me. Thin smoke rolled on the floor, and the beams from three spinning bulbs were barely visible in the fully lit auditorium. I walked across the carpet to the cage. I knew two of the three people who screamed, and this was with ten of my friends in the audience.

I took off my T-shirt, handed it to my brother, and stepped into the square cage. Within seconds I had Hunsaker in a bear hug and lifted him clear off the duct-taped mat. "Up! Up! Slam him down!" Mark screamed, the most excited person in the building. When I punched Hunsaker in the face, the cheers began. That was what they paid for. It was ninety seconds of violence, up close and personal.

"Let's hear a nice round of applause for both of these fighters," the announcer said. He got it, with even a few hoots. I went backstage and stood around, laughing with Mark until it was time for the semifinals an hour later.

My next opponent, Dave Menne, wouldn't be a cakewalk, but I wasn't too worried about him either. Again Mark and I walked out through a layer of smoke, as Alice Cooper's "No More Mr. Nice Guy" played through the weak speakers. The applause ended before I reached the cage, twenty steps away.

I slammed Menne within seconds and took the fight to the ground. "Hit him in the ribs!" my brother barked. I worked on Menne for five minutes until the first round ended, then I walked back to my corner. Between rounds Mark tossed me a bottled water over the ten-foot wire cage. I had a minute to catch my breath and then we went back at it. There were people in the back of the room who were standing. It was not that they were excited; they just couldn't see. For three rounds I slammed Dave Menne and punched him. The decision from the judges was unanimously in my favor.

Then it was time for the finals. "Let's get it on," the ref

said. Dennis Hallman went for a kick. I grabbed his leg and he wrapped his arm around my neck. I swung him around and then went unconscious. It was like a switch went off in my head, like when you count backward when getting ready for an operation. Choked out in eighteen seconds.

I woke up and didn't know what was going on. I saw my brother and the ref standing over me, and then it all came back to me. Mark had a sort of smirk on his face, which made me smile. I looked up at the ref and the first thing I said was, "I guess I lost, huh?" The crowd saw that I was fine. They were glad, if not exactly relieved. Some were probably even disappointed.

I got up and stood there grinning while Hallman got his hand raised. I left the cage and watched as they gave him some sort of a belt. He looked at it with a bit of surprise. He was probably worried that it would be coming out of his paycheck.

The crowd filed out of the halls quietly and calmly, more like they were leaving a museum tour than leaving a live blood sport. They spoke about what they would do the rest of the week, or what errands they had left to run. They discussed the fights that day in the same tones that they wondered, seconds later, where they had parked.

The people who saw me get into my car didn't smile or nod in acknowledgment, because the only things separating the audience from the fighters were thin cage walls. Maybe it would have bothered me if I had been a football player instead of a wrestler. But wrestlers are used to the indifference.

"You all right?" Mark said as we started to drive away. "You sure didn't look all right." He was laughing at me and I kind of grinned myself.

"I'm fine. I'm just thinking."

"'Bout what?"

"I'm thinking that I need to start learning these submissions."

In March of 1999 I was at Eastern and I heard from Monte. "Hey Matt, how's it going?"

"Hey, Monte Cox! I love hearing your voice," I said. "I'm not doing too bad, Monte. And yourself?"

"I'm fine. Listen, I got a big one for you. Are you ready for this?" Even one-on-one he was a promoter. "Japan. There's a buzz around you in the Japanese small circuit." It was the buzz of a housefly: You would only notice it if you were really close to it. "The promoter for Shooto wants you to fight a guy by the name of Akihiro Gono."

"Do you know anything about him?"

"Not really," Monte said. "But he's Japanese, so he's probably pretty technical."

I got some more details about the fight out of my manager and then got off the phone. I pumped my fist and could not stop smiling. A real organization was paying to fly me out for a real fight in a real foreign country. This sounded like a big deal, and that meant I needed to get serious about this thing. I had an open invitation from the world welterweight champion, and now would be a good time to use it.

The three-hour drive to Bettendorf from Illinois is just high-
ways. I wasn't rehearsing what I'd say to Pat Miletich or wondering what the workout would entail. I was just thinking about
mundane things.

Bettendorf is an industrial town. Freight trains bullet through
on giant metal overpasses, and the Mississippi River swallows
the rust and grime that the factories spill out. Meth labs, yes;
sushi bars, no.

Pat was the UFC's world welterweight champion, the best
170 pound fighter on earth. So where does the Ultimate Fighter
train? At Ultimate Fitness, of course. The two-story brick building
was the simplest thing you could still call architecture. I walked
in, wondering if there were some fancy machines to train us at
the intensity we needed. There weren't many fancy machines.
There weren't many not-so-fancy machines, either. Ultimate Fitness should have been called Racquetball Fitness, because the
entire space used to be racquetball courts. Even though there
was equipment everywhere, there hadn't been much of a transi-
tion. The clients were women who wanted to lose weight, businessmen who worked hard and played hard, and, in one old
court, guys training in mixed martial arts.

I had to bend over to get through the racquetball half-door.
There were about thirty people in Pat's room, rolling around
on the ground on thin wrestling mats. There were no windows,
and while the fourth wall was mirrors, the steam kept them constantly fogged.

Gray and navy blue T-shirts turned black from the sweat
pouring out of the athletes. The kicks striking the pads were like

gunshots: sudden, loud, and sharp. Pat walked around noticing things out of the corner of his eye. "Watch the arm!" he yelled, predicting what would happen two moves from now. "Don't give up your position! Hand control, hand control!" He was like the cornerman to everyone in the room, all at once.

Pat remembered me when I came in. "Hey, go with Ben," he said immediately. Ben Inwood looked kind of benign; I wondered what I was supposed to do with the guy. Ben started out on his back, in the turtle position, and I jumped on top of him. We didn't say anything because after five minutes we'd each understand the other as an athlete. And five minutes after *that* was when I tried moving his legs out of the way, came down, and accidentally banged one of his knees with my teeth.

My front tooth was like it was on a hinge. I could feel it with my tongue as the blood poured onto the floor. I went quickly to the bathroom to take a look. It was a bad deal. I stepped out of the bathroom. "I need someone to take me to the hospital," I told the girl at the desk, blood soaking a towel. Just ten minutes at Pat's led to several hours of oral surgery over the next two days.

There's a lot you can get done in five minutes, but flying to Japan is not one of them. A few days after my oral surgery, I was on a plane to the Far East. I spent the time on the plane either looking out the window or watching the in-flight movie. I never could sleep on planes, even when I wasn't this excited—which meant that the whole first day in Japan I was passed out from exhaustion.

Yokohama wasn't like Tokyo, with the neon and the skyscrapers. It had a sense of traditionalism about it, and I wondered if this was their version of the Midwest. I sat in strange restaurants in uncomfortable positions, trying to eat weird meat, and not realizing that I wasn't supposed to tip. I would have killed for just one country breakfast.

My red hair and big shoulders should have made me a walking freak show, but no one bothered to stare. Even in Yokohama, the short people were so busy going places that they barged right into me. It was good practice keeping my balance as I was elbowed and shouldered from every possible angle. If I fell, I would have been trampled to death by tiny feet.

The arena where we were going to fight had two levels of seats, with bleachers overlooking the ring. Dave Menne was also there, nicely healed from when I took him on months ago at the tournament. I hadn't flown in a cornerman so I used his guy. I couldn't understand the ring announcer except for when he called out, "Matt-ah Hugh-see."

I took that as my cue. I walked down the long ramp, my face projected onto huge TV screens hung above the crowd. I waited in my corner as the lights dimmed and some Japanese house music came on. The people clapped and cheered, but in a subdued way, like at an opera. The announcer in his tux made some comment into the mike and Gono threw his T-shirt into the crowd. I stood there against the ropes, staring right at my opponent and seeing what I could figure out.

His stubble was carefully groomed and he had a scar running all the way across his stomach. He looked fairly big. My hands were sweaty in my gloves as I waited, just like everybody else, for the fight to start.

It took a minute or so of us scrambling until I had him up for a slam. Only now did the crowd react. *"Ohhhhh!"* It sounded like I had insulted his mother. I got Gono up again and slammed him down, better this time. *"Ohhhhh!"* No cheers, no applause. Librarians don't work in places as quiet and well-behaved.

We both got up and paced the ring. The crowd clapped. I don't know if they were glad he was standing or if they were endorsing good sportsmanship. I was busy watching out for Gono's submissions. After three five-minute rounds it went to a decision. "Matt-ah Hugh-see!" I lifted my hand in acknowledgment to the crowd.

When I got back to Illinois days later, Monte called. "Congrats on your win." He didn't sound too surprised, to be honest. "You're ranked on the Shooto board now."

"What does that mean?" I asked him. "I'll get to go to Japan again soon or something?"

"Better," he said. "I've talked to John Peretti, the matchmaker at the UFC."

"I know who John Peretti is, Monte. You explained it the first time he set up a fight for me and then canceled, and you explained it the second time he set up a fight with me and then canceled."

"I really think I can get you in the UFC this time."

"That's fine," I told him.

Monte paused for a second. Mentioning the UFC to a fighter was usually like bringing a woman to a prisoner. There should have been *some* reaction. "You don't sound too excited," he finally said. "That's where the big money is."

"I know, I know. If you can make this happen, that would be great. And I know you're doing your best. But I'll get excited when it actually happens, you know?"

"You mean like Mark actually settling down and getting married?"

I chuckled. "Yeah, something like that."

But that day did come, that fall. Everyone standing around–the groomsmen in their suits, the bridesmaids in their dresses–was uncomfortable enough already. Though the air was chilly under the orange leaves, we were all beginning to sweat, not being used to the monkey suits.

"I'm not doing it," Dad said. "I'm not going to be in any pictures with *her*."

I rolled my eyes. It's hard to shake your head when you've got a necktie strangling you. "Is this really such a big deal, for the guy to get photos of all of us together? It's a *wedding*," I told him.

"I know it's a wedding," he snapped. "I'm not doing it."

"I'll be right back," I said. I went to find the lucky groom, my brother. He was joking around with Tommy and some of the other guys. "Hey, Mark, Dad's not wanting to take pictures with Mom in them."

"Okay!" Mark said with a smile. "We'll just have the pictures without him." So we stood in groups, and individually, and in pairs, as the photographer snapped pictures for posterity and Dad watched it all with his arms crossed.

When people attend public ceremonies, they always take an

accounting of their own lives. At worst there's a sense of envy, that your friend is getting married and you're not. Otherwise there's an evaluation, wondering in general if you are where you need to be on your journey. I remembered what my mom had told me: "Fighting isn't a sport that you just dabble in. If you're going to do it, either get in with both feet or get out. But don't have one foot in the fighting scene and the other foot in the coaching scene."

I watched my twin say his vows, the groom in his tux who looked just like I would when I would be a groom. I looked at Emily, magazine sharp in her white dress and done-up hair. I thought about my Janelle. She was low maintenance—almost *no* maintenance—and pretty, and we had spent three years together. Living with her was practically like being married already.

When we all ran to the limo and popped open the champagne, I poured it down my throat as quickly as I could. "The best man's got to give the toast," Mark laughed, hugging his new wife tightly. "You keep on drinking there, Matt."

Emily looked at me, wanting to say something but knowing that would make it worse. She opened her mouth but then she closed it and just poured herself a glass instead. She was thinking that I was going to tell the story of how she and Mark got back together: how they had broken up, how Mark had broken into her new boyfriend's house and found them there together, how Mark was prepared to throw the guy out the window if they were up to anything (they weren't—just sleep), how Mark made her give him her driver's license so she'd have to see him the next day. She hated that story.

"You do not want me to have that mike," I let her know. I grabbed the bottle and polished off all I could. *I better get some alcohol in me so I can muster up this speech,* I thought. I hoped that as the champagne flowed, the words would follow. But I was just getting drunker and not any more eloquent.

By the time we got to the reception everyone was stumbling as they walked. The tables were covered in the best, if not most expensive, bouquets that Mark could get. No one would have noticed if we had wasted money on pricey liquor. I poured some wine and then pulled my buddy Tommy aside and half-whispered in his ear. "I'm worried about the speech."

He chuckled and put his hand on my shoulder. "Just don't rag on her too badly."

"No, I mean, how do I this? What am I supposed to say?"

He looked at me for a second and then snapped his fingers. "You know what you should have done? You should have had a bunch of keys made and given them out to a ton of girls and then said, 'You know my brother's married now, so anybody who's got a key to his house, I'd like for you to come up here and give it back to him and let him live his married life.' And then all these girls would come up and drop off the keys. An old lady or two would be even funnier."

I gulped down some more wine. "Well, it's a little late for that." I wandered the reception like a lost son, pulling people aside.

The guys with the thick necks and the cauliflower ears had little to offer in terms of speech-making advice. "You know what, Matt?" Sammy finally said. "You just need to speak from the heart."

He's right, I realized. I shrugged my shoulders, letting out some of the tension.

Then I had some more wine.

When I got the mike, guys elbowed their girlfriends, who then held their breath. Those who knew me knew that I was loopy, and those who didn't could guess from the silly grin I couldn't shake. "Emily," I said. I paused as everyone wondered what was going to come next. "Today we've gained something in our family," I told her. "I speak for everybody here when I say that we welcome you with open arms. Mark is very lucky to have found someone like you." I don't remember what I said after that. Maybe it was the wine, maybe it was because it was the same thing that brothers say every day at weddings. But that didn't mean that it wasn't true, and that I wasn't speaking from the heart. I watched her listening to me. At first she fought it, and then, not caring if I made fun of her, Emily started to cry. Following her lead, so did other people in the crowd.

We all drank until the old people left. Then we drank some more. "Hey, would you mind getting a keg?" Mark asked me.

"It's my brother's wedding," I said. "Of course!" I walked over to the bar. "Tap a new keg!" I told the guy, and then wrote him out a check. I was already too drunk to think about how much this keg was costing me.

My niece Sami came up to talk to me. "Hey, Matt, there's a guy outside hitting on us girls," she said, not really complaining but just letting me know what was going on.

I walked outside to the bushes, took a pee, and saw two

college-age guys on the other side of the parking lot. "Hey, where's the young girls at?" I asked them.

They leered at me like we were in a gang together. "Yeah, these girls keep coming out here and we're trying to get with them."

I stood there looking at this kid and I thought, *You piece of trash. That's my niece.* Everyone knows what you do with trash: You take it out! I just hauled off and hit this kid, and he fell right to the ground. His head barely missed one of the concrete parking blocks. His buddy looked at him, looked at me, and slowly backed away.

I walked outside at the end of the night and there were fights all over the place. The reception ended in a battle royale, Emily's guests from Kansas versus Hillsboro, in the parking lot. "Matt! Matt!" I heard my brother call me.

He was between two vehicles with a troublemaker kid. Mark turned to me and simply said, "Take care of this." The kid looked at me and took off running. I was quick enough to reach him and grab his shirt, ripping it right off of him. I chased him inside and all around the hall; he couldn't shake me. He ran into the bathroom and locked the door.

Mark had not thrown a punch the entire time. He had promised Emily that he would not fight at the wedding. He loved her enough to make a commitment, and he kept it. I went back inside and smiled at Janelle. If Mark could do it, so could I. I wondered if I was ready to take that next big step.

CHAPTER 6

For the Money

I knew this UFC 22 thing wouldn't happen. I just knew it.

It was September of '99, and we had made it down to Houston just fine from Iowa. The next leg of the trip, from Houston over to Louisiana, was going to be tougher. Our flight, of course, was canceled. The businessmen in their suits and the kids with their Discmans didn't look twice at us four guys from Bettendorf waiting around in the airport. Jeremy Horn leaned back in his chair. He was tall, skinny, and slouched in jeans and a T-shirt, with a brown crew cut growing out. You would have suspected the man knew his way around a skateboard or a surf-board. By sight, he should have been the kind of guy who you wouldn't let bump into you on a sidewalk. Being the number two guy from Miletich Fighting Systems would only sound impressive if the name Miletich meant anything to you.

Pat, sitting to Jeremy's left, did not exactly look like a fighter. In jeans and the cleanest dirty shirt he could find, he was annoyed because the airport people had already told him not to spit his tobacco juice on the floor. Every so often he put a cup to his mouth, irritated. "How long are we going to be here?" he asked Monte.

"Let me go check," our manager said. He went off to talk to the girl behind the counter. If he told her we needed to get onto a plane because we had a fight to get to, she would have probably called the police.

I looked around, holding back the exciting feeling that maybe, just maybe, this whole UFC 22 fight thing was actually going to happen. Assuming I could get on a plane.

I noticed a short, thin guy sitting off to the side a bit with wavy hair that looked familiar. He was bopping his head to some music. His eyes were two different colors and he kept sneaking glances at us. "Hey, Pat, do I know that guy? Is he a fan?"

"Jens Pulver," Pat said. "He's thinking about coming down to Iowa."

Monte came back, shaking his head. "They can get a few people on this flight, but everybody else has to wait and go a couple of hours later."

"Matt's cutting weight," Pat pointed out. "We've got to let him go so he can weigh in and start eating."

Monte nodded.

"I'll see you guys soon, I hope," I told them, grabbing my duffel bag.

"Yeah," Pat scoffed, spitting into his cup. "We all hope."

When I arrived in Lake Charles, a van was waiting for me, ready to drive me to whichever hotel I was staying at. Monte and the UFC had worked it all out, which was fine by me. Even when

I dropped my bag off in my room, I still was kind of in disbelief about the whole situation.

I went straight downstairs and there, in the flesh, was a big guy I recognized right away. Despite his nickname, Big John McCarthy wasn't particularly huge in person. Only when I shook his hand did I accept that I had entered into the world of the UFC. The Big Show. The fights where your friends don't have to drive; they can just turn on their TVs and watch you on their sofa, the way Mark, Janelle, and our buddies would be watching the next day. Mark was throwing a party and I was having to go to work.

"Weigh-ins happened earlier today," Big John said.

"Yeah, I got stuck at the airport," I explained. "I haven't even been able to cut weight really, just sitting there."

"Not a problem. I'll take you over here," Big John said, ushering me into a room. "You can weigh in right now." Since all these fighters think they know him from watching him on TV—and in a way, they kind of do—Big John makes it a point to treat them like they're one of the UFC guys already, even if it's their first fight. Or at least, that's how it was for me.

I stripped down to my underwear and got on the scale, my first official weigh-in for the UFC. It was just me, Big John, and another UFC person in a tiny room. Big John calibrated the weight. It was almost like this wasn't really that big of a deal, like I was weighing myself in my own bathroom. "You're a pound and a quarter over," he said.

"*Shoot.* I knew it. I can go run this off right now. Will you be around?" I asked, the adrenaline already going.

"Don't worry about it, Matt," he said. "You have until tomor-row."

"But I need food in me tonight. I'll be right back." I put my sweats on and stepped outside. The weather was mild and humid. I ran and ran and ran, as far as I could in one direction, until I got tired. I didn't have a rubber suit on so I ran some more just to make sure. Then I ran back. *You're in the UFC,* I told myself. *You've got to make weight. You've got to prepare your body to fight tomorrow night.* I ran back knowing that I had sweat it off. Big John was waiting for me. He understood.

The next morning Pat and Jeremy arrived at the hotel. Jeremy had a fight of his own coming up the same day, and Pat was there to corner both of us. Pat and I went over the strategy backstage. "This guy Val Ignatov is a Sambo champion," he explained. "Big on ankle locks. You're a wrestler, so you're going to be fine. Guys just don't get your ankles. Wrestlers are bad for ankle-lockers, because they just never see your ankles. Just stay on top, because if he gets on top that's how he's going to try and submit you. He's about your size. Says he's got a wrestling background."

"Well, I'm not worried about that." I already knew everything he was telling me, but it calmed me to hear it again. At this point it wasn't advice or knowledge; it was a mantra, repeated over and over, so that everything else was forgotten and my opponent became just a skilled obstacle made out of muscle and bone.

Pat looked me in the eyes. "Just relax and you'll do fine. It's going to be a fight just like any other fight."

I heard weird synthesizer music playing as I waited for

Ignatov to make his entrance. After a minute it was time for me to come out. The same strange theme music started to play for me, sounding more like an introduction for a *Star Trek* actor than for a fighter. But the smoke filled the entire doorway, and flashing lights illuminated the darkened arena. Already it was unlike one of Monte's small shows.

I walked out, slapping the hands of the few fans who bothered to stretch their arms out. Pat followed directly behind me as I made my way to the octagon. The fence was a little lower and the cage a little smaller than it is now. There were thousands of fans, but hundreds fewer than they had hoped for, judging by the empty seats. On the floor of the octagon itself was a cheesy drawing of a muscleman holding a belt—the UFC mascot or something. But there was Bruce Buffer in a black shirt and black suit making the announcements. This was it. This was the Big Show.

The fight was three rounds of me throwing the guy around, getting some ground and pound, and doing some damage. After fifteen minutes, they called us in the center and Bruce Buffer announced my win by unanimous decision. The fans cheered politely and then waited for me to get out of the ring. They were there to see Tito Ortiz fight Frank Shamrock, not some nobody from Hillsboro beat some nobody from Bulgaria. I hadn't expected a huge reaction, but I hadn't expected it to be like Japan, either. I thought about Mark and my buddies watching on TV back on the farm. They'd be excited. I knew they were jumping up and down back home, even if people in the arena weren't.

I followed Pat out of the octagon. He had been right that this was a fight just like any other fight, yet the consequences would be huge. I wasn't thinking about tomorrow or my next fight. I was thinking about everybody seeing me on TV back in Hillsboro. The first thing I did when I got back to the hotel room was pick up the phone and call my brother.

He picked it up after one ring. "Hey man, great job, just a great job!" he told me. He was even more pumped than I was, but then again I was crashing from the adrenaline.

"What was it like?"

"Nerve-racking!" Mark blurted. "Everybody was really getting into it over here. I should have set up a camera on top of the TV so you could watch us watching you."

I laughed. "Hey, so what did everybody say?"

"I'll tell you the truth. I think a lot of people had heard of you fighting, and had known this was something that you were doing. But then seeing you on TV, it kind of made them take a step back and realize this was something real. I mean, I don't think that guy really did anything to you at all, did he?"

"No," I said. "But I hurt his neck pretty bad with that one slam." The truth was that Val would never fight again, but I didn't know that at the time. "Say hi to everybody over there for me, all right?"

"You got it, brother. Listen, congratulations again. I'm real happy for you."

Several weeks after my fight I waited in our apartment for Janelle to come home. I looked around our place one more time. Nothing had many memories for me. The furniture had been things people didn't want to take with them after they graduated college; our sofa was meant to last four years, no more. I noticed all the refrigerator magnets from the places I'd been to. *Make sure to take those,* I thought. When she walked in the door, I couldn't deny how much fondness I felt for her as a person. "Hey, there's something that I've been wanting to talk to you about," I said.

She nodded. This had been a long time coming, and we both knew it. "Okay. Let's talk."

"I'm moving to Bettendorf, to train for fighting full-time," I told her. "This is something I think I can do. I'm pretty good at it and it's a chance to compete."

Janelle let out a deep breath. "Are you sure this is what you want?"

"Yeah, I'm sure."

She heard what I was saying, so I didn't really have to say it. "What about work?"

"I told them I couldn't coach anymore. The electrician gig will be here if I ever need to come back."

"Do you think you will? Come back?"

"I don't know," I admitted. "Monte told me that I"—*not we, Janelle*—"could stay with him until I"—*there it was again*—"get on my feet. Hey, you always said you were going to move back with your folks in Chicago when you were done here at Eastern."

It was a lot for her to take in. She sat there making arrangements in her mind about the future, rather than making arguments with her boyfriend about the present. But even though we both knew this relationship wasn't one that would last forever, I'm sure she had to be a little shocked that she was losing her man to anybody—even if it was the great Pat Miletich.

Musicians have showcases, businessmen have conventions, and fighters have tournaments. Since Pat was the UFC welterweight champion, there had to be some way to get other fighters recognized. Monte called all his toughest 170 pounders and decided to name his next tournament the "Best of the Best." If you couldn't be champion, at least you could be *that*. Fine by me. The event would be held in Wisconsin, a couple of months after my UFC debut.

It was a year since Dennis Hallman had choked me out in mere seconds. Monte had the event in the same exact place, eight fighters competing once again. I wasn't thinking about my only defeat, because I wasn't the same Matt Hughes anymore. Twice a day at Ultimate Fitness, we learned things the hard way—and my favorite way. Not listening to lessons, but with intense exercise. Like the shirts say, you sweat so you don't bleed.

Before the fights Monte set us up in a room and put a video camera in our faces for an interview. The lights felt intense and the chair I was sitting on felt too small. I don't know where my saliva went, but it sure wasn't in my mouth.

"So what do you want me to say?" I asked Monte.

"Just introduce yourself and talk a bit about the fight."

"Okay," I said. I noticed the camera and then glanced away. "My name is Matt Hughes. Wrestling background. I have, uh, Joe Doerksen the first round. Um, don't know a whole lot about him. I'm going to try and stay on my feet, box with him." The floor must have been interesting because I couldn't stop looking at it. "Should be a good tournament. To be honest I don't know who's going to win. Uh . . . to be honest it could be between four or five different guys." Now I stared up at the ceiling. "I think I, uh, need to be relaxed out there."

"Thanks, Matt," Monte said.

"Great!" I said, leaping off that chair.

This time when I was introduced in the cage, two people whistled in addition to the dozens cheering. The UFC fight had made a big difference. Joe and I hit the ground very quickly, and I got in a few solid punches which led to a big toss. I was surprised by how much I was dominating, because I knew Joe was no pushover. The one-sided first round ended and I walked back to my corner.

"Remember," the announcer took the opportunity to tell the crowd, "the more you cheer for your favorite fighter the harder he will fight! So make as much noise as possible." There was a burst of cheering.

Less than a minute into the second round I kneed Joe in the head, got in two jabs, and knocked him down. The ref stopped the fight and raised my hand.

"That first punch you threw knocked me out," Joe told me backstage.

"Really?"

"Yeah, but the second one woke me up!"

While we watched Dave Menne and LaVerne Clark rack up wins, Mark whispered some info about my next match. "This guy Tom Schmitz doesn't have much heart. When things get rough he's going to bail. So you know what you have to do."

"How do you know that?" I asked him.

"Some of the guys, they was telling me." Just like in high school everyone knows who the "friendly" girl is, and in business everyone knows who the meanest boss is, in fighting word gets around without you even realizing how it is that the information got there.

I nodded at my brother and stepped into the cage. The ref kept lifting his hands in the air to get the audience to cheer. A few guys in baseball caps and jeans hooted.

Tom and I tapped gloves. Then I came at him like a ball of fire, throwing punches and backing him against the cage. He fell to the ground and I stood over him, trapping him in the corner and raining down punishment. The second he kicked me away he called the ref over. The ref stopped the fight, and I was announced the winner. "I got a thumb in the eye," Tom explained to me later. "I couldn't continue." I didn't say anything. I had my win, and backstage people told me that they knew exactly what had really happened.

Then Mark and I sat and watched who would be fighting me in the finals. For two rounds LaVerne had his way with Dave. By the time the third round came, Dave had a softball growing out of the side of his head. It looked as if an alien had laid an egg in his face, the swelling was so bad. Now he was trying to take LaVerne down, not to win the fight, but just to keep Laverne from punching him so much. Then LaVerne began to float more like a caterpillar than a butterfly—he lost his footing and fell down. Dave saw it through his one good eye and was instantly on top, where he choked LaVerne out. The ref and the announcer didn't have to say anything to get the audience screaming. It was the kind of fight people hope they'll see when they pay good money to watch the sport.

I'm going to fight this guy that can't even see out of one eye, and he's tired. He's beat up, I thought. *It's going to be one easy fight.* Then Monte came up to talk to me. "That eye's real bad so Dave's not fighting in the finals," he let me know. "We're putting LaVerne in against you."

"That's fine," I said. MMA is not like boxing, where you can only use your fists to strike within a certain area, and you only try to knock your opponent out. You can knock a guy out, or submit him, or make him bleed until the ref steps in. MMA is a thinking man's sport. LaVerne "Fists of Fury" Clark trained at Miletich, but he didn't train very much. He remained pretty much a straight boxer that you can't really take down. And he definitely did not become a thinking man.

One strange thing LaVerne had shared with me was that he was under the impression that cats, somehow, were Satan. It didn't matter if one was walking across the street, a pet in the next house, or a picture on a calendar–he was terrified. Even the kitten in the "Hang in There!" poster either was the devil or had something to do with the devil, I'm not sure which; there are certain things you don't ask people to explain.

"It's going to be hard, but I think my wrestling credentials are enough that I can take him down," I told Mark. "Then I'm going to submit him. The only thing I have to worry about is him hitting me, because if LaVerne hits me with those thinly padded gloves, I'm going to be in trouble."

We tied up the first round until my foot hit something—it must have been what LaVerne's hit when he slipped. I lost my balance and he was on top of me for the rest of the round. I knew all I had to do was to keep him from hitting me. I played it safe and waited the round out, instead of trying to stand back up and giving him the opportunity to strike. Two minutes into the second round I took him down, and he made the most basic mistake people make when they're new to the sport: He gave me his back.

I got him in a rear naked choke, and he tapped out.

Immediately after, Monte was waiting for us outside the cage with a camera and a mike, getting us to talk big to get the crowd excited. "Normally in a sport you don't get two world-class fighters unless it's for millions of dollars. In this case it wasn't for that. What's next for you?" he asked.

"My promoter Monte Cox takes care of all that," I told Monte. "So I'll have to talk to him." I didn't get a belt like Dennis Hallman had. After winning three fights in one day and being named "Best of the Best," all I had was a handshake, a small check, and a bedroom in my manager's house in Bettendorf, Iowa. Some athletes would have felt at that moment like they were rich beyond their wildest dreams, but I couldn't when my bank account told such a different story.

A couple of months later I was in Georgia. This was the WEF, World Extreme Fighting: a big show but not the Big Show. Their deep pockets allowed them to pull in guys from all over the world, so I was not supposed to win this fight. I was just a wrestler training under Pat. Jorge Pereira was a Vale Tudo champion training under Renzo Gracie.

I was in the ring when I felt my elbow hit Jorge in the face, bone against bone. I hit him again and again. I saw the skin pop open and like a bull I aimed for that red. The ref tapped me on the shoulder and the round ended.

I watched what was going on from my corner. The ref stood close enough by him in case Jorge's knees buckled as he tried to see where his people were. The blood poured down Jorge's face from his forehead in neat lines, like bad stage makeup. The doctor held a towel to his face, waiting to see what was going on underneath the gore. A Renzo Gracie guy doesn't submit. If he was going down, it would have to be a doctor stoppage. Once the guy with the latex gloves got to see how bad the injury really was, he shook his head to the ref. The fight was over.

"I'm very satisfied with how the fight turned out," I told the ringside interviewer, barely winded.

"What comes next?"

"I have no idea. You'll have to talk to my promoter, Monte Cox," I said, to someone other than Monte for a change.

Backstage, some computer people were waiting for me. I stood against a white background as they took photos from every angle and used tape measures to find out my exact proportions. They said it would take a few months, but I would be in the first UFC video game. Kids all over America and the world would be able to skip over me when picking Mark Coleman or Kevin Randleman to be their character.

The rest of our crew did not fare so well that night. Jeremy

Horn lost a decision. Pat, with a messed up disc and a cortisone shot, couldn't coerce his back into round two. "You, you no longer campion!" Pele Landi yelled at Pat in his broken English. "You no longer campion anymore!"

Later that night I asked Pat, "What was Pele going on about?" All of us were in Mark Hanssen's room, waiting to pile into a van and drive back to the airport. "You've still got the belt."

Pat shrugged and reached for his cup. Stretching out his arm made him wince. "Yeah," he just said, shaking his head to himself.

"Your back's really messed up. You probably shouldn't have fought at all."

"Let's just go," he said.

"We're full," I heard Mark Hanssen tell some guy on the phone. "Well, I'd get a taxi if I were you."

"Who was that?" Pat wanted to know.

"I don't know, someone asking for a ride."

We dragged our luggage downstairs with the energy of factory workers at whistle-blowing time. As we loaded our stuff into the van, we saw Jens Pulver walking by, fresh off his thirty-three-second knockout win. "Hey, Jens!" Mark Hanssen yelled.

I could see Jens's lips moving, but he didn't look up and he didn't slow down. "What's that about?" I asked.

"Let me go see." Mark ran up to Jens. "What's going on? You all right?"

"You guys don't have room for *me*," Jens snapped. "Don't worry about *me*."

Mark Hanssen did kind of a double take. "What are you talking about?"

Jens looked up at him, annoyed that he had to explain what was so obvious. "I called the room to ask for a ride to the airport and you guys don't have room, right?"

"Jens, I didn't know it was you," Mark explained. "You could have been someone random or a fan or whatever asking to mooch a ride."

"I'll scoot over," I yelled out from the van. "We've got room for *you*. It could have been Jorge Pereira for all we knew."

"Yeah, okay," Jens grunted, following Mark to the van. He got in and slid the door shut.

"Are you going to be comfortable like that?" I asked him.

"I'm fine," Jens said. "There's plenty of space."

"Don't you need to change your diaper before we head out?"

"Shut up, Matt."

"Oh, I think someone's cranky! Hey, Mark, do you have this baby's bottle?"

A few months later I was in the United Arab Emirates with a bunch of other MMA fighters for the Abu Dhabi Combat Club. I wandered the lobby of our hotel looking for a phone. I picked it up and pressed a crazy amount of numbers to get my manager. There was a whistle in the phone that made me think Monte couldn't hear me. "Did I wake you up?" I said.

"No, I'm awake," he told me. "What time is it in Abu Dhabi?"

"I don't know. It's tomorrow. Or yesterday. Whichever. The thing is, they've got me in the wrong weight class."

"I already told you that they wanted you at 185."

"I *know* that," I said. "But they thought I was *starting* at 185 and they bumped me to 205, so now I'm bumped up *two* weight classes. Not only that, but Jeremy and I are in the same bracket in the tournament. The least they can do is put us on opposite sides of the bracket, you know?"

"All right, I'll see what I can do," Monte promised. "But I don't think the sheik's guy is going to be very cooperative."

And he wasn't, which was no surprise. The Abu Dhabi Combat Club tournament was open to the sheik of Abu Dhabi, his selected guests, and the fighters who would grabble on mats for their amusement. Striking was forbidden—too barbaric, I guess. The fighters wrestled on three big white mats in a huge room that could have been a hanger, while a few dozen men in T-shirts or robes looked down from the bleacher seats. Three matches would go on at once as we flopped around on the floor for His Excellency's enjoyment. Ringling Brothers had nothing on us.

Standing between me and recognition—and a big check—was Ricardo "The Big Dog" Almeda. Jeremy walked me to the mat. "He's a Renzo Gracie black belt," Jeremy told me. "Big time grappler. Watch his submissions and don't let him get anything started."

Ricardo didn't have a cornerman, and that made the difference. While he had to struggle in silence, trying to out-think me and out-maneuver me, I had a steady stream of advice pouring at me from Jeremy like an angel on my shoulder. "Lift up your hip . . . He's trying to get a triangle, don't let him . . . Move your head on out of there." He was the only guy speaking English in a room of men chattering in Arabic to one another and, from time to time, glancing down to see if anything interesting was happening.

My match went the whole time and I took the victory by points. The referee raised my hand. Four people noticed and they all applauded.

I returned the favor and cornered Jeremy for his quick submission victory. We sat down on benches carved of pure granite. I wiped my hands; the sand was everywhere. "Looks like it's you and me, buddy," I told Jeremy. "And then the winner has to take on Tito."

"You got the good wrestling," he pointed out. "I think your wrestling is better than his. You can get the takedown. I can't throw my elbows if this is no striking. I can't cut people here."

"He's really good defensively," I said. "I don't think you can take him down and I don't think you'd be able to submit him."

Our trainer buddy Matt Hume came over, having heard what we were talking about. "You're forgetting two things," Matt said, smiling.

"What's that?" I asked.

"Quickest submission gets $1,500. Best throw gets $1,500. If I were you guys, I'd just fake that fight."

I ran through the fastest combinations in my head. "Here's what we do," I told Jeremy. "I land a big throw right off the bat. After that I go for a submission and choke you out. At least we'll get to split $3,000 that way, and maybe if I get through Tito, even more."

Our grappling looked as real as day. The choreography was almost too good for the WWF. Unfortunately, we only got to split one check. One of Renzo Gracie's fighters basically walked into Renzo and Renzo got him in a guillotine in seconds. It looked to me like they didn't even have the decency to pretend.

Tito and I nodded at each other and touched gloves. His hair was freshly bleached. I wondered, *Is it L'Oreal, because he's worth it?* When I was locking up with Tito, I was surprised that he wasn't as powerful as I was. But the man had leverage, and technique, and after a ten-minute round the two of us were all tied up. Now it was overtime. The match got stopped and they restarted us. Tito got into a lot better position and I was forced to go for a guillotine. He picked me up and got the takedown, the points, and the match.

And the most important thing: the check.

CHAPTER 7

Nadir

"Take your right arm," Jeremy told me through the octagon wall. "Grab his left wrist, throw your elbow at his forehead, and never let go of the wrist."

I tried to imagine what Jeremy was seeing. I did exactly what my cornerman said, and the cut over Marcelo Aguiar's eye burst open. The ref pulled us apart. While Aguiar was getting looked at I got a towel and wiped his blood from all over my chest. The doctor barked at the ref. It was June of 2000 and my second UFC fight (this one, in Cedar Rapids) was over.

When I walked into our locker room backstage, the guys all applauded. No matter where I kept wiping with the towel, there was always some more of Aguiar's blood on me somewhere. "I'm going to hop in the shower," I told Monte.

I closed my eyes and let the water pour over me. I started singing "Folsom Prison Blues" to myself, not really caring if anyone could hear me or not. As my fingers ran through my hair I could feel the bumps where I got hit. I winced. *That one should have hurt.* The adrenaline was gone, and it was like I was waking up after a drunken night out. I had bruises all over, and I couldn't remember where they came from to save my life.

Afterward Monte and I got into his four-door Lincoln Mercury. The car had so many miles on it from traveling to shows that it deserved its own pension. "You know," Monte said, "it's getting harder to find guys to take you on."

"Hey, I'm training hard. Would you rather I lose?" I said, with a grin he knew too well. "You got my brother a couple of fights. He doesn't have my record."

"Mark doesn't have the reputation you have. And we both know his heart's not in it. He just tried it out."

"Yeah, you're right. He's got Emily now." I leaned back in the passenger seat, thought more about what Monte had just said, and then I got totally confused. "If people see me on TV, doesn't that make it *easier* for you to promote me in shows? Isn't that kind of the point?"

Monte sighed. "I can't put you in a show and have you fight nobody. Don't you get it? Remember that guy last month?"

"Sure do. 'Pain' Peters. A lot of people came down from Hillsboro to watch me beat the crap out of that guy."

"He was from Canada, okay? He had to drive down all the way from *Canada* to Illinois for that match. I couldn't find anyone closer to take you on. That's just how it is. Look, let me explain it to you like this. It's not just that you're winning. That's not the problem. How many of your fights have gone to decision?"

I went through my matches in my head. "Like four, I think."

"Right. And you've got over fifteen wins. You're physically beating people up. I'm not paying someone to go in there and lose; I'm paying someone to go in there and take a beating. There's a big difference. No one wants to walk out of a cage with black eyes and a bloody nose for a few grand, Matt."

"So what are you going to do?"

"I'm going to do what I've been doing. I'm paying these guys more than I'm paying you. You're still my investment. You're still my star. But in the short term, I've got to have bodies in there when I put on shows."

"I understand," I told Monte. But I could feel the tension building in my neck and shoulders.

Every day there were new people entering Ultimate Fitness, trying to throw down with me, Jens, Pat, and Jeremy. Some were short, some were tall; some were built, some were lean. It was like we were training in a clown car and we never knew the size and shape of the next clown we would be seeing.

I watched the biggest doofus I had ever seen in my life try to enter the fight room. Jens and I looked at each other and then back at the spectacle. I had to give it to the guy; he sure knew how to make an entrance. He had to bend over almost double to squeeze through that half-door.

He came right up to Jens and me. "Hey, are you Matt Hughes?" he said, eyes wide open. I'd seen puppies that were less needy and excitable.

"Yeah," I said. I shook his hand very quickly and tried to turn away. But he needed more.

"Hi, my name's Tim Sylvia," he said.

"Uh-huh."

"I just wanted to say that it's a big honor to meet you and to train with you here. I think you're awesome."

"Just be careful not to be a flailer and you'll be fine," I said, looking up at him and looking down on him at the same time.

"What's a flailer?"

"A flailer is a training partner who does stupid stuff," Jens interrupted. "They end up cutting you with an elbow or a head butt or a knee or something. So try to be careful."

"Yeah, yeah, sure, man. Hey, you're Jens Pulver, right?"

"I know who I am," Jens said, and walked away. I went after Jens and sat down by the mat. We started to wrap our hands. "I mean, I get how every idiot thinks that they're going to be a fighter," Jens said. "I get it. I just don't get why they have to come here and think they're going to train for a week and then become champs. Look at that guy."

"Don't sweat it," I told him. "If it's not him it'll be another one. And another, and another."

If I had to go all the way to the other side of the world to avenge my only loss, then so be it. It was UFC Japan, and even though there were hundreds more people in the audience this time, the sound level was very much the same as it had been at Monte's show. The cage had eight sides instead of four. But that didn't matter. What mattered is that I was looking into the eyes of the only man who had ever beaten me in a fight: Dennis Hallman. But that had been two years ago. Two years where my life was a cycle of training in the morning, then lunch, a nap, and back to the gym at night. Never missing a session.

It's one thing to know that you screwed up. It's another thing when somebody else knows you screwed up, and gives you a chance to fix it. "Everybody says that the first fight with Dennis Hallman was a fluke," the UFC matchmaker had told Monte. "Matt didn't know anything. Let's do the rematch. Matt's well known enough now."

Hallman and I paced by our corners in the octagon, anxious. We had waited two years just fine, but waiting two years and five minutes was intolerable. Even from across the octagon I could see the acne that riddled his back. There was no steroid testing in the UFC back then. Hallman liked to jump around in weight classes. I assumed he was using steroids, but I didn't care. If he felt like he needed them to take me on, to even the playing field, then whatever he had to do was fine by me. I was going to do whatever *I* had to do, in the cage, to get my loss avenged. I was going to lift him, ground him, and beat him in every sense of the word.

I ran into him, picked him up, and slammed him. I saw openings that I wouldn't have been able to see two years ago. I saw that he could get me into a triangle if he wanted, but this was my cage tonight. We'd only be doing what *I* wanted. Hallman wrapped his legs around my neck and I picked him up, again, and slammed him, again. Hard. As hard as I could.

There's a term in Brazilian jiu jitsu for someone who notices an opening and leaves that opening there for their opponent to exploit. That term is *idiot*.

Hallman slapped on a triangle and switched from that triangle to an armbar. I tapped and the fight was over. It hadn't even taken him thirty seconds to beat me. Again. Hallman started doing flips in the ring, literally.

I stood backstage with my hands on my hips. Even Mark, my cornerman, didn't have anything to say. Or whatever he said might as well not have been said, because what happened was so obvious and ridiculous I almost couldn't believe it. A camera light caught the corner of my eye and brought me back to reality. "Get him out of here!" I yelled to Mark, pointed at the cameraman and the friendly journalist who simply wanted an interview. "I just don't want that freaking camera here."

My brother kind of gestured and they nodded in understanding, maybe even in pity. If I had been overpowered and bloodied by a superior fighter, that just meant that he was better than I was that day. But to lose in seconds said that I didn't know what I was doing, that I didn't belong in the cage.

It said that I might be tough, but I wasn't a fighter.

A couple of weeks later I was at home in Bettendorf. I finished reading a letter that I had gotten in the mail. Then I went to the living room and handed it to Monte. "Take a look at this," I said. The envelope's return address said UFC.

He read it in front of me. Then he made as if to read it again, because he was thinking of how to make me feel better about it.

"They're telling me that they're done with me," I said. "Just like that. One fight and I'm cut from the UFC. How about a little bit of loyalty?"

Monte paused. "You know that that was part of your contract. This is a business."

I kept crossing and uncrossing my arms. "I know, I know," I eventually said.

"I'm going to give them a call about this," Monte told me.

I went upstairs and laid down on my bed. I looked at my feet, a good three inches higher than my head because of my crappy mattress. I glanced at my dresser, the only other piece of furniture that I owned, with drawers half-full of shirts I had gotten for free. I thought about how all the people back home in Hillsboro cheered when they watched me on TV. I wondered what Mark would tell them, what *I* would tell them, when they asked why I wasn't on TV anymore. *Because Matt had his chance and he blew it,* is why.

Monte knocked on my door and stepped in, leaning on my dresser. "I've got some good news and some bad news."

I turned around on my bed and looked at him. Good news is good, usually. "What'd they say?"

"This was a mistake. This paper got sent by mistake."

I just kept blinking. *"Really?"*

"Not so fast," he said, holding up his hand. "It's a mistake, but they're 'not going to rectify it at this time,' they told me. I talked to the guy and maybe they'll let you back in if you go out and prove yourself. You've got Kuwait in a couple of months. Go there, get the win, and it'll be like this whole thing never happened."

* * * *

Several days later we were training at Ultimate Fitness when Jens pulled me aside. "Her name's Brandy," he let me know. "I asked around with the guys. And let me tell you, she's a bit *different.*" We sat at the corner of the mat. I wished our room had a glass wall, so I could look out and see if she was there. I was never sure if she was around or not.

"Different how?" I said. "Well, there's Jens different and then there's Bobby different. Is she more like you where she likes drama and makes things crazy, or is she more like Bobby where she's crazy and drama is the by-product?"

Jens rolled his eyes, then considered a second and answered. "I don't really know. And the thing is, I think Bobby has my handwraps." Jens "Little Evil" Pulver just sat there, weighing his next move.

I looked across the room at Bobby Hoffman. Six foot two, 240 pounds of pure force. "If something happens, I've got your back," I told my little buddy. "Heck, everybody's got your back in here."

Jens kind of nodded, and kind of gulped, too. He stood, walked over to Bobby, and looked up into his face. I had never seen Jens so polite. "I think you've got my handwraps."

"What?" Bobby snorted.

Across the room I was spring-loaded to strike. I played through the scenarios in my head: *I have time to grab a weight and smash Bobby's head in if I have to. He'd only be able to hit Jens a couple of times. I'm pretty sure no court would convict me.*

"My handwraps," Jens repeated as calmly as he could. "They're smelly and they're hard to work with so I just leave them here."

Bobby shrugged. "A lot of people leave handwraps here. What's your point?"

"Mine say 'JP.' I wrote it on the end."

Bobby rolled his eyes. He grabbed the wrap and started unfurling, tossing out fabric like he was a mummy. "There, you see?" he told Jens. "It doesn't say your name. Are you fucking happy?"

"Actually," Jens said, forcibly calm, "I only wrote it on one. So it could be the other one you have."

Bobby scowled down at Jens, getting more wound up as he unwound the second wrap. Jens looked back at me and saw that I was there, arms crossed.

There it was on the wrap: JP. Jens Pulver. Bobby threw it on the ground. "I wasn't stealing them," he growled.

"I didn't say that," Jens replied.

Bobby began to pace. I hated when Bobby began to pace. "Now everybody's going to think I'm a thief!" he yelled.

"It was a mistake," Jens said, not taking a step back but not cocking a fist either. "I needed them for practice. If I'm not using them you're more than welcome to them. I don't care."

"This is fucking bullshit. I thought those were mine, and now I don't have any fucking handwraps! What the fuck am I supposed to do?" The other fighters kept on wrapping their hands, paying Bobby no mind. The sound of him screaming was like the sound of a guy hitting a pad. Loud, violent, but commonplace and irrelevant. "I can't do shit here, so I might as well go home and do nothing there!" He stormed for the door, and soon stormed into a life of violence, warrants, and judges.

When Bobby was gone, Jens turned back to me. He saw the serious expression on my face and started to laugh a little bit. That made me laugh too.

The health club members were not as used to the commotion as we were. They stared at us like men staring at wild dogs, careful not to make eye contact but making sure they knew where we were at all times. Among them was that good-looking girl from around the gym. I gave her the elevator eyes—checking her out from top to bottom and then back up from bottom to top. From the stomach up, she was really put together well. The boobs were fake, but not in an obvious way, and she had long, straight, brown hair down to the middle of her back. She had a great complexion—not tan, but not as pasty white as me. She did have a little bit of hips on her, but here she was doing something about it.

Screw it. I hunched under to get out from that half-door and just walked up to her. "Hey, I've been seeing you around here a lot. I'm Matt."

"Hey, Matt," she smiled, one of those smiles you give to people you've known for a while—or been wanting to know for a while. "I'm Brandy. What was all that yelling about?"

"I wish I knew!" I said, smiling right back.

"So you're one of them fighting guys, huh?" she said. "It seems pretty intense."

"It is, it is."

"I don't know too much about it."

"Well, I think I can show you some moves."

*   *   *   *

A few weeks later I was on the plane to the Middle East. Mark sat next to me. He sniffed hard like a dog, trying to clear his nostrils so that he could breathe. "You'd think that if you pay one thousand dollars for a ticket you wouldn't have to smell smoke on a freaking plane," he declared.

"It's not like we're in the smoking section," I said.

My brother sat up in his seat and turned around. Two rows back sat a dark-skinned man, puffing away and looking out the window. Mark turned back around. "Two rows back. Do you see that, Matt?"

"Oh, it's terrible, just terrible. Hey, you're getting a free trip to Kuwait, so you sit there and you be quiet."

"I don't even know what Kuwait *is*."

"You just worry about helping me take this tournament."

The plane could not land soon enough for us. We got our luggage from overhead and filed out with Monte, Pat, and Jeremy. As soon as we got into the airport we saw our contact, dressed in those robe-dress-shirt things they have over there. "Please come with me," he greeted us. "The sheik has arranged for a special room at the hotel for you all."

We followed the guy to our waiting town car. I held back and grabbed Monte's arm. "The sheik of Kuwait is behind this? Is that like a prince or something?"

"They're big into the word 'sheik,'" he said. "There're hundreds of them. This guy just happens to have a training facility, so he wants to see a fight."

As we drove by the hotel, it looked like something out of

a magazine that no one in Hillsboro would ever subscribe to. The style of it was completely foreign, very much looking like it belonged in this other country, but at the same time it was clearly a place where millionaires from all over the world would feel at home.

Our hotel was the other one. The *kind of* nice one. The carpeting, the beds, that lamp that's in every hotel room but nowhere else—it might as well have been the Best Western, or maybe the Best Middle Eastern. Jeremy sat playing his Game Boy while Pat spat in his cup. "When's weigh-ins?" Mark asked Monte. "I bet the guys want to eat before the fight."

"Let me call and find out," Monte said, going for the phone. He picked out a little piece of paper from his wallet and began dialing.

"Wow, Mark, you're earning your keep already," I told my brother. "That's pretty good. Always thinking!"

Monte got off the phone. "Hey, listen up guys." Jeremy hit pause and looked up. "They're saying that they're not even going to have weigh-ins."

"That's bullshit," Pat said. "We want weigh-ins. You don't fly eight guys in from all over the world, tell them that there's going to be weigh-ins, and there's no weigh-ins. We want to see where everybody's at. You tell them that we're not fighting unless there's weigh-ins."

"You guys okay with that?" Monte asked.

"Absolutely," I said.

"Go for it," Jeremy added, going back to saving Zelda.

*   *   *   *

Later that day we all got together with our "peers," so to speak. Pele Landi was standing around, keeping to himself. The American guys were all in a corner, almost in a huddle. The weigh-in room wasn't filled with excitement; it was more like a group of people trapped in a blackout. People craned their necks trying to listen in on conversations, in the hopes that someone received some information on just what it was that we were supposed to do, what the exact rules were. "I saw Big John here," Pat said. "It can't be that different."

"I just don't want anybody to pull my hair," Carlos Newton said. "Make sure nobody pulls my hair."

"Nobody is going to pull your hair, Carlos," I told him.

"I just want to be sure. I don't want anyone grabbing my hair."

"Look at the size of that Russian guy," I said, pointing to Monte. "He's got to be way over."

"That's the sheik's main man. They moved him here from Russia and I think they think this tournament is going to make an easy name for him."

The Russian finally got on the scale. My prediction was right: He was way heavy, at least fifteen pounds over.

"You think they're still going to let him fight?" I asked Monte.

He just looked at me as if I were a slow learner. Monte was a promoter. He knew how these things worked. "Yes, Matt. I'm pretty sure they will."

*   *   *   *

The following day Pat leaned over and whispered in my ear right as I was getting into the cage. "You can't stand up with him!" he insisted. "You *can't* stand up with him."

I remembered Pele Landi beating Pat and yelling in Pat's face, "You're no longer campion!" in his broken English. As we circled each other in the octagon, I held my fists up and looked for an opening to take him down. We rolled around on the ground, neither of us doing much damage. When we stood up, he did a little dance like some sort of Brazilian bird. But I only thought about taking it back to the ground.

I tried shooting in to take him down, and he brought his knee up a little bit, catching me in the head. I dropped to the floor and, before Pele could get a third punch in on me, Big John stopped the fight.

Pele had now beaten me, too.

Pat jumped up and leaned over the cage wall. "That's not a fair stop!" he screamed. "You shouldn't have stopped that! He didn't even fall down!" Then Pat looked into my eyes and kind of shivered. "Okay, I see," he told Big John.

Pat put his arm around me and he and Mark walked me back to the dressing room. "What did he stop it for?" I asked Pat.

"Pele got you with a knee. You're going to be fine."

"How long did it go?"

"About five minutes. Have a seat."

I sat down and Pat and Mark looked at each other and back at me. It was like I was drunk and they were wondering if I was going to puke. My head felt light so I rested it on my hands. "Your shoes, Mark."

"What's that, Matt?"

"You got those shoes at Christmas."

"That's right, Matt. I did."

I looked back up at Pat. "How long did the fight go?"

"Five minutes, Matt," he said, very, very, slowly.

"Oh. And why did Big John stop the fight?"

"You got kneed in the head," Pat repeated. "A flash knock-out."

"He's on Queer Street," Mark said. "Is he going to be all right?"

Pat stared into my eyes, looking for something—only he knew what. "He'll be fine," he assured my brother.

"Your shoes, Mark. You got those at Christmas!"

A week or so later I was back in Bettendorf. I had recovered enough from my flash knockout that I could actually have a serious conversation with Monte. "I've never seen a guy this depressed at Hooters," Monte said.

I don't know if the waitress smiled extra hard because I was being so sullen, or if it just seemed that way because I hadn't been around a smiling woman for weeks. Or maybe she was smiling because I was the first guy in a while to look her in the face. "Monte, the more I think about it, the more I think I've made a big mistake."

"With what?"

"With everything. With this whole fighting thing. Maybe this sport's a lot tougher than I thought. Maybe I'm not the fighter I thought. Don't get me wrong, I like you and I like your family. But it's not the same as living in my own place. I gave up coaching and a well-paying electrician job, and for what, you know?"

For once, Monte the promoter who convinced people for a living didn't have words. "Come on, don't think of it like that," was all he could offer.

"Maybe I'm not training hard enough. Maybe I'm not training right. Maybe I'm not training in the right place. Two years of training twice a day and this Hallman guy submits me again in under a minute. I think I'm getting so much better, but it's like it's a *joke*, Monte. I don't blame the UFC for dropping me. I don't. A guy who can't carry a fight for them past the first round doesn't deserve it. Do you really think they'd let me fight there again?"

"Yeah," he nodded. "I sure as hell do."

I shook my head. "Who knows if there's even going to be a UFC?"

"The UFC isn't going anywhere. It got bought out. And you know perfectly well there's plenty of money to be had in smaller shows. You need to fight to get your confidence back. You're good at this."

"I just need to think about some stuff." When we drove home we talked about other things, but those same questions kept bouncing around inside my head. On the machine at home was a message from Brandy. I picked up the phone and dialed her.

"Where were you?" she demanded.

"I went to Hooters with Monte. Is that okay with you?" I asked sarcastically.

"I told you I didn't want you going to that place," she said.

"You know, you can't always be wanting to know where I am and telling me where to go and who I can and can't see."

"I just like to know where you are. That's not weird. It's not weird that I don't want you going to *Hooters*, Matt."

I wanted to slam down the phone, but I held myself back. "You know what, I'm in a really rough patch and I don't think we should see each other for a while."

Silence. "Are you sure?"

"Yeah, I'm pretty darn sure."

Even though days passed between the time I hung up the phone and the next time she called me, it almost felt like I hung up and then picked up the receiver a second later. There was something that she needed me to know.

She needed me to know that she was pregnant.

CHAPTER 8

A New Hope

It wasn't hard for me to figure out where I needed to be when Brandy told me the news. Like any wounded animal, I went back to my home to see what I could do to make things better. I went back to stay in Hillsboro.

Dunn's Real Estate has the best view of Hillsboro's Main Street—all three blocks of it. The two-story buildings have flat fronts, almost like a Hollywood stage set. I had my feet up on the table, leaning back in a chair, and was trying to talk to the two Dunn's ladies like I was normal, like everything was fine. From the window I saw a familiar face on someone walking into Sullivan's pharmacy. The woman looked just like my "kid sister" Audra. Or, to put it another way, this was the woman who Audra had grown up into. Her little son, Joey, wasn't with her right then, and Joey's dad wasn't with them ever.

I got up and followed her into the pharmacy. She was dressed in jeans and a loose T-shirt, but from the way it hung on her I could see she still had a tight figure. Her brown-blond hair was long and straight, the same way she always wore it. I waited until she was distracted, looking at some greeting cards, before I struck.

To get her attention, I smacked her hard right on the butt. She jumped a bit and then turned around, pissed. But she quickly smiled when she saw who it was. She wasn't a little girl anymore–twenty-one years old is a lot different from thirteen or fourteen.

"I haven't seen you in a long time," I said.

"Yeah? And whose fault is that?"

"Maybe we can go somewhere and talk."

"Okay. My car's right out there," she suggested.

We sat down in her teal green Honda Civic. "I don't know if you heard, but my girlfriend's pregnant," I told her, flat-out. "*Ex*-girlfriend."

"I take it this was unplanned?" she said.

"You could say that," I answered immediately. Then I thought for a second. "Actually, scratch that. She told me she was on the pill. I mean, yeah, sometimes things happen . . . But I don't know. She's keeping it. We talked a bit, and there's no two ways about it. She's keeping it."

"So are you going to marry her or something?"

I considered that idea for the hundredth time. "I can't. I mean, we're just different people. For an example: One time she came home and gave me a 'Property of Brandy' sweatshirt."

"What's a 'Property of Brandy' sweatshirt?"

"She took a sweatshirt, turned it inside out, and instead of 'Property of Lincoln College,' it said 'Property of Brandy.'"

Audra made a face. "Yeah," I said, "we're different people."

But Audra and I weren't so different. We were still family, even if we hadn't seen each other in forever, and having family hear what I was thinking and listen to me, just really listen, made me feel like I was finally catching my breath.

"I've got to go . . . ," she said eventually, totally apologetic.

"Maybe we can talk a bit more. You can come on over. Do you think your mom would watch Joey?"

"I'm sure she would, but I thought you were in Iowa?"

"I'm staying with Mark and Emily while I sort some things out."

She nodded. "Okay. Well, give me a call." I got out of the car and shut the door. I didn't bother watching her drive away; I knew I'd be seeing her again soon enough.

A few days later I was at Mark and Emily's house. I'd noticed it was decorated all Emily, and no Mark. The fridge was covered with photos of people who looked just like her, and there were little trinkets with warm sayings hanging on walls, sitting on counters, filling up shelves. The pillows had patterns on them that matched the drapes.

Audra and I lay on the couch, side by side, with my feet by her head. She was watching *Bounce*, but I was staring right at her. Her jeans had a hole down by her knee, and I took my hand and put it in the tear. I started playing with her skin. She hadn't shaved her legs and I could feel her tense up with embarrassment. I didn't care, and I didn't pause. At the end of the film I asked her, "Do you want to go upstairs?"

She thought about it for a second. "Um . . . I guess," she said finally.

We went upstairs to my little bedroom, me leading the way. The hardwood floors were scuffed, there was a window through which we could see the trees and fields, and the bed in the corner had crisp white sheets. I sat down on the bed, and she sat on top of me. "So what's your favorite color?" I asked her.

"Green," she said.

"Mine, too." Then I made my move, putting my arms around her and leaning in for a kiss. Audra kissed me back. It felt good to be with someone and not think about anything, just for one night. I held her, and all we did was talk. But it was the first night in a long time where things were going in my direction.

In early 2001 I was fighting at a Rings show in Iowa. "Take the arm!" my opponent whispered in my ear. "Take the arm!"

He had left his arm exposed and wanted a quick submission from me. I was the one dominating the fight, and he wanted the punishment to end—so much so that he was telling me how to end it. I had entered the sport to compete and to make money, but my opponents weren't any competition and they were earning more than I was. I still had a little more aggression to get out before I was going to let him off the hook.

I got up, forcing him to get up as well, and I delivered a hard jab right into his face. I shot in and took him down. Only after a few more elbows was I ready to take his arm and submit him.

I felt him tap and another ref raised my arm again. Pat and

Jeremy came into the ring and patted me on the back. They congratulated me as enthusiastically as if I had just finished a jigsaw puzzle. This victory had been inevitable, unmemorable, and pointless.

In May of that year we were backstage for UFC 31 in Atlantic City. "How you doing, buddy?" I asked Pat.

He rolled his shoulders and tilted his head from side to side. "Neck's still tight," he told me.

I put my hand on his neck and gave him a brief massage. "Do you want me to get some Bengay for that, Grandpa?"

"Maybe later."

He looked confident walking out to the octagon to face Carlos Newton, and Jeremy and I proudly walked behind him in his shadow. I watched the fight from Pat's corner.

Pat didn't resist much as Carlos went for takedowns; once they were on the ground, Carlos couldn't do anything. I watched Pat dance circles around Carlos's limbs on the ground, almost literally. They stood up and Pat started firing away punches and kicks. I knew Pat well enough to understand that he was having fun, doing what he loved, and doing it well. Carlos's strength was his grappling knowledge, but Pat's grappling knowledge was so great that it overflowed into other people and spawned an entire camp of fighters in Bettendorf.

By the third round, Pat was bored. If the fight had stopped right there and went to the judges, it would have been a unanimous decision. But Pat wanted the knockout—not the submission and *definitely* not the decision—and he was confident he could get it. Pat got up quickly. It was time to put the nails in Carlos's coffin.

A lot of times in sports movies you'll see the underdog pull off some amazing play and defeat the champion, the overwhelming favorite. Through this one-in-a-million stroke of luck, through this miracle, he pulls out the impossible victory. All the spectators can do is drop their jaws in slow motion. I definitely felt mine drop that night.

Carlos grabbed Pat's neck and held it as if to give him noogies or something. He squeezed as hard as he could. I'd seen a lot of things, training twice a day for two years in a fighters' camp, but I had never in my life seen the move that Carlos pulled on Pat—nor have I seen it since. The move, I found out much later, is called a "bulldog choke," and it's such a freak move that the first thing you'll find when you Google it is Carlos Newton versus Pat Miletich.

I saw Pat tap his fingers against Carlos, and then I thought, *Pat just tapped out.* I watched them raise Carlos's hand, and my eyes must have been spinning like slot machines because of my total shock. I looked over at Pat. He grabbed his mouthpiece out of his mouth and yelled, "*Fuck!*" He threw his mouthpiece as hard as he could. They put the belt around Carlos's waist.

Pat Miletich was no longer the only man ever to be UFC welterweight champion.

A few minutes later the only sound in the locker room was Pat pacing and muttering to himself and to us. "I just wanted to get up," he said, "because if I got back on my feet I was going to get him. Things were coming together. My next combination was going to land and he was going to fall."

I thought back on all the times I was coaching and things didn't go right for one of my guys. But there was nothing I could have said, and especially not to Pat. It wasn't a mistake. It wasn't a lack of strength or endurance or stamina. It was a fluke, plain and simple. I almost wanted to ask Pat what that move even was, because if you had a question about fighting, he was the person you asked. But I just stood there, trying to make sense of what I had just seen.

One week later I was in Omaha and I was still somewhat dazed by Pat's defeat. One of the fighters, John Cronk, seemed to believe that he could knock out either me or Pat in the first round of a fight. He was stupid enough to believe this and stupid enough to tell people. I didn't care how stupid he was; I was going to have to beat the facts into him myself.

There were two locker rooms backstage. One was sort of big, just a room, and the other was also an empty space, but smaller. I was sitting with Jens and Jeremy when John Cronk walked in and made himself at home. I looked around and no one seemed to notice or care. *Do I say something or not?* It was like I was in *Seinfeld. If not for me, at least for Pat,* I decided. "What are you doing?" I barked.

John ignored me, pretending not to hear.

"I said, *what are you doing?*" He slowly looked up at me, like a kid caught shoplifting. "You can't be in here. This is our locker room.

There's another locker room you can go sit in, I don't care. You can sit out and watch the show. But you're not going to sit in here."

Cronk got up, walked out without looking at anyone, and went to sit in the hallway.

Jens managed to wait until he left the room before bursting out laughing. "Ah, ha, ha, ha! Did you see the look on his face?"

"Hey, my opponent's not going to be in my locker room, watching me buddy up with my friends and have a good time."

"Yeah, but did you see him?" Jens said, in hysterics. "Ah, ha, ha, ha!"

Right before the match started, I pulled the ref aside. "This is a guy that said some things about me and Pat," I told him. "This is a guy that's probably going to need to tap out. If he gets in a bad situation, make him tap out; don't stop the fight."

The ref nodded. The fight began, and I did my job: I made John Cronk bleed.

For the next few months Monte made sure I kept fighting, winning, and earning. Bruce Nelson. Scott Johnson. Chatt Lavender. Then it was time for Kanehara, in Japan.

Before the fight Jeremy told me, "He's kind of a big deal over here."

I grinned. "You've been watching those tapes again."

"I've been watching my tapes," he confessed. "His style is, he's not quick throwing punches, but he always counters with punches. So be aware of that. I think he's got like ten pounds or so on you too."

"I'm not worried about that," I told him. I'd been throwing weights around for weeks, pushing all my tension out through my hands and into the steel. I was stronger than I'd ever been, benching 305 pounds, and I knew that meant that I was stronger than Kanehara had ever been too.

When I faced him I could see that he was massive, but massive doesn't mean anything in a fight—especially in MMA. Right off the bat, I got hold of his leg and swung him around and onto the ground.

"Untangle your left arm," Jeremy called from my corner. "Untangle your left arm."

I ignored him. I was aware of Kanehara pulling me, but my arm wasn't going anywhere I didn't want it to go. I pushed him around on the floor. When we stood up I picked him up and flung him. I flipped him over so hard he landed on his head, vertically. For fifteen minutes, I tossed him around the ring like a cat playing with a mouse, winning the decision. I returned to the United States $20,000 richer—cash.

"Some important people saw that fight," Monte told me.

"Oh, yeah? No one in Hillsboro could see it. No one in Bettendorf could see it."

"The UFC called, Matt. They want you back after what you did to that guy. You're going back to the Big Show."

When I got back home a couple of days later, there was a letter from Audra. I put down my luggage by the door, tossed my jacket over a chair, and tore it open.

> Matt,
>
> I have been giving our relationship some thought. For Joey's sake, I don't think this is going to work out. My life is perfect.
>
> Audra

I reread it several times. Then I almost laughed. Does she think it's going to end just like that? Like I'm not going to fight for her?

I took out the present I had gotten for her, a rose encased in crystal. I sat down at the table, found a piece of paper, and thought about what I'd write. I knew she'd be reading it over and over, just like I had.

> Audra,
>
> I was thinking about you on this trip & I saw this Rose & thought of you. Your mom would say that it is just something to dust around, but I still want you to have it.
>
> In your letter you say your life is perfect. Don't you think it could be better?
>
> Love, Matt

* * * *

"Hey Matt, it's Audra."

"Hey."

"My mom told me to call you and thank you for the rose."

"Did she say it would just be something to dust around?"

"Yeah," Audra admitted. She waited for me to say something else, which meant she wanted me to keep talking. "So how's everybody?" she asked finally.

"They're thinking of bringing in Dennis Hallman to fight Jens for the title. You met Jens, right?"

"Yeah."

"He was in the back of Monte's car and just went crazy. 'No, I will not fight him. I won't fight him. I'll give up that title not to fight him.' Then in the same sentence, the same breath even, 'Ha! Dennis Hallman thinks he can beat me? You know what? I *will* fight him! I'll just knock him out! One punch, and I'll knock him out. Yeah, yeah, they think I'll fight him? I'd rather retire and never fight again than fight that Hallman. He thinks he's going to make it big trying to fight me, and I'm not doing it. But he better watch out, because my one punch . . . !'"

She started laughing. "Stop. You're making this up."

"I'm no psychologist, so I can't tell you where he's at mentally. I don't know if he's bipolar, tripolar, or . . . Hey, how about I give you a call next week and we can get together?"

"That's fine," she said.

"Okay, great." I hung up the phone, more than a little

excited. *Most people would think she didn't care at all, but that's her version of enthusiasm,* I thought. *It's funny knowing how someone thinks, reading between the lines.* I stopped for a second. *I'm thinking about how she thinks, all the time. Is this what it's like for Mark with Emily?*

CHAPTER 9

Zenith

Tim Sylvia walked over to me during practice. His back was hunched a bit, like Pat's is, but Pat I could look in the face. "Can I talk to you for a second?" he asked.

"Sure thing." He led me into an office and we sat down on two chairs.

"No one here's got a problem with me except you," he began. "When I first started, Jens would say I'm a fat piece of shit who's never going to amount to anything, and he'd get me crying, but now even Jens likes me. Is there a problem?"

He was waiting for me to tell him that it was a big misunderstanding or to apologize, like I wasn't aware of what I was doing. "Yeah, I really don't like you," I told him.

"Is there a reason why?"

"I don't think you're a team player and I don't think you work very hard," I said.

"How am I not a team player?"

"Remember that whole thing with that girl?" I reminded him.

He waved those ridiculously long arms of his in the air. "They weren't even going out!"

"Yeah, but you knew that your teammate had a thing for her and you went for it anyway. But I don't even care about that. I'm talking more about training. When somebody's got a fight coming up, everybody tries to make sure the guy's got some training partners to get ready. Everybody tries but you. Your first priority is always Tim, and I don't think that's a good attitude." I wasn't angry or even annoyed. I had as much emotion as if I were talking about the contents of a fridge. "I don't think you work very hard, either. You're a little sore and you don't come in. Jens, who's a champion, has been sore and he's come in. Pat, who's a champion, has been sore and he's come in. I can't tell you how many times I've been sore. No one's ever going to be 100 percent. You just suck it up and you do it, period."

I didn't care one way or another what he said in response–I assumed he'd get defensive or angry. But he didn't; he was reasonable. "I'm actually hurt to hear you say that. I've been a huge fan of yours for a long time and I've been trying to model myself on some of your work ethics, and the way Jens works out and stuff like that, and it's too bad you feel like this. There's nothing more that I want than to be accepted by you and the rest of the guys."

"You don't become accepted by buying yourself a ticket to Vegas, following us around while we're there when no one really invited you, and then crying–again–when Jens calls you out on it."

"Is there anything I can do to be friends with you?"

"Well, right now I have enough friends and I don't need any more friends," I said. "Is that it? Are we done here?"

He let out a deep breath. "Yeah, I guess."

"Good." I got up and left.

Soon enough it was fall, harvest time at the farm. I drove the combine through the acreage, doing beans. The fields were knee high with the brownish dead plants, low to the ground but not so low that I was gathering up dirt. I scanned the rows for rocks or any junk that might have fallen in. The hum and the vibration of the combine felt like a massage. I stopped the combine and pulled its auger over a wagon. I pulled the lever and the bin began unloading. I walked around and saw some of the beans spilling out. *Shoot, it's got a leak.* I drove the combine up to our workshop and got two wrenches. I was taking the cover off when the phone rang. I picked it up and cradled it against my ear.

"Hey Matt, it's Monte. I've got you back in the UFC and I've got you back in a big way. You ready for this? They want you to take on Carlos for the title."

I didn't stop looking over the combine, and I could hear its engine running. "What about Pat? When does he get his rematch?"

"They don't want to give him one, but they are giving him a say as to who gets to take on Carlos," Monte explained. "You're next in line from the gym."

"So, what, they're trying to force him out and I'm supposed to help them with that?"

"Matt—"

"That fight's not mine," I said, cutting Monte off. "That fight's Pat's. I don't want to fight for it. Heck, it's not just Pat's fight, it's Pat's *belt*. Now, everyone knows that fight was a fluke, and that's why Pat needs to get in there and settle this. There's one world champion and that's Pat Miletich."

"Jens is a world champion too," Monte pointed out.

I put down my wrenches and thought for a second. I remembered Jens after he defended his lightweight title for the first time and they rebelted him in the octagon. He walked around the airport with both belts strapped around him like sashes: Miss Teen Ultimate Fighting Champion.

Mentally, the world champion title was like the four-minute mile for me. The four-minute mile was considered to be impossible, but after it was accomplished for the first time, someone else did it again just six weeks later, and then lots of people did it because they knew that they *could*. Now I started to think that *I* could.

"You know what?" I told Monte. "If you can get Pat to call me himself and tell me that this is what he wants, then I'll consider it."

Less than a day later I was on the phone with Pat. "You've got to take this fight," he told me. "If you don't take this fight, someone else is going to take this fight and they're going to become the world champion. You *have to* take this fight."

"Okay," I said. "I'll get off the farm and start training."

A few weeks before Thanksgiving 2001, I was in Vegas for my UFC 34 fight. Backstage, I noticed the souvenir program when

Mark and I were cowboys at an early age. Mom couldn't tell us apart in this picture.

From the collection of Linda Hughes

I am the one wearing number 19.

From the collection of Linda Hughes

Mark and I play with our big sister Beth.

From the collection of Linda Hughes

From the collection of Linda Hughes

While celebrating our fourth birthday, Mark and I see
who can blow out more candles. (I am on the right.)

From the collection of Linda Hughes

The Hughes family poses long enough for a family photo.

From the collection of Linda Hughes

The culmination of my first IHSA state wrestling championship.

Courtesy of Ken Meade

Yearbook photo of the senior football players at Hillsboro
High School in 1991. (I am wearing number 40,
and Mark is number 42.)

From the collection of Linda Hughes

Wrestling in the IHSA state wrestling championship.

Courtesy of Ken Meade

MARK R. HUGHES   MATTHEW A.
                   HUGHES

SENIORS ⟨21⟩

Our senior pictures as found in our Hillsboro High School
yearbook. Mark's senior quote: "Born to be an athlete, Live
to defeat, Born to be the best. Live to shame the rest."
My senior quote: "Wrestling is my favorite sport,
but girls are my favorite."

From the collection of the Hughes family

Graduation from Lincoln College in the spring of 1994
(from left: Mark Hughes, Marc Fiore, Chad Red, DeMarco Suggs, and me).

From the collection of the Hughes family

Competing in college for Eastern Illinois University (EIU).

With my coaching staff at the
NCAA Division I National
Wrestling Championships
(from left: Vladimir Anoshenko,
Joe Daubach, me, and
Ralph McCausland).

From the collection of Linda H.

From the collection of the Hughes family

Toasting my brother
and new sister-in-law,
Emily, at their
wedding.

One of the most memorable pictures in my fighting career. I am shown just before slamming Carlos Newton to the ground in UFC 34 to win my first UFC welterweight title.

Photograph provided by Zuffa, LLC © 2007. All rights reserved.

Photograph provided by Zuffa, LLC © 2007. All rights reserved.

I am preparing to enter the ring for my bout with Sean Sherk in UFC 42.

From the collection of the Hughes family

Audra and Emily held a suprise birthday party for Mark and me for our thirtieth birthdays (from left: Robbie Lawler, Mark, Tim Sylvia, me, and Pat Miletich).

From the collection of the Hughes family

A favorite time at the Hugheses' house—dessert time.

ERDOG·COM

Photograph provided by Zuffa, LLC © 2007. All rights reserved.

Sinking a rear naked choke hold that ends my first fight with Frank Trigg in UFC 45.

Mark and I pose with my new brother-in-law Tommy Moore at my wedding.

From the collection of the Hughes family

Helping with a concrete pour at Rancho 3M in Guadelupe, Mexico, near Fabens, Texas

From the collection of Nathan Rosario

Playing with the children during one of my trips to the Rancho 3M orphanage.

From the collection of Nathan Rosario

Photograph provided by Zuffa, LLC © 2007.
All rights reserved.

UFC president Dana White stands between me and UFC hall of famer
Royce Gracie at the weigh-in prior to UFC 60.

Photograph provided by Zuffa, LLC © 2007.
All rights reserved.

UFC referee Big John McCarthy prepares to stop the fight during UFC 60: Hughes vs. Gracie.

From the collection of the Hughes family

The family visits Disneyland with
Willa Ford and Chuck Liddell shortly
after my victory over Gracie in UFC 60.

From the collection of Steve McLaughlin

The Orpheum marquee in my hometown of Hillsboro
is changed after my defeat of Royce Gracie.

From the collection of the Hughes family

Did someone call for a doctor? I prepare for the birth
of my daughter, Hanna.

From the collection of the Hughes family

Hanna brings out Dad's softer side.

Photograph provided by Zuffa, LLC
©2007. All rights reserved.

BJ Penn is finished by ground and pound in UFC 63.

From the collection of Steve McLaughlin

I am being interviewed by Scott Pelley for a *60 Minutes* special on mixed martial arts.

From the collection of the Hughes family

Like father, like son: Looks like Joey and I could use a visit to our dentist, Dr. Chiles.

Courtesy of Ken Meade

The first family photo taken since new addition
Hanna was born.

From the collection of Michael Malice

Here I am caught spending another long night at the typewriter, finishing
the manuscript for this book.

I was getting ready for the fight. Carlos was on the cover alone, shooting a ball of electricity from his hands. Giving his goo out. The UFC even made a little cartoon for him. He was the man who beat Pat Miletich; he was the next great welterweight champion. If he could beat Pat, obviously I–"Pat Jr."–would be a cakewalk.

We walked out to the cage and Pat started giving me advice a mile a minute through the wall. "He's the type of guy where it's a fight if he's on his feet, but as soon as it hits the ground it's a grappling match. Throw a punch at him to disrupt his ground game. When he was on the ground, he was looking for submissions, but if you threw a punch at him it would throw him off his game. The best defense for an armbar is a good punch to the face."

I could barely register what he was saying. I turned around. "Pat," I said curtly. "*I feel good.*"

He got the message and quieted down.

Carlos and his crew came out with giant afro wigs, dancing down the aisle and kissing on some girl. I knew I could pull off wearing the belt, but the hair was a different story. *Good,* I thought. *The more you focus on putting on a big show, the less you'll be focusing on the fight.*

"Let's get it on!" Big John said.

I slammed Carlos down a lot in that first round. I took him down and got on top of him, and then he was able to reverse me. He got on top of me for a little while and then I was able to stand up. Then I took him down again. Now I was one round ahead.

The second round I had a big slam right off the bat. It was me with my body weight on top of him, over and over. I was scoring with the judges and I was taking something out of him, both physically and psychologically. I knew he could tell things were slipping away from him, because they were. As I wound up to throw a punch, his leg came up between my neck and my shoulder, and he put me in a triangle choke. *Pick him up,* I thought. *As soon as you pick him up he's going to know he's in danger, and he'll release the hold. Then you're going to come back down and he's still going to be on the bottom.* I lifted him all the way up. Nothing.

What do I do now? I walked him over to the wall. Carlos's left arm tightened up the choke even more, while his right arm reached outside the cage for leverage. It was an illegal move but a natural reaction on his part. "Let go of it!" Big John said. Carlos released his hold on the wall immediately. *What do I do? Can I stand here until his legs get tired?* The choke was getting tight. I could feel it cutting off my blood. *I've got to do something. If I slam him and it doesn't do anything, then I'm done. But if I slam him and it breaks the hold, then the fight continues.* I bridged back on the fence, shifted his weight onto the cage, and locked his legs. I took my right leg, took a step back, twisted him off, and slammed him with all I had.

Carlos was out.

I looked at him and he was asleep, cold, for like twenty seconds—a long time to be knocked out. He woke up, and he didn't know where he was. I wasn't quite sure either. I don't know what happened with me coming down. Maybe the blood ran into my head or maybe it was just the choke, but when I hit, his choke had done enough to me where I was loopy.

I had convinced myself that I was going to win: Anybody who walks into the octagon and thinks they're going to lose are that much closer to it already. But I hadn't thought about what would happen a second after winning. I had been concentrating on the fight. I ran over to Jeremy and said, "What's going on?"

"You just won!"

A light bulb went off. *I'm world champion!* I jumped on the fence and pointed to where I thought the Hillsboro people were. I spun my head around and found Jens in the commentator booth. I jumped the fence and practically tackled him with my hug. I got back in the ring and my cornermen hoisted me on their shoulders. They put me back down and Pat Miletich literally gave me the shirt off of his own back. (Carlos was less generous when he later filed a grievance asking that it be declared a draw, that we were both knocked out.)

I didn't do anything that night, including sleep. I was sharing a room with Mark and Emily, and I was the first one to get to bed. I wished Audra could have taken time to come see it happen. I didn't even stare at the belt—I'd seen Pat's, I'd seen Jens's. I lay in bed, thinking about what it all meant. My eyes were on that hotel room ceiling all night. *You've got to stay the same person. When you leave the sport and when you come down off this high, you're going to need to be able to look people in the face. When you pass them on the way up, treat them the same as when you're on your way down. Look at Randy Couture. That's the kind of champion, the kind of man, you want to be. Now the UFC has to give you fights. Monte won't have to scramble. Three or four fights a year, and more money. That belt—Pat's belt,* your *belt—means you can fight for a living. It's all coming together for you.*

Maybe it's time to move out of your manager's place.

That Christmas Audra and I were on the floor at her mom's house, leaning against the sofa. The tree in the living room was heavy with Hallmark ornaments. The woods in the backyard looked like a forest through the huge deck windows. Giant block letters over the TV read BELIEVE.

"Merry Christmas, Mr. World Champion," Audra said.

"Hey, I like that. You can call me that anytime you want."

"So where's the belt?" she asked.

For a second I didn't realize what she meant, because I was wearing overalls on top of a sweatshirt. "Oh, I threw it under the bed," I said.

"What, that disgusting bed at Monte's? Matt, you can't do that. You should hang it up or something. I don't know. Do *something* with it."

"I'll try to find a place for it when I move into Tony Fryklund's apartment. I told you I'm taking over his lease in Bettendorf, right?"

"*Yes, Matt.* Don't you remember anything?" she said. "I bet Monte's going to miss having his houseboy around."

"Yeah, well, he's got that deck I built him to remember me by." I got quiet for a second and thought about Brandy. I thought about how I found out secondhand that she had had a boy. That I was to have nothing to do with him. I wondered if his name, "Brandon," was short for "Brandy's son."

I thought about taking steps and knew I was ready for the

next one. "I got you something." I turned around and pulled out a little black box. I popped it open. There was a gold band with two white gold stripes on each side; it was the one that we had picked out together.

"I didn't think I was going to get this," she said. "You gave it to Mark to wrap."

I laughed. "I wanted it to be a *little* bit of a surprise." I took the ring off and slid it on her finger. "You know I asked your dad for permission?"

"You asked my dad?" She stopped for a second and tried to imagine the scene. "What did he say?"

"He said, 'Well, it's about time!'"

She put her arms around me and leaned in for a kiss. "I can't believe this," she whispered. "Do you know when you actually want to get married?"

"I'll make a deal with you," I told her. "You can pick out the month and the day. But I get to pick the year."

"Ha, ha," she said. "Very funny."

But every time she heard me tell someone that, it got a little less funny for her.

In spring of '02 I was back at the farm planting. The phone rang. It was Joe, one of the UFC guys. "Hey, Matt, how's it going?"

"Joe, before I forget, I was wondering if I can change my music."

"Well, we can do 'Let the Bodies Hit the Floor.' Because you're always slamming people."

"I was hoping for 'Country Boy Can Survive.'"

"Matt, I told you that it was too slow."

I thought for a second. "What about 'Folsom Prison Blues'? Johnny Cash?"

"You said you wanted 'American Badass' because it sounded more patriotic! I can ask again, if you like, for Hank Williams."

"Thanks, buddy."

"Oh, you saw that Carlos took out Pele, right?" he said, quickly changing the subject. "You beat Sakurai, you'll probably get your rematch."

"I sure hope so."

"You nervous about the fight?" he asked.

"Not really."

"The guy's tough. He's like a god over there; he's got an amazing record."

"Oh, I know. He beat Frank Trigg. He's a stud, no doubt about it. But I think I'll do all right. I'm probably a bit stronger than he is."

"Well, he's a little nervous, I think." Joe paused and waited. He had something good. "The guy doesn't want to be around you."

"He doesn't want to be around me? How do you know that?"

"He told us. He said, 'I don't want to see Matt Hughes. I don't want to be in the same room as Matt Hughes before the fight.'"

It must be hard being the most famous athlete in your country. People stop you to take pictures; fans have your photo on their wall; newspapers report your latest night out. Wherever you go, that is the place to be.

Except, of course, when you leave your country.

Then, the "Michael Jordan of Japan" becomes the Mach Sakurai of America, and the Mach Sakurai of America can walk around unnoticed, even in Vegas. Unless, of course, he's got someone looking for him specifically.

I flew into Vegas on Monday and checked into the hotel. I went upstairs to drop my stuff off in my room. And then I went out to hunt.

In the cafeteria: "Hey, Mach, how's breakfast this morning?"

In the elevator: "Isn't this hotel great, Sakurai?"

In the lobby: "Did you get a good night's sleep?"

He nodded and mumbled friendly responses, but kept looking away and not making eye contact. I was on him the entire week like white on sushi rice. He looked smaller than on television, and on television he already looked smaller than me. I could tell he was thinking the mirror opposite of what I was thinking—that I was bigger in person than he had expected.

At the end of the week it was time for our match. I entered the octagon, and stared at Sakurai. He looked back with a certain sternness. It wasn't like he was trying to be tough; it was like he was a tough person naturally and his expression just reflected that. Seconds into the first round I got him with a jab right into the face. He threw one of his fancy spinning kicks and I caught him and took him down. When we got up I took him down again, throwing him around the ring. As the fight went on I kept picking him up and slamming him into the ground, over and over. The Michael Jordan of Japan was still just the Mach Sakurai of America. The fight ended exactly how I wanted it to. By the climax of our match, when I was grounding and pounding him, I really felt like he shouldn't have even been there against me. It wasn't a challenge.

"If you win a belt, that could be luck," I said to the interviewer after the match. "But if you defend it, it's yours. I'll tell you one thing. Carlos Newton just beat Pele, and we need to come here and we need to straighten things out. *We need to have a rematch.*"

A couple of weeks later, Audra was sitting in the passenger seat as we drove to her house. "So I'll probably be down next weekend," I told Pat. "I'm wanting to get started early." I lowered the cell phone for second. "I'll just be another minute," I let her know.

"That's fine," she said, looking out the window.

"So it's set for July?" Pat asked. "Is that right?"

"Yep, me and Carlos. In London. We can go over details when I get down there. I'll talk to you soon, Grandpa."

"Yeah, okay," Pat grunted.

I hung up the phone and squeezed Audra's thigh. She tensed up, so I shook her leg. "What was that all about?" she asked.

"Oh, it was nothing."

"No, I'd like to know."

"Don't worry about it," I said. "I don't know what you're talking about."

"Matt, I'm serious."

"I can see that!" I said, laughing.

"I need to know what you guys were talking about."

"If I want you to know about something, I'll tell you." I pulled my hand back from her leg. "I guess you're just going to have to be in suspense a little while longer, then."

I could feel her eyes boring into the side of my head. From the corner of my vision I saw her take off her engagement ring. I felt it hit me in the chest before it bounced to the floor. Twenty-two years old is a lot different from thirteen or fourteen, but in some ways it's a lot the same.

When I pulled up to her parents' house, she got out of the car and slammed the door. I bent down and felt around on the floor for the ring, and then I put it in my pocket.

I waited for a couple of days before calling her. I was used to my dad and to Mark—people who need to regroup after they've reached that angry point. "Hey, Audra, it's me," I said.

"Yeah," she said. I knew the tone. It reminded me a little of Brandy.

"Are you still pissed off over what happened in the car?"

"Yeah, I am," she said. "If we're going to be getting married, we can't be having secrets from each other."

"It was just *Pat*, Audra. I was just messing around. It was a *joke*. What could Pat and I possibly be talking about that's a secret?"

"I just think that if I'm asking you about something, I've got a right to know."

I sighed. "Look, do you want me to keep this ring?"

"For now I do, yeah."

"Okay, if this is what you want, this is what you got. You've got to be careful of what you ask for. I'll talk to you after you've calmed down a little bit." I hung up the phone, got in my truck, and went over to see who was down at Trails Inn. There's a lot you can get done in five minutes. Breaking off an engagement is one of them.

For two months we kept in touch. We'd known each other for so long, and I'd known her family so well, that it really couldn't be otherwise. Two weeks before the Carlos rematch I swung by their house for dinner. It was the first time I felt a bit uncomfortable there, as if I didn't know where I should be sitting or how I should be talking to everyone. As I was leaving I hugged the family and lingered by the doorway a second. "Aren't you going to give me a kiss for luck?" I asked Audra.

She came over and kissed me on the cheek. Her lips felt warm. I got in my Jeep and began the drive to Bettendorf.

Almost two weeks later I was in London for UFC 38. I was in a big ballroom, with a little stage set up for the fighters to get on the scale. Half the seats were filled with reporters and photographers, calling out to us to pose for their shots. There were no fans around, just people doing their jobs.

The commission guy shook his head. "You're over," he told me, pointing to the scale.

"There's something not right here," I told the guy. "I don't think I've not made weight."

"Matt, I'm sorry, but you're about half a pound over," he told me in his British accent.

"I think your conversion from pounds to kilos is off or something," I insisted. *The idiot doesn't know that I've weighed in more times than he's shown up to work every day. It's his first UFC and he thinks he knows everything.*

The guy just shrugged and turned away.

Tito Ortiz got up from his chair. "Did you not make weight?" he said, with a huge smirk on his face. "You're the champion and you didn't make weight?"

"Tito, it's no big deal. I'll come back and make weight in a second."

"I can't believe you didn't make weight," he said. "I'd never do that. I mean, come on, man. How can you not make weight?"

That really ticked me off, but I shouldn't have been surprised. Ever since the UFC had made him a star, it was always something with Tito. "Tito, it'll be *fine*."

After I ran long enough, I came back and made weight. Then I went out to look at the venue. It kind of reminded me of a silo. It was like a small circle and it rose five or six stories. *Man, everybody's got great seats,* I thought. *The higher you are the better, because now you're looking down instead of having to look through the cage. I bet even the people at the highest tier could spit on us.*

The next day I was scheduled to fight Carlos, and I wasn't even nervous when the time came. I wanted to settle things once and for all, but I wasn't too concerned about how things were going to go. Right when the match started, I took him down and slammed him, but he got me in an armbar. I rolled to clear the armbar, but in the wrong direction. I immediately rolled the right way; it cleared the armbar but messed up my elbow at the same time.

That was the last damage Carlos Newton would ever do to me.

For three rounds I had my way with him. At the end of the third round I got to my corner. Pat got on the inside of the cage with me. My guys were throwing water in my mouth and putting some Vaseline on my face to make sure I wouldn't get cuts. I watched Pat out of the corner of my eye. He looked at me and then he looked over at Carlos—me, Carlos, me, Carlos, like he was a crazy person. "Do you see what they're doing over there?" Pat said.

"No . . ."

"They're putting him back together!"

You know what? He's right. Across the octagon Carlos's team was using an ice cold piece of steel, an endswell, on his face to break up the bruising under his skin. They were like a bunch of doctors trying to get him to go back out for another round. *I can be a little bit more reckless now because Carlos doesn't have the energy to catch me,* I realized.

During the fourth round I got him pinned beneath me. I kept punching him in the face as hard as I could, and his head bounced along the ground. There was nothing he could do about it, and it felt great. *How much is John going to let me give this guy?* I wondered. I felt the referee hovering nearby. We both heard Carlos's last words. "I give! I give! I give!" The fight was over. I had beaten Carlos, again.

The UFC had a van to take us all to a club for the after-fight party. The fighters poured Red Bull and vodka down their throats, but I only had a few. "I know everybody wants to go have fun," I told Pat, "but I just want to relax."

"You crashing?"

"Yeah, I'm going to go pass out. I'm exhausted."

"Congrats, man," he said, smacking me on the back.

I took a cab back to the hotel and got to bed. Our flight was leaving early in the morning. I got woken up a couple of hours later by Pat knocking on my door. He was smashed. "Pat, what's going on?" I said, grinning to myself. He could barely stand. "What time is it?"

"It's, like, five. Don't worry about it. Just sit down and fucking listen. You will not believe what just happened."

I laid on my side on the bed. Pat plopped into the chair in the hotel room and leaned his head back. "So it's four o'clock in the morning and they had everybody leave the club, right? Well, the UFC had bussed us all over there but they didn't have a bus to take us back. It's down to Mark, me, Tony Fryklund, Chuck Liddell, Tito, and Lee Murray. Lee Murray's crew was still there, Tito's crew was also still there.

"I walked out the back door to go in the alley. Tito's buddy jumped on my back. He jumped on my back and acted like he had me in a chokehold, just messing around, you know? Then I felt him get ripped off of me. I turned around and Tony Fryklund had *him* in a choke hold, and was really choking him. The guy looked like a mouse that just got trapped in a mousetrap; his eyes were popping out and obviously he wasn't breathing. Tony thought he was actually attacking me—that's the only reason he did it. So I turned around and I told Tony to let him go, and Tony let him go. Then Tito's buddy turned around and basically said, 'What the fuck are you doing?' to Tony. Well, when he said that, one of Lee Murray's buddies, that one guy who kind of took care of us all week long, thought this guy was actually trying to fight us, so he ran out of the crowd and cracked this kid with a right hand and knocked him out cold."

"Are you serious?" I asked Pat.

"Hold on, it gets even better. The entire alley erupted into a huge brawl. I was just standing there, and there were bodies flying all over the place. I was confused how it all happened, because it happened so fast. I was standing there with my mouth open, like, *What the hell is going on?* I looked over and Chuck Liddell was with his back against the wall, knocking people out that were trying to go after him. Then I looked over and there's Tito directly past me, taking his coat off, going after Lee Murray, and Lee Murray's backing up the alley taking his jacket off. Both their jackets come off, and Tito throws a left hook at Lee Murray and misses, and right as he missed, Lee Murray counters with, like, a five-punch combo, landed right on the chin, and knocked Tito out. *Out.* Tito fell face-first down to the ground, and then Lee Murray stomped him on the face a couple of times with his boots.

"Then Tony Fryklund and I grabbed Lee and pushed Lee and said, 'Get out of here!' And Lee said, 'I'm sorry, I'll see you later,' and took off. And Tony Fryklund helped Tito to his feet.

"Then these English bobbies showed up and they were threatening to spray the entire crowd with huge canisters of mace. 'You think you've got problems now?' I said. 'You spray this entire group of fighters with mace and we'll all be in a heap of big trouble.' So I talked the police out of doing that. And then Tony and I got a cab and we headed back here."

"That's insane, Pat."

"Long story short, Matt: I'm ready to get on that plane, pronto."

I didn't know that Audra was sitting in her teal Honda in the lane by the farm, waiting for hours for me to come home from Europe. I didn't understand she thought our kiss meant that we were back together. I didn't even have a chance to see her there when I returned to Hillsboro, because instead of going home, I was too busy spending the night in someone else's bed.

CHAPTER 10

Reunions

On August 13 I woke up and realized that it was Joey's birthday. He was turning three years old. I wanted to go over to his house and give him a hug, pick him up, and take him out for a ride. I wanted to give him a new toy and wish him a happy birthday. I wanted to get down on the carpet with him and pretend we were farming fields with our John Deere toy tractors. But I couldn't do any of those things because he was Audra's son and I wasn't Audra's man anymore.

I knew that Audra was still in school, getting her teaching certificate. That meant she would be gone most of the day, and he'd be at home with his grandma. I waited until Monday afternoon and drove up to her mom's house, where they were all living. I knocked on the front door and came in just like I had been doing since high school.

Kathy, Audra's mom, was in the kitchen, leaning over the counter and reading a magazine. I noticed how her arms were long and thin, just like her daughter's. Joey was on the floor playing with some of his action figures. He looked older, like an entirely different person. "Hi, Matt," Kathy said. "Audra's not here. Was she expecting you?"

"Oh, she isn't? Do you know what time she'll be back?"

"Probably not until five."

I looked at the wall clock and did the math. I crouched down. "Hey, Joe."

"Hi, Matt!" he said.

"Listen, I'm going to Wal-Mart to pick up a few things. Do you mind if I take Joey with me?" I asked Kathy.

"I don't know," she said. "You'd have to ask him. Joey, do you want to go with Matt to the store?" He nodded up at her. "He's all yours, Matt."

I grabbed the boy and picked him up. "I'll bring him back here before Audra gets home."

"Take your time," Kathy said, smiling to herself.

For the next couple of weeks, I would go by their house and sort of kidnap Audra's son. Then one time I came over and the look on Kathy's face was different. She felt embarrassed. "I can't let you take Joey anymore," she told me. "Audra found out and she got mad."

I looked down at the boy. "Joey, I told you not to tell your mom."

"I didn't!" he protested.

"No, I told her," Kathy said. "I thought she'd be glad. Well, she kind of wasn't. She said I can't let you take him anymore."

I stood there and thought about Audra's letter to me. I understood where she was coming from. "I'll fix this. I'll see you soon, Kathy."

"Sorry about that, Matt."

"Don't worry, it's fine." I drove home and waited until it got dark, and then I waited until I was absolutely certain that Joey was asleep. I picked up the phone and called their house.

"Hello?" It was Audra.

"Hey, it's Matt," I said. "I was wanting to come over and see Joey. Is he still up?"

She laughed a little. "Yeah, come on over."

"Okay, I'll be right there."

While I drove back to their house, Audra went upstairs and shook the poor kid out of his sleep. "Joey, wake up! Wake up! Matt's coming over and he's wanting to play with you."

When I came into the house he was yawning, but he walked over and gave me a hug. I hugged him back and tousled his hair, the blondest that I have ever seen. He plopped down on the floor and started messing around with the growing army of John Deere farm toys I'd been buying him. Audra and I plopped down ourselves on the sofa. "So how have you been?" I asked her.

"I've been good." She was smiling. We missed each other and didn't bother hiding it, but we didn't bother saying it either.

"Well, how's school? Tell me all about it."

It was November 2002, a year since I had beaten Carlos for the first time. I was fighting at UFC 40 in Las Vegas. During the first round I realized that my head knocked into Gil Castillo's, but I certainly didn't feel anything. I doubt he did, either, even though a cut popped open over his left eye. I completed the takedown. I threw elbows and punches at his face for the rest of the round. When the bell rang I returned to my corner, panting.

Gil summoned Big John and then sat down on a stool. The doctor came in and took a look at his cut. It wasn't bleeding much, if at all; it was about the size of a staple. But the fight still got stopped. The fans booed, and loudly. Gil walked back and forth, squeezing his eye shut when he could remember to do so and making faces like he was in pain.

Mark and the Miletich guys came into the ring and gave me high fives. Then came that microphone. "Who do you think is going to give you a run for your money?" the interviewer asked me.

"Nobody can give me a run for my money," I said, just like the UFC had told me to. "But I tell you, Sean Sherk's going to be trying here. So Sean, let's bring it on, boy."

We headed back to the locker room. I grabbed a quick shower while the guys sat around, laughing about who knows what. When I was finished, Big John was standing around with everyone.

"Hey, what happened there?" I asked Big John.

Big John shook his head. "He was sitting down and I'm walking to him. I asked him if he was okay and he looked at me and told me he couldn't see. Then I squatted down to look him right in the eyes and he told me again that he couldn't see. I had to call the doctor in and he told the doctor that he couldn't see either. They couldn't find anything wrong with him. But when a fighter says he can't see, I can't send him back out there, you know?"

I nodded. "Well, I'm just glad it went like it did. I didn't train at all for this and I knew that if it went five rounds I'd totally gas. Gil's a great guy but he doesn't have a lot of heart. I thought that if I made it rough for him he would give up and fold, and that's what he did."

Big John smiled. "All right. Well, congrats to you."

"Thanks." The fight was over; the fun was beginning. It was time to go out and celebrate.

Coyote Ugly is a bar in Las Vegas that is based on a bar in New York City. A coyote will chew its leg off if it gets caught in a trap. And "coyote ugly" refers to a woman so hideous that you'd rather bite your own arm off than wake her up by pulling it out from under her the morning after, when you wake up in her bed. But I doubt if there was a single girl who was actually coyote ugly at the bar. It was shoulder to shoulder silicone and denim, with dudes in carefully unbuttoned shirts wondering who would be their Vegas sweetheart that night. The best ladies made it easy by getting up on the bar and dancing for everybody.

The Hillsboro crew found ourselves a corner and picked up where we left off five nights before: drinking. The music came on, the girls got on the bar, and the entire room cheered. Again and again.

Six beers later Mark said, "Hey, Emily, why don't you get up and dance on the bar?"

"That's all right," she said. She stared at him. After three years, she was still trying to figure out when he was kidding.

"Come on, it'll be fun. I'll tell them to put on a song for you, whatever you want."

She realized he wasn't kidding. "Mark, I'm not dancing on the bar! You know what? You're drunk. I'll see y'all back at the hotel." She got up and left us.

Mark watched her go and finished his beer. "Hey, do any of you guys know where the bathroom is?"

"You've got to go outside, go all the way around, and then go down the escalators," our buddy Dan explained.

Mark got up and began the long journey. I knew I'd have to go next, but I waited until Mark got back. "Was it as far away as it sounded?" I asked Dan.

He nodded. "It sure is."

"Well, for every move there's a counter." I polished off my beer and went up to the bar. It was dark, and the place was packed, so I figured I was safe. I opened my fly, pulled it out, and started pissing against the bar. "Let me get another one of these," I said, showing the bartender my bottle. She went to get me a beer while I emptied what was left of the last one out of me and onto the floor. Then I tucked it back in.

"Here you go," she said. Her timing was perfect. My system was foolproof.

My buddy Graham came back into the club. "Where'd you go off to?" Mark asked. "I didn't even notice you were gone."

"Tommy's passed out on the street and his girlfriend couldn't budge him. By the time I got there to help, people were putting hats on him and cigarettes in his mouth and taking pictures."

After many, many trips to the bar—and the growing puddle right in front of it—it was time for us to return to the MGM. We walked out in pairs like some sort of beer-drunk centipede, with the Hughes brothers bringing up the rear. We had our arms wrapped around each other, doing a balancing act on level ground.

Mark stumbled and I caught him. He looked right at me. "Hey man, you make me real proud," he said. Mark's face got even blurrier to me as I sort of began to well up. "I love that you're my brother, and I wouldn't trade that for anything."

"Hey, I love that you're my brother too," I said to him, as best as I could manage. We shuffled all the way back to that hotel—Mark to his wife, and me to yet another girl that I knew wasn't the one.

A month later I got a call at home. "Hey, Matt." It was Audra. "Listen, I've got kind of a big favor to ask you."

"Anything, Auggie. What do you need?"

"I went with Missy to the consultation."

"Yeah, she told me."

"Yeah . . . so I'm finally getting my boobs done and I kind of need someone to take care of me for, like, an entire day." She said it really quickly, like she'd been saying it to herself out loud beforehand.

"Hey, nothing would make me happier." It was the truth. I was glad that Audra, not one to ask for favors, felt so comfortable asking me to help her; I was glad she'd finally have the body she'd always wanted; I was glad that she knew me well enough that she knew I would agree to take care of her, no questions asked.

And I was glad because I missed her and I knew that she

missed me, and if she really wanted to she could have asked somebody else. I was her go-to guy, and that was a role I was thrilled to play.

The doctor was about an hour and a half from Bettendorf, in Cedar Rapids. We drove out in the morning straight to the hospital, joking about her future wardrobe. I watched her fill out the forms, writing as fast as she could to get it all over with. She kept looking up to make sure that I was still there.

I left her in the hands of the doctor and went to check into our hotel. We had to stay within ten minutes of the hospital; surgery was surgery. Then I found a grocery store and bought some frozen peas for her. Three hours later she was ready to leave.

Audra was slouched in a wheelchair, her eyes half-open and her skin a weird greenish color. She felt even worse than she looked, but all I was noticing was that someone I cared about was uncomfortable and in pain, and I was going to do my best to make sure she'd be all right. I brought her downstairs where I was parked. I pulled her by the back of the neck to help her get up, just like they showed me to, and I helped her out of the chair. I listened to the noises she was mumbling, trying to figure out which were requests meant for me and which were just sounds of suffering meant for no one.

When we got to the hotel I put her right to bed. I filled the sink with ice. Every hour, on the hour, I took the bag of frozen peas from her chest and replaced them with another, refreezing them in the sink. She couldn't use her arms, so when she needed something, anything, I was the nurse who got it for her.

"I need to go to the bathroom," she eventually said. I led her in, slowly, and helped her ease down on the seat. I turned away so that she would get some amount of privacy. I heard her sigh. "I need you to wipe me," she said. "I can't use my arms." She didn't even have the strength to be embarrassed. It was the first time I had seen her totally naked. She had always kept her shirt on in bed, or she took it off underneath the covers. I led her back to bed where she slept, and all night I kept up with the peas.

She woke up in the late morning and we made our way to my car. I drove her back to my apartment, chastising myself every time we hit a bump in the road. "I want to take a shower," she said. She was already much less groggy than the night before.

"That's fine."

She didn't shuffle as slowly to the bathroom. I turned on the water and tested it to make sure even Goldilocks would have been comfortable with the temperature. Audra didn't stiffen when I completely undressed her and led her into the water and got her clean.

I toweled her off and walked her back to the bed. She looked at me the way she used to look at me at night, when we were at her house and Joey went to sleep. I leaned in at first, but I saw that she couldn't really lean back. I leaned further and kissed her, being very careful that my hands didn't brush up and hurt her. In fighting, you always want to be on your back. But some-times it's good in other situations too. I barely felt her weight as I eased her on top of me. As we moved together on my bed her stitches ripped a little bit and her blood drizzled across my chest. I lived in a world where people were bound by their blood, roll-ing in practice rooms and in cages. It was the first time I'd had that kind of a bond on bedsheets. We were together again, and it felt wonderful.

We got up and got dressed, just in time to see Barbara drive up to take Audra home to Hillsboro. Barbara Adams, Esq., was Audra's stepmom, with long, white hair, a quick smile, and an even quicker tongue. I got up and opened the door for her. "Hi, Matt!" she said.

"So, you wanna see them?" I asked Barbara.

A few weeks later I was back training in Bettendorf. I went to a hotel room to film interview footage for the UFC. A bunch of the crew already had the lighting, the backdrop, and the stool set up when I walked in. All of them were wearing jeans or sweats, and they were ready for me to sit down and talk for a couple of hours about the upcoming fight.

I gave UFC director Anthony Giordano a pat on the back as I sat down on the stool and faced him. He looked a bit like Tony Soprano, and he was in a good mood as usual. I saw that Anthony had his pad of questions ready for me. "When'd you get in to Bettendorf?" he asked as one of the techs miked me. Another one started to position the boom over my head. It was like being at the dentist, but not as fun.

"Just yesterday," I told him.

"*Yesterday?* But the fight's in two weeks."

"I'm ready. I'm more worried about your questions than about the fight," I said, chuckling.

"Okay, okay. Remember, I need energy from you."

"You got it."

"So, tell me what you think about Sean Sherk," Anthony asked.

"Well, Sean and I are both from the Midwest. We've known each other since before I was a world champion, so we've got a lot in common, and I think he's a good-natured guy."

"What's your strategy for the fight?"

"I saw that he's not comfortable when people are on top of him. I'm going to try to do that and then do some damage."

"People say Sean's a very tough guy," Anthony said. "Do you think he's as tough as people say?"

"I think Sean's a very tough guy. Now, tough's not always good in our sport because tough means you can take a bunch of punches and survive. If I'm good and I'm fighting somebody that's tough, they're going to take a bunch of punches but they're not going to give up. So how is that good for them? That means that they're probably going to go to the hospital with aches, pains, and bruises and still lose. I'd rather be good, or technical, or strong, way before tough, because tough just means you get beat up. The name of the game is not 'how much punishment can you take.' But Sean is definitely going to be a tough opponent, no doubt about it."

Anthony let out a long breath. "Matt, most fighters would have taken that as an opportunity to say that the guy they're about to fight really isn't that tough after all, you know what I mean?"

"Oh, okay." I shrugged my shoulders and waited for the next question.

Anthony nodded at me, leaning forward hopefully. "Do you predict that you'll submit Sean?"

"I doubt it. No one's ever submitted him and I don't think you *can* submit him. He's really compact, so you can't get a choke on his neck–he doesn't even have one–or get that arm stretched out for an armbar. How's that, Anthony?"

He didn't answer. I could tell from the way he scanned his list of questions that he was wishing–once again–that Tim Sylvia was sitting on that stool.

It was April of 2003, and we were backstage at UFC 42 in Miami. "Hey Pat? You want a water?" Mark asked.

"Sure!"

"I bet you do!" my brother yelled out. The entire locker room was in hysterics while Pat kind of looked away, pissed that he had fallen for that line–again.

Michael Moorer's eyes darted in every direction, like he was in a swarm of bees or something. "Michael, what's going on in your head?" Mark asked him.

The boxing champion said, "Man, you guys are *weird.*"

"What are you talking about?"

"In my locker room we're serious, and you guys are joking around, doing this and that."

One of the clipboard people soon came in to tell me to get ready. I stretched and moved around a bit to get the blood flowing and walked out to the curtains with Tim, Mark, Pat, and Jeremy. I started to tell myself, *This is my home, and this guy thinks he's going to come here and beat me in my home.* My face became hard, a look I wore for maybe ten minutes a year, and I walked down the ramp as fireworks exploded all around me. The crowd cheered because they anticipated that this wasn't going to be a quick knockout or a quick submission. Sean and I were going to go to town on each other, no question.

Sean and I stared each other down. He looked like a wrestler even more than I did, if that was possible, with his head attached directly to his body. *When I get on top of him it's going to be over,* I thought. *First round, and that'll be the end of that.* Soon after the ref started the fight, I got a cut opened above his left eye. But he didn't quit. In the second round he pushed me with his feet and threw me across the cage. I hopped right back on him like a bull-frog and went back to hurting him. By the fourth and fifth round that cut of his was painting the octagon floor red. But Sean was like a vampire: He just wouldn't die. After about half an hour of being tough and taking punishment, Sean went from looking as sleek as a shark to looking like Sloth from *The Goonies.* I won by unanimous decision.

Immediately a microphone got shoved in my face. "Is there anybody who can take your title?" they asked.

"There's a guy out there running his mouth. Frank Trigg. I'd like to give him a shot." *To the face.*

That September I was back at my house and had read the bad news about Tim on my computer. I thought about the stories I'd heard about Tim in high school, and I thought about what it must have been like for him. The jokes at his expense, meant to hurt rather than to tease. I got his number from Pat and gave him a ring. "Hey, Timmy. It's Matt. Matt Hughes."

He sniffled a bit. "Hey, Matt. What's going on? Are you

calling about the test?" he asked. A failed test for steroids. His belt would probably be taken away from him, that belt that he wore like a policeman wears his badge, to tell people that he was somebody. That he should be respected.

"Yeah," I said. "What's going on?"

"It's true," he said. "I did it, I knew it was the wrong thing, and I did it anyway. I have no excuse."

"Listen, I just wanted to tell you to hang in there. Maybe I've been a little hard on you in the past. When you got the belt, when you stuck to Pat's game plan and kept it standing, you did us all proud. When you support everyone from the team in your interviews, you do us proud."

"Matt, I've let everybody down." His voice was hoarse. I don't know how long he had been crying, how long he must have been pacing in his house, wanting it to end. "The entire gym, I don't know how I'm going to look everyone in the face, you know?"

I'd been where he was mentally, and I'd been there as a coach. You think everyone sees you as a failure when everyone knows that you're a success. Everyone but yourself. "Let me tell you something. Champions are not made; they're born. No one in the gym is going to treat you any differently. I guarantee it."

CHAPTER 11

Winning the Prize

Back in the gym in Bettendorf, we set up a fighting conveyor belt. I stood still on the mat and one training partner after another came at me. Pat stood over us and watched. "Keep him tight, Matt," Pat said for the third time. "Trigg can't punch if you've got him tight."

The guys did their best to tap me with their gloves, making little noises to make it sound like they were hitting me hard. I wrapped my legs around their waists and held them close. They pushed against me, trying to get distance so they'd have leverage. I did the same maneuvers over and over, machinelike, dozens of times.

"Next guy," Pat said, beckoning.

Another fighter angled for position. I got my knees on his abdomen, keeping him at a distance so he couldn't reach me. His gloves touched me, but with no force whatsoever.

"All right, good," Pat said. I stood up and now Pat himself

assumed the Trigg role and tried his best to take me down. I was getting winded but I still went for more. As long as there were more "Triggs" ready to take me on, I was ready to throw down with them.

During this training period the UFC had me come back to that hotel room for some more footage. Anthony wasn't fidgeting with his paper while I was getting miked for my interview this time. As I sat on my stool he had almost a smirk on his face—the kind of look you have when you've got the winning hand in poker and are just waiting for your opponent to go all in. "I did things a little differently this time," he informed me. "I talked to Frank Trigg, and I thought I'd ask you questions based on what he said."

"That's fine."

"Are you ready?" I was ready, but I wasn't exactly prepared, though the cameras were rolling all the same. "Frank Trigg says he has a better upbringing than you."

"Wait, he said that?"

Anthony nodded. "I've got the transcript right here."

Suddenly, I was aware of all the techies in that hotel room. For once, they were listening to an interview, instead of just recording it. "I don't know that that's true," I said, "and I don't see how that matters."

"He said he's going to, quote, 'kick the shit out of you and take your title.'"

"Huh. Well, there's talkers, and there's doers. Frank's done a lot of talking but I don't see how he's actually done a lot of doing."

"He also says he's a better wrestler than you."

"Okay, let me clear that one up. Frank Trigg was never a Division I All-American. I was a two-time Division I All-American wrestler. He does not have wrestling credentials over me. He wasn't anything for Division I. I don't think he even broke the starting lineup for his squad." This wasn't really a debatable point. I felt my breath going in and out through my nose, like I was a bull pawing at the ground.

Anthony read the next claim from the list. "He says he has greater functional strength than you."

"I don't think that's true," I said flat-out. "You know, it sounds like he's his own biggest fan."

"Trigg says he's finally going to bring some personality to the welterweight division."

I thought about all the crazy times and laughs I'd had with Pat; I thought about screaming with Pat; I thought about drinking with Pat. I remembered the time Pat vomited out his bridgework on the streets of New Orleans and went looking through the puke to find his teeth, and then poured beer on them and put them back in his mouth. Pat and I were far from plain vanilla. "If by 'personality' you mean someone that everyone hates, then Frank Trigg is your man." *People are going to see this,* I told myself. *Calm down. You don't want to start cussing at the camera. If things get real bad, you can stop the interview and tell them to use some old footage.* For the next two hours I came to understand what it felt like to be cross-examined by a good attorney. I could not get that mike off of me quick enough.

*   *   *   *

That weekend I went back to Hillsboro. We were having dinner at the Canton Inn, Hillsboro's version of the Four Seasons. The women there wore hairstyles like 1970s' beauty queens, while the men's button-down cotton shirts were faded from the wash. The restaurant had a bar when you walked in, an aisle of booths, and a special room in the back that was clearly added to the main building afterward—the ceiling was low, the space constricting. My brother and I were polishing off a plate of lamb fries, a popular appetizer made of breaded lamb testicles. Emily and Audra were talking with Joey.

"Mark, I cannot lose to this guy," I said. "I absolutely cannot lose to him. It's not like losing to a Sean Sherk, who's a nice guy. This guy is a jerk running his mouth. He's just an *idiot*. On a scale of one to ten, he's a Tito."

"That bad, really?"

"I mean, and Tito's at least got some credentials, and some money, and a little bit of fame."

"Is this because Trigg beat Dennis Hallman?" Mark had that little smile on his face.

"Mark, I'm serious."

"Matt, I don't think there is one thing he's better at than you. I don't think he has better takedowns, I don't think he's better striking on his feet, I don't think he's better on the ground. And I *know* you're going to be in better shape than he is. We were there when Sakurai beat him, and you beat Sakurai no problem."

I thought about Trigg's fight with Sakurai more than a year before. Trigg came out in the first round and looked good, probably winning it. When the second round started, Sakurai threw a hook and knocked Trigg down. He got a standing ten-count because those were the Shooto rules. After the ref said go, Sakurai's first punch knocked Trigg down again. The third punch was the third knockdown, and it was all over.

"You know what you've got to do? Call Fiore," Mark said. "Fiore's been around Trigg in tournaments, and he'll tell you exactly what you need to know."

"That's not a bad idea."

I dialed Fiore's number as soon as I got home. "Hey, Fiore. It's Matt."

"Hey, what's going on, buddy?"

"Listen, I've got this Trigg fight coming up, and I was wondering if you had any advice for it. I know you were around him when you were doing your Army Greco coaching."

"Yep, yep," Fiore said. "Well, he likes to be in body locks, but he really doesn't do a whole lot from them."

"Do you think you can swing by and maybe show me some of his tricks?"

"Of course I could show you a few moves, and that's fine and whatever, but I can tell you some stuff right now that's even more interesting."

"Like what?"

"Like that the guy's basically weak-minded. Seeing him wrestle in tournaments, if he loses, he drops out. If you ever get him in a situation where he's under duress, he'll quit. He'll find some way to quit. That's just the way he is. Either he gets dirty, or he claims to be injured."

As soon as Fiore started talking, I realized how useful he

could be. "Hey, I've got an idea. How about you come down with me to the Mohegan Sun that week and corner me for the fight? Mark's got work and he can't be gone a whole week, but you're retired."

"Matt, I'll be more than happy to help you any way I can. You just name the time and the place."

It was late November of 2003, and I was in Connecticut. The basketball hoops were still up, but the arena floor had been cleared at the Mohegan Sun for UFC 45. In a few hours there would be an octagon where we stood, and then the next day thousands of fans in the seats would be screaming for blood. My legs were pumping as fast they could, easily outpacing my training partner, Jeremy. We ran back and forth, sprinting as fast as we could. "That was a good one," I said, doubled over and panting.

"Hey, uh, Matt?" I looked up. Fiore stood there in a sweat-shirt and nodded to Jeremy. "Anytime you want to stop sprinting is fine with me," Fiore said.

"Sorry, buddy. I just love to work out to the last minute so I know I've done all I can." I still hadn't caught my breath.

"I get that," Fiore said. "I just don't want your legs to be sore tomorrow. You've got weigh-ins and then we're going to start rehydrating you. You've got an interview scheduled at six. Over the phone, no big deal."

I nodded, and the three of us headed back to the hotel room. It felt weird not having to worry about my schedule or when I could drink fluids. Fiore was taking care of everything, and I was thinking about taking care of Frank Trigg. I was able to keep my head clear. My mind and my body wanted to be in that cage as soon as they could. And soon enough, that's where we were.

I paced back and forth, listening to what Jeremy and Pat were telling me through the cage walls. I knew that somewhere among the thousands of people in the seats were my friends from Hillsboro—and Audra.

I went to tap gloves, but Trigg turned that into a takedown. No matter what direction he tried to go, I was there blocking his path. We struggled on the ground until I managed to hoist him over my shoulder. Then the bodies hit the floor. We jockeyed for position until he had me on my back and stood over me trying to throw punches. I felt the soft leather of his gloves reach me with no force, just like in Bettendorf.

In the crowd, Audra became so upset that she got up out of her seat and took off running toward the exit. She tripped on her way up the stairs, pissed at herself for wearing high heels. She picked herself up and kept going.

Then Trigg turned his back to me. I climbed on his back and wrapped my arm around his throat. I wrapped my other arm around his head and he stood up, as if he were giving me a piggy-back ride. I cinched up as hard as I could. *How long can he take this?* I wondered. I didn't let myself get excited. For every move there's a counter. The crowd was hysterical. No one had been choked out while standing before. Audra heard them, turned around, and ran back to her seat. I felt Trigg tap on my thighs, but I wasn't going to give him any way of talking himself out of a loss later. He was going to tap, the ref was going to stop it, and that's how it was going to be declared. Those were the rules when you came to play in my house. Trigg passed out and fell backward, and both of us hit the ground. Big John quickly pulled us apart.

It was over. I hadn't thrown a single punch.

Trigg woke up right away and looked straight at me. I smiled at the guy. The fight was over, and what had been said or done before the fight was over with. We had come into a cage and settled matters like men. Maybe he had felt the need to hype things and let his mouth get the better of him. I didn't know and I didn't care. I just hoped that now he was going to act like a normal human being.

Fiore and Tim Sylvia rushed into the cage, even happier than I was. "That was awesome, little buddy!" Tim said.

"Thanks, Timmy, thanks."

As I did the postfight interview Fiore stood over my shoulder, staring directly into the camera and checking himself out on the big screen. The adrenaline started to recede as I waved to the fans and walked to the backstage area. "Man, I can't believe he gave up his back like that," I said, shaking my head. "It's one thing if a boxer does it, but a wrestler?"

"Matt, do you really think someone can be competing at your level and make such an obvious mistake? That's like MMA 101, that's the first thing you learn," Fiore said.

"So what, you think he didn't know about that?"

"No, man, it was like I told you. That was him breaking. That was him saying that he was done, that he can't find a way to beat you."

*   *   *   *

My next fight was only two months later in Vegas. On paper this meant that I shouldn't have had time to breathe. That would have been the case if my opponent were someone other than BJ Penn. When I was running through the snow in Iowa, I was thinking about how his soft feet were running over even softer sand on the beautiful beaches of Hawaii. I remembered his belly-aching after Jens kicked his butt, claiming *he* had actually won. And now he was going to go up a weight class to take me on. Was this spoiled rich kid for real?

I ran into the gym and strutted into the training room. "Do you want to figure out a game plan?" Pat asked me.

"Oh, I've got a game plan," I told him. "I'm going to grab this guy, I'm going to throw him up against the fence, he's going to slide down, I'm going to get on top of him and just beat him up. End of story. I mean, come on. This is a gimme."

Pat didn't say a lot. I was still in shape from Trigg, so when I practiced my grappling and my striking, I didn't really need much focus. I didn't need much enthusiasm, either. I had just taken out Frank Trigg in one of the most popular MMA fights ever. This match was like a free gift from the UFC.

On January 31, 2004, I was at Vegas's Mandalay Bay Arena. When I was leaning back against the cage during the introductions, I felt something I hadn't felt in over two years in the cage: I was bored. *Hey, let's get this thing started,* I thought. *I wanna go watch some TV.*

The ref waved us in, and I hit BJ with a stiff jab right off the bat, snapping his head back. Then I went for a takedown, but he took me down instead. I was on my back. He tried to pass my guard; he couldn't. He tried to improve his position; he couldn't. BJ backed out of my guard and came in with a big haymaker punch. He connected, hard. He took advantage of that, we scrambled, and then he caught me in a choke. *He's got me good,* I realized. *Hey, I can't get out of this. I can't get out of this!* I had no choice. I had to tap.

It hadn't even taken him five minutes. BJ Penn was the new welterweight champion.

I went backstage, sat down on a bench, and rested my head on my fists. I looked down on the ground. My knee would not stop bouncing up and down.

"Don't even worry about it," Pat told me. "Jeremy's been there, Jens has been there, I've been there."

I looked up at him. My face was still as red as when I was getting choked out. "This isn't the same as you, Pat. This wasn't some flukey move. He got me with that punch and he took me out. Fair and square."

Pat kept talking, saying the things I didn't bother to say to him after his loss to Carlos. I had always focused on winning the fight, never preparing to deal with what happens five minutes after. This time, I hadn't even focused on the fight.

I didn't feel angry, or annoyed, or depressed. That would come later. When I was sitting in the locker room, all I could feel was numb. For two years, I had been Matt Hughes, welterweight champion. Now I didn't know who I was anymore. But the more I thought about it, the more I knew who I wanted to be.

A couple of months later I was driving with Audra in Hillsboro and the idea just sort of appeared in my mind. Audra and

I were living together; I loved her, loved her son, and got along great with her family.

I was ready to pick the year, and that year was 2004.

I turned to her and said, "You know what, Audra? We should just go ahead and get married."

"Yeah, I think that's a good idea!" She got a smile on her face and her eyes opened up wide.

"Let's just do it." I put my hand on her knee and squeezed. "You can make the arrangements." It took her all of a week.

Not that many weeks later, I crouched a bit as I worked my way around backstage at a UFC event, looking for my prey. Scurrying around in every direction, men with laminated badges, clipboards, and headsets made what I and people like me do possible. Out of the corner of my eye, I saw my victim talking to one of his employees. His employee saw me over my victim's shoulder. I shook my head and flashed my eyes at him. He got the message and pretended not to notice me.

I heard the music from *Jaws* in my head. Closer. Closer. I crept up on my tiptoes. My victim still didn't see me. I bent over and pinched him on his very upper thigh, squeezing him with all of my strength. He jumped so high it's a wonder he didn't get a concussion from the ceiling. *"Motherfucker!"* he yelled. To preserve the man's anonymity, I'll just refer to him as "Mr. White."

"How's it going, buddy?" I smiled.

"Ow!" Mr. White rubbed his leg with his palm and hopped a bit. "That's going to leave a fucking bruise." He punched me in the shoulder.

"Hey, if Matt Hughes is around, you need to watch your back."

Mr. White winced again. "Have you heard about this shit with BJ?" he asked me.

"Yeah, I read a bit about it," I said.

"I think we're going to have to strip him of his title," he confided to me. "Lawsuits are flying everywhere. It's fucking nuts, man."

"Why, because he's wanting to fight in other places?"

"Yeah, and we're like, 'Dude, you can't fucking do that.' He just doesn't understand why we won't let him. It's like, 'You're our champion. Our champion can't go lose on another show. If you're going to lose, it's going to be on our show.'"

"Well, I got Renato Verissimo next and we'll see how that goes," I said. "I'll see you around, Dana."

On June 19, 2004, I was back at Vegas's Mandalay Bay Arena for my UFC 48 bout. There were rows and rows of fans who had waited hours just to be able to see me. Not even to see me fight, but to simply see me in the flesh right in front of them. When I was called, I pulled back the curtain and stepped out on the stage. I got on the scale, made weight, and flexed my arms for the crowd. From the cheers, I gathered that this was entertaining for them.

Verissimo had already weighed in and was standing on the far side of the stage, waiting for our picture to be taken. I went up and made a move like I was going to punch him. He jerked back and laughed, and I laughed right back. We posed for our photo and then hugged. All I could think about was that this was the first fight in a long time—maybe ever—where the outcome didn't matter. I could relax, compete, and not have to worry about the belt. Or worry about my career, or the money. It was like I was back in college or even high school. It felt more like Hillsboro than Vegas.

I swung by Mark's hotel room on the way back. I knocked on the door. "Come in," I heard. I pushed the door open. No one was there except Brian, Mark's buddy from church, lying on the bed with a book. He looked like a younger version of Dennis the Menace's father.

"Is Mark around?"

"He and Emily stepped away," Brian said. "Should be back soon."

"What're you reading there?"

"The Good Book!" Brian said, holding up the cover and chuckling.

"Yeah, Mark said you've done a lot with helping him be a Christian."

"Well, I'd say Mark should get the credit for that, or God. I'd be a distant third. Why, is that something you've been thinking about?"

I walked over and sat down on the chair next to the bed. "I'd like to know more about it. I mean, if this is something that my brother is serious about, I'm interested in it for that reason alone."

"Well, where would you say you are, spiritually?" Brian asked.

It was such an obvious question, but as soon as I started to answer, I knew the answer would be inadequate. "I'm not sure, to be honest with you. I mean, I go to church with Audra because she thinks Joey should be raised in a church, and I totally agree with it, 100 percent. But, how do you know that there's really a God?"

Brian put the bookmark in the Bible and put it on the nightstand. "Well, the best metaphor I've heard is this: If you were walking on the beach, and you found a watch, that would lead you to think someone made that watch, right? I mean, a watch can't come together from pieces of metal, randomly. So if you look at the universe, and how it's designed and how it's run, that tells you that someone or something has to be there, in the background. And that person or energy or whatever you want to call it, that would have to be God."

I looked out the window at all the Vegas lights. *I might be in the wrong city to be having this conversation.* "That's interesting," I told him. "I never heard of that before."

"Well, would you consider yourself a Christian?"

"Am I a Christian? Yes, definitely. Am I sure Christ is God? Well, no. But I think he's a good role model and definitely someone everyone should model themselves after, whether they're a Jew or a Christian or an atheist or whatever."

I could see Brian frown for a second but I didn't say anything else. "Well, that's not really a tenable position," he said. "Christ said He was the risen Son of God. So either He was telling the truth, and He *was*, or He was lying, or crazy, or both. And if He's lying or crazy, He's not exactly a good role model."

"Yeah, but every religion has their guy that they follow, and you don't necessarily have to believe he's, like, some spiritual holy person."

"True, but the difference between Christianity and the other religions is that Christianity's teacher is still living, and that is the Lord Jesus Christ. Muslims can go worship at Mohammed's tomb and all these other religions pray to dead people, but Christianity is the only one where your savior is still alive and still out there."

I sat there for a while. "You know, I haven't given a lot of thought to this stuff, so I don't want to offend you or say something ignorant, you know? This is very interesting, and I think it's also very important."

"I agree," Brian said.

So we sat, talked, and argued until it was almost past time for me to get to the arena and fight Verissimo. It was kind of a comeback fight, so I went back to my roots of wrestling. I thought that I was a better striker than he was, but I wasn't going to play that. I didn't want to go into where my strengths were and where his strengths were. I was going to go back to what was winning my fights. Verissimo is an excellent submission artist, and he wanted the fight on the ground too. We rolled and traded for the full three rounds, and when the final bell rang, I immediately shook his hand and helped him up. He gave me a hug. It was a unanimous decision for me, and that's still a win. Now I could focus on what really mattered.

On July 9, 2004, I stood at the front of the church in a blue cotton shirt and a tie that I had borrowed from Audra's stepdad.

The audience sat quietly, clad in denim jeans. Matt Ferguson, our pastor, stood behind me. We all watched Audra being led down the aisle by Joey, her son—*our* son, now. Her ivory dress was $90. It was the second one she bought, because one of our dogs had gotten a hold of the first one and ruined it. The ring was a $500 band with some diamonds.

She kept her eyes locked on mine, looking uncomfortable that everyone was staring at her. The day before, she had even joked that she wanted us to simply be standing at the front so she wouldn't have to walk down the aisle. There was no smoke, no pyrotechnics, and no Kid Rock blasting from speakers, but her entrance still captured everyone's attention.

"Before I get started," Matt Ferguson said, "Mark has some words to say to the new bride and groom."

"Are you kidding me?" Audra whispered in fear. But he was kidding. We put rings on each other's fingers and kissed. Less than eight minutes later, she was Mrs. Matt Hughes. One hundred of our aunts, uncles, and cousins, siblings, nephews, and nieces—and our friends—headed downstairs to the church basement for the meal. They watched us cut the cake. They covered their mouths with their hands so they could whisper about how there didn't seem to be any wine.

"We'd better get going," Audra said to me.

I glanced at the clock. "You're right," I answered, looking at her all gooey-eyed. I got a mike and thanked everyone for coming. It was time for the honeymoon.

We changed into shorts and T-shirts in the bathroom, got into my silver Jeep Grand Cherokee, and put Joey in the backseat.

Forty-five minutes later, we pulled up to the hotel in Springfield and parked. It was time to get wet.

The hotel had a pool, and we wanted Joey to swim as much as he could—that meant until closing time, ten o'clock. While our son did his laps, Audra and I sat there and watched, like we were on vacation on a beach in Florida. I thought about growing up with Mark, thought about racing with him in the water and splashing with him. I thought about what it would be like not to be a twin, not to always have someone there for you to play with. I knew that Joey would never have that problem if I was around.

At ten he got out of the water. We went to our room, dried Joey off, and got into the car to drive to a restaurant for a nice steak dinner. A nice Steak 'n' Shake dinner. The diner looked like something out of *Happy Days*. I read over the menu for no real reason, because I knew it by heart. "You know what?" I told my wife. "I may be watching what I eat, but this is my wedding day. I'm going for the steakburger."

After dinner we got back into the car, just blocks away from the hotel. "Let's drive home and spend the night in our own bed," Audra suggested.

I put my foot down. "No, honey, we're going to live on the wild side a little bit. We're going to go ahead and spend the night in this hotel because we already paid for it and it's our wedding night."

The next morning I drove back home to Hillsboro, with my family.

CHAPTER 12

The Sublime and the Ridiculous

I looked at Brian from across the poker table. "I don't want to go to some orphanage down in Mexico and live that lifestyle for a week," I told him.

"The thing is, Matt," he said, "we could sure use some tool belts down there, and you and Mark are real handy."

Mark turned over the card. It was a three. I raised anyway. "What kind of work is it?"

"We've got to lay concrete, and Mark's got experience with that." Brian tossed his cards on the table, folding.

I took the pot, tossing my cards over to my brother. "Well, if Mark goes, I'll go. If we're doing manual labor, I guess I can have a good time."

"Then I'll go if Matt goes," Mark said.

"You guys can go back and forth all night on this," Brian said, cracking his knuckles. "Just let me know what you think. It's not that bad."

"I'll tell you what," I said. "Let me check my schedule."

*   *   *   *

A couple of weeks later I was in Mexico with Mark, Brian, and the church youth group. The water in the orphanage shower had a different smell from the water in Hillsboro, and from the water in every hotel I'd ever been in. I stood with my back against the showerhead and tried to get the dirt out from my nails with my teeth. The dust and dirt were everywhere in Juarez. I put my hand up against the wall and the water felt tingly across my back and arm. I rubbed my bicep with my hand and let out a deep breath. I leaned against the wall again to scrub my leg and felt it tingle again. *That's not the tingle of relaxation,* I realized. *There must be an exposed wire behind this wall. I'm getting electrocuted.*

I got out of the shower, scrubbed myself dry, and put on a T-shirt and some cutoff jeans. I stepped out into the hall of the orphanage. The water cooler was humming in the other room, the closest thing they had to an air conditioner.

I headed to the cafeteria, a small room with long white plastic tables. The orphan kids were running everywhere, smiling like they were something out of *The Sound of Music,* but dressed like they were something out of Old Navy from five years ago. A little girl came up to me and said something in Spanish. I shrugged my shoulders. She laughed, and then I laughed, and she ran away. I walked over to the kitchen and grabbed breakfast. They had warmed the milk and cut up a banana into a bowl of cereal. I picked up a spoon and sat down next to my brother and Brian. "Aren't you eating anything?" I asked Mark.

"No," he said, all intense for some reason. "I'm not going to eat today."

"You're crazy," I told him. "Why aren't you eating?"

Mark made a little noise and looked away. I turned to Brian but he didn't say anything either; he just ate a spoonful of warm mush. Mark sat there the whole breakfast, looking around.

I got up after I finished eating and put the bowl and spoon in the kitchen. I started poking my head in different rooms, looking at all the bunk beds where we had been sleeping. Teenage kids from the youth group ran up and down the halls, almost knocking me over as they turned the corners.

I walked into the chapel. It was empty and quiet. It seemed like it was just a small room. There was nothing holy-seeming about it at all; it was hot, and it was dusty, and I was already sweating again and it wasn't even eight o'clock. Then I saw a big poster framed on the wall. It was of a bunch of different types of people on a rock in the middle of the ocean. A storm surrounded them, but they were busy playing guitar or talking. Some were in the water, helpless; a few of the others were trying their best to get them ashore. I stood there, looking at every single person drawn, and wondered what it was all about. I forced myself to look away and walked, quickly, back to the cafeteria. "Hey, can I show you something?" I asked Brian.

"Sure." Brian followed me back into the chapel, back to the painting. When he saw where I was leading him he tightened his lips and got serious. "Were you wondering about the picture?" he asked me.

"Yeah. Do you know what this is?"

He explained, "It's called *Who Cares?* The guy who founded the Salvation Army had a vision, and they made a painting based on it. Then they updated the painting at some point, and the idea is that you're supposed to see yourself as one of the people."

"That's what I guessed." I nodded and looked back at the wall. "Who do you think you are in the picture and who do you think I am?"

"Well, obviously you're the weightlifter," he said.

"That's what I thought at first, but no, look again." I folded my arms and I unfolded them.

Brian kept staring at *Who Cares?* "I can't tell you who you are, Matt, really. I don't even know who *I* am, but I'd like to be that guy on the dock helping people out."

"Me too! That's who I want to be. And I think you are that person."

Brian turned his head to me. "Well, that might be just another obvious answer."

"What are you saying?"

"I'm not saying anything. I just mean that that painting is the kind of thing you can look at for hours and not be sure of where you stand."

I considered what he said. "I've got an idea. Next time we do the Bible group with everyone, why don't we make copies of this and pass it around and everyone can say who they are in the picture. I'd be interested to hear what everyone thinks."

The next night, on the way back from dinner in Texas, the wipers were wagging hard on the windshield of the Astro van like the tails of two excited dogs. "We get five inches of rain a year," Dean said, staring out into the downpour from the driver's seat.

Dean ran the orphanage. He had the build of a former athlete and a haircut right out of the Beach Boys. "It looks like we're getting a couple of inches right now, easy. We should have been back an hour ago." The streets were not roads; they were practically canals. We could see a truck lodged on the center median, which had been submerged.

In the back seat, Mark, our buddy Scott, and I were digesting steaks from the restaurant in El Paso, as was Brian in the passenger seat. Our backs leaned into the seats at an angle like we were on recliners in our living rooms. "I think the road's blocked. I know a back way." Dean turned the wheel and we went onto what had been a dirt road, and was now a mud road. Every so often we'd get jostled, but we were going so slowly it was like we were on a boat getting knocked by an occasional strong wave.

Dean looked at me in the rearview mirror. "Matt, where would you say you are right now?"

"Mexico? Texas? Did we pass the border?"

Everyone laughed. "I mean spiritually."

"Well, I think I'm in a good place, spiritually."

"Oh, I had thought so at one time too," Dean explained. And he talked about being a partier at Loyola, and about how his path led him to move his family to run an orphanage in Mexico, about the time his kids asked him when they're moving back "home." Then Brian talked about how his divorce led him to Christ, and Scott went on about how something that happened to him at a deer stand brought him to salvation. Finally Mark talked about his promise to Emily and how that had brought them together as a family.

I listened very politely in the backseat for close to an hour. I was glad it was so dark because they couldn't tell how red in the face I was getting. I was turning red because I realized they had planned this.

"I'll ask you again, Matt," Dean finally said. "Where are you at, spiritually?"

"Look, I appreciate all these stories, and please don't get me wrong, I'm glad you told them to me. They're very interesting. But I just don't see what they have to do with me."

Four sets of shoulders seemed to sag at the same time. "Matt, what are you waiting for?" Mark demanded.

I sat up in my seat and my voice got a little louder. "You know what? I came down here for three reasons. Number one, to spend time with my church buddies; number two, to do some work with my hands. And the third reason was to help people. I'm all about having a good time. Now, I appreciate what you guys are trying to do, I really do, but I didn't come here to find Jesus."

The way Mark looked at me you would have thought I was lying to him. "Can you honestly tell me that you're content where you're at?" he snapped.

"Yes, Mark, I am!" I snapped right back. "Right now I'm asking questions, I'm reading the Bible."

"Matt, the time is now."

"Mark, I just got married, I'm still learning about God. My life is pretty much perfect as it is."

"Don't you think it could be better?"

I turned and stared out the window. I couldn't see much

through the rain, but I remembered what those words looked like when I wrote them to Audra. I remembered how I felt when I mailed her that flower.

"Let's talk about something else," Brian interjected.

"Let me just say one more thing," Mark said. "I fasted the whole day on Wednesday because I wanted God to hear me so that you would become a Christian."

I didn't respond. I stared out into the downpour but couldn't see anything for all that water.

It was our last night in Mexico, and we were all at the top of McKelligon Canyon. We could see the lights of El Paso in the distance. The sand still swirled around in the wind but the trees and plants gave us some space. Twenty-eight of us—the kids in the youth group, me and my brother, our buddies from Hillsboro—stood there in a circle. The sun was beating down and any humidity that the rain might have brought was gone like a week-old dream. Our sneakers were dirty from working all week, and we were sore.

We went around the circle and we talked about *Who Cares?* Teenagers talked about things that they would never tell their parents; our pastor from Hillsboro had to leave the circle when he broke down in tears, discussing his sons. People were saying the kinds of things that were so personal you couldn't possibly repeat them. You'd miss the nuance. The point of the stories were told by people's expressions as much as by their words. We held hands in that circle and we talked about who we thought we were in that painting.

By the time it got to my turn the sun was beginning to set, the golden hour. "The first time I looked at the painting I thought I was the weightlifter," I began. "Then I started to understand the picture a little bit more, and I thought, *I wouldn't be up on that platform.* Then I thought, *I'm a helping person. I'm the guy on the boat. I'm in the water but I'm helping people.* Then I thought a little bit more and thought, *I'm not as saved as that.* Now I realize that I'm not saved at all. I'm one of the guys under the water, and I'm not a Christian." I thought about how I had been literally under the water years ago, until somehow I got an idea that ended up saving my life.

I felt both my hands get a squeeze from the people on each side of me. I squeezed back, just a little bit, to thank them. When I finished I felt everyone's face on me. No one was judging me, but from their eyes I could tell that more than a few were praying for me.

Soon it was Mark's turn. "I think I'm one of the guys reaching out on the dock. I'm reaching out to help, you know, the best way I can, to pull people out of the water. You people that know you're not saved, *please*, do something about it. *The time is now.* Don't wait until you get back to Hillsboro."

I stared at my brother, but he wouldn't make eye contact with me. I couldn't hear the next person talking. I put my head down and thought about where I was, about who I was, and about who I wanted to be. I thought about God, and His Son. I thought about my wife, and the husband I knew I should be; I thought about our son, and the father I knew I could be. I put my head down and said a prayer for forgiveness. *Jesus, I know You died on the cross for me. I want You to take me in and I want to walk in Your footsteps.*

Then it was like I was a candle which had just been lit for the first time. I could sense an energy pouring out of me, as if only now I had become what I was meant to be. I saw the faraway twinkling lights of El Paso, and suddenly they seemed like they were stars, and I was floating above them looking down. I was convinced I could make it there in two steps. When I exhaled I held on tight to the people by my sides. I didn't want to sail away, on a breath.

We said a prayer and then broke the circle. I walked over to Mark and Brian. They looked at me like I was the same person, and I was amazed that they couldn't see what had happened to me. "I've made a decision," I said. "I'm a Christian." My brother grabbed me and hugged me so hard that he lifted me clean off that mountaintop. He had pulled me out of the water at long last.

A couple of days later I was back in Hillsboro, sitting on one of the wooden chairs at our kitchen table. To my right I could see our deck, and past that the backyard. I was looking for John Deere stuff on eBay on my laptop. Audra walked in with the mail and started going through it piece by piece. "What's this?" she said.

"I forgot. I sent you a postcard when I was in Mexico."

She put down the rest of the mail on the kitchen counter and started to read it. I watched her face because I remembered what I wrote and I was excited to hear what she thought. She held it up in the air and looked at me. "What's this?" she said again. But this time her eyebrow was raised, her lip was curled, her voice was sharp.

"What don't you get?" I asked her.

"'I've made a lot of changes and you'll see that most of them are for the good,'" she read. "What kind of changes do you mean, Matt? What, you're going to be on your high horse now because God spoke to you on a mountaintop?"

"You know, just because you believe in God doesn't make you a Christian. You know that? Satan believes in God. Do you know that?"

"No, Matt, I don't. I don't know that," she said, crossing her arms. "Whose idea was it to go to church anyway? Who said that we should raise Joey in a church? Was it you?"

"Mom, I don't know why you're getting so upset. This is a good thing. It means being a better husband to you and being a more honest person. Praying more and giving thanks."

She stared me down. Then it was like someone had whispered in her ear the exact thing to say. "You're being honest, huh? Okay, Mr. Honesty, tell me this: Did you or did you not hook up with that Nici girl?"

"Yeah, Momma, I did. You and I weren't married, but I'm not making excuses. There is no excuse."

Over Audra's shoulder there was a mantle of photos of our family: me and her, her and Joey, me and Joey. Her expression made those pictures seem sarcastic, like the idea that we would be smiling somewhere together had to be some kind of a joke. "I knew it. I freaking knew it. I bet you there's a list of them. I asked you about her before," my wife said.

"I know, Mom. All I can tell you is that I promise it won't happen again, and I'm sorry about it."

"Didn't you get a good look at that face of hers? What the fuck is the matter with you?" Audra took the postcard and held it up to me. She ripped it in half, and then ripped it into quarters. Then my wife tipped open the garbage can lid and threw the pieces inside.

"Maybe you shouldn't cuss so much," I told her sternly.

"You've been a Christian for a few days and now you're going to be telling me how to fucking talk? Are you freaking kidding me?"

"Mom, all I'm saying is that there's going to be a big difference around here. You'll see."

"Oh, yeah?" she said. "How do you know that?"

"I don't know that," I admitted. "But I have faith that there will be."

"I've got to go pick Joey up from school," she said. She turned around and walked to her car. I would have liked it better if she had slammed the door. I gave her some space for the next couple of days. Then when I was getting dressed in the morning I noticed my postcard on the dresser, taped back together.

I closed my eyes and said a quick prayer of thanks.

On October 22, 2004, I was at Trump Plaza in Atlantic City for UFC 50. Georges St. Pierre had a shaved head and he was toned, but when I looked at him across the octagon I could find nothing else that reminded me of Frank Trigg. Georges looked me in the eye, not timid and not cocky. *Let's hurry up and get this done before he gets another minute more experience,* I thought.

We touched gloves. I threw punches and made sure to work my angles, to keep my feet moving like my boxing coach Matt Peña taught me. Georges hit back, and he hit hard. *This guy's pretty strong. I'm taking this to the ground.* I shot to take him down and he defended a bit, but I got him. If he had pushed his left hand on my knee and brought his leg up and around, he could have gotten guard back. But he didn't.

Georges tried tying me up with his arms, but I still got some punches in. He tried to go for a keylock, but I spun around and got him in an armbar. Less than a second before the end of the first round, Georges tapped.

The crowd exploded and I jumped up. "Did he tap? Did he tap?" Mark yelled from the corner.

I looked down at GSP. "Hey, Georges, you okay?" I asked him.

"Yeah," he said.

"You tapped out, right?"

"Yeah." From the look on his face I knew what was going through his head, because it had been going through mine when I was there. GSP was no longer undefeated.

A month later I was driving from Bettendorf to Hillsboro. I pulled the CD out of the drive and looked at the label. It said "Mark" on it. I put it on the seat next to me. The trees that lined the highway were turning orange, which meant that there were things to do on the farm. But I was driving in the other direction, to Bettendorf.

With my right hand I felt around on the passenger seat for the first CD I had listened to. I grabbed the disc to see if it said "Mark" also. It said "Matthew." I tossed it back down, stuck my earpiece in my ear, and called up Brian. "Hey buddy, what's happening?"

"I'm all right. How about yourself?"

"Good, good. Hey, I'm driving down to Iowa and I got the Bible on CD here and I think I got a bad set of CDs."

"What do you mean?"

"I finished listening to Matthew and then I popped in Mark and it's the same exact story," I explained. "Is that how it's supposed to be?"

"Um . . . yes. They're telling their perspective on what they saw in their walks with Christ. Luke and John are also going to be similar."

"What's so funny?"

"Nothing," he said, wheezing a little.

"Oh, it sounded like you were laughing there for a second."

Several weeks later I was at Park 'n' Eat in Hillsboro. The restaurant probably used to be a trailer. There were eight seats around the counter and that's it. Above the counter was the menu, with black plastic letters spelling out the choices next to the low prices. Below were Pepsi stickers, the logo from when I was a kid now faded to orange and sky blue.

The three men in the place had hats and jeans on, and all of them chewed tobacco. I had gone to school with one or another of their kids. "So when's your next fight?" one of them asked me.

"I'm waiting for that call any day now, buddy," I told him. Ring tone music started playing out of my pocket. I sat down, took out my cell, and looked at the screen. Dana. "What's going on, DW?"

"I've got your next fight for you. It's going to be Trigg again."

I spun the bar stool away from everybody. "What? Dana, I'm not going to be able to beat this guy any better than I beat him last time."

"Well, we don't have anyone else to throw at you," he explained.

"All right," I said. "I'll do it."

I got off the phone and dipped my fries into some ketchup. I scarfed them down with the burger, threw down five bucks, and waved goodbye.

On April 16, 2005, I was at the MGM Grand Arena in Las Vegas. I was finishing getting my hands taped backstage for UFC 52. The room was shaped like a bottle, with the doorway in the exact center of the wall. I was sitting with my back to the entrance. All around me were the Miletich guys, wearing white, black, or gray sweats and T-shirts that they had gotten from sponsors and sneakers, with one or two in flip-flops. It was like we were waiting for a movie to start: We were kind of quiet, but ready for something to happen.

We were watching the undercard fights on the smallish TV, with duct tape holding its wires to the wall. "What did Eddie Bravo just say?" Robbie Lawler asked. He looked like he was someone's younger brother, and had that energy like a freshman who couldn't believe he was hanging out with the seniors.

"Now, Robbie," I told him, "you know the only reason Eddie Bravo is there is to keep Joe Rogan on time, and you *know* that Joe won't do the show without him. It's not an easy job; trust me."

Robbie shrugged and looked up. I felt someone walking into the room from over my shoulder. Pat lurched in and leaned against the wall across from me. He started smiling, the kind of smile a crocodile would have if it's just ready and waiting for its next meal.

"Hey, Old Gray Mare, what's going on?" I said. He pointed behind me with his chin, and standing there was my brother. "*Mark?* You told me you had to–"

He gave me a big hug. "And you believed me? You think I was going to miss this? Hey, I guess we know who the smart one in the family is." I squeezed him tight. I felt silly for thinking he wouldn't come. I started to well up and I shook my head a second to clear my eyes. "We've got a jerk out there to take care of," Mark said.

The rest of the people in the room turned their heads or started to get into their own conversations. I pulled away from my brother and stood in front of him like I was looking at a fun-house mirror, one that made me look a little chubbier and a lot more scruffy. "Did you hear what he's been saying in interviews?" I asked Mark.

"What, you mean about him having something that you want?"

"He means that Nici girl," I said.

Mark looked down at the ground and scowled. Then he snapped his fingers. "That one you went out with? He's with her now?"

"Yeah," I said. Mark's eyes opened wide and he let out a deep breath. "*Yeah*," I said again.

Minutes later, when we were in the octagon, Frank Trigg looked at the ground even while Bruce Buffer announced his name. All I could do was stare at the tattoos he had on his lats. He was giving up his back already, and the fight hadn't even started yet.

The ref looked over at my opponent. "Frank!" Mario Yamasaki yelled. Trigg turned around and walked over to meet me in the center of the cage. And then he kept walking, even though I was right there. *What's this guy doing?* I felt his lips against my face and I shoved him: I knew where those lips had been. From across the octagon, Twinkle Toes started blowing kisses at me.

When the bell rang he came at me hard. We traded a bit and then he landed a knee, right in my groin. Fortunately it only hit my cup, so instead of a sharp pain it simply went into me and left me numb. I lost my breath and knew that the ref had to have seen it. I turned to him to see what he'd do. But Mario did nothing, and then Trigg did something.

His first two punches connected, but they didn't really hurt. After the third or fourth hit, I wasn't feeling much of anything anymore except for my back against the floor. The next thing I knew, Twinkle Toes was mounted on me and I had gotten a hold of his waist. He was balancing himself with one hand on the mat and using the other to try to hit me again. *I've got to get out of here, and there's got to be a way out. I've just got to figure out what that is. Just catch your wind and think.*

I got my foot on the fence and tried to flip him. I couldn't do it, and he started to try to choke me out. I raised my hips and turned into him. Now we were face-to-face. *This is the guy who hit me in the nuts, and kept hitting me. Even if the ref didn't call it, he knew it was a foul.* I looked at that queer expression of his; it was the first time I was truly angry in the cage.

I grabbed him, lifted him up, and carried him across the octagon to my corner. My cornermen stood up and started to cheer. I slammed him down and began to hurt him as much as I could. I passed right through his guard, got mounted, and started throwing elbows.

Trigg buckled, again. He gave up his back, again. But I didn't take it this time. I would never have a chance to be in a cage with this person again, and I needed him to hear the things my fists wanted to say to his face. I hit him and hit him and hit him again. He tried to scramble away from my punches and gave up his back yet again. I took it and choked him until he tapped.

His eyes were all over the place, trying to get his bearing. I lay there on the mat waiting until he looked at me, and then I threw him a huge smirk. The Matt Hughes–Frank Trigg story was done.

A few weeks later, driving home from Bettendorf, I shoved my earpiece in and hit a button on my cell. "Hey, Mom. I'm driving back right now and I should be home before dark. How are you?"

"I'm fine," Audra said.

"What's going on? You don't sound like everything is fine."

"When I went to pick Joey up at school, I had to talk to his teacher. He got in trouble for fighting with the other kids at recess."

"Is he there? Put him on. Let me talk to him." I heard her pass the phone over to him. "Joey, what happened?"

"Us kids were playing," he explained in his soft voice, "and we started kicking and pushing. Everybody was doing it!"

"Joey," I said, angry, "were you using your toe? Or your shin?"

"Toe . . ."

"Joey, you can't do that! If you're going to kick somebody, you've gotta use your shin. You're going to break your toe!"

"I know . . ."

Then my wife snatched the phone from him. "Matt, I'm trying to teach him that he shouldn't be getting into trouble, not which way he should be hitting the other kids!"

Dial tone.

CHAPTER 13

The (Other) Big Show

I got on my red Yamaha four-wheeler and took a ride around the farm. On my left were trees and on my right were acres of corn. The stalks were coming in nicely—no bare spots. I sped up. The wind pulled my T-shirt against my body and blew some dust into my face, and when the path was a bit uneven I jumped up a bit in my seat. In my mind's eye I could see two little red-headed twin boys running around and wrestling each other, and I could see certain trees that were no longer there. I made a wide turn and tore back up the hill to the house. My sneakers and the bottom of my jeans were muddy. I kicked off a little of the dirt.

I took off my shoes, walked into the kitchen, and poured myself some water from the pitcher in the fridge. The fridge door was covered with pictures of friends and family and notes that Mark and Emily had written to one another. By the refrigerator were glass bowls, filled with candies. I saw my cell phone on the counter. I had missed a call from Dana. I picked up and called him back. "What, is it going to be Trigg III?" I said, first thing. "I can only choke the guy out so many ways!"

"Ha, ha," he said. "How are you? You been good?"

"Yeah, I'm good. How're Annie and the kids?"

"I think you're going to be seeing a bit of them this summer," he said, dangling something in front of me.

"How's that?"

"You ready for this?"

"Go for it, DW! What do you got? Come on now!"

I could hear him licking his lips over the phone. "We want you to be a coach on *The Ultimate Fighter*, and we want the winner of Franklin versus Tanner to be the other coach. Then you fight the other coach at the end. Pack your bags, buddy, you're going to Vegas for the summer." He waited. I guess he thought I had put down the phone and was jumping up and down for joy. But my feet were still planted firmly on the earth.

"I'm not fighting Rich," I told him.

"What? You said that you'd go up a weight class if I needed you to."

"Yes, and I will. But I know Rich, he's a buddy of mine, we have the same manager. I'm not fighting him."

"How about Evan?" Dana said.

"That's fine. I think he's in a good place now, so we'd get along, but I'll fight him, sure."

"So you in?"

"Let me think about it," I said. "I need to talk to my wife first, okay?"

"Well, call me back right away."

I hung up the phone, put my shoes on, and got in my truck to go home. I was worried about how I was going to let Dana down easy. When I got to my house, Audra was wearing a gray T-shirt with pajama bottoms and had just set a tray of Rice Krispies treats on the counter. She was cutting a corner off for herself. "This is for Joey," she said, kind of apologizing even though she was so skinny. "I'm just having one piece."

"That's fine, Mom." I put my arms around her and shook her around a little bit.

She pushed back against me, giggling. "Stop."

"I'm not doing anything," I said, swinging her from side to side. I let her go and she went back to grab the knife and cut some more squares for herself. "Listen, Dana called and he wants me to be a coach on *TUF*."

She chewed for a second. "I think you should do it. You'll get a lot of exposure."

"Well, what about Randy, Mom?"

"What *about* Randy?"

"When he was on the show he found that girl and he ended up leaving his wife for her. I don't want anything like that to happen."

Audra leaned back on the counter, resting on her elbows. "You're not Randy, Matt."

"I know! I'm no Randy. But Randy's the guy who I *wanted*

to be, and if this can happen to him, it sure could happen to me. What's my favorite Bible verse?"

"It's the only one you know," she said, smirking.

"Come on, Momma . . ."

"About Jesus coming into the world to save sinners."

"Of whom I am the worst," I finished. "I don't want to be away from the farm, I don't want to be away from Hillsboro, and I don't want to be away from you and Joe. I'll do the show if you come out there with the boy."

"Well, when is it?"

"It's six weeks in June, into July."

"Joey's got baseball, Matt. And what am I going to do out there, anyway?"

"Do you hear yourself? You love Vegas. Come on, we can go to Raffles any time you want. It'll be our anniversary, Momma."

She rolled her eyes. That meant she was annoyed at herself for giving in. "*Fine.* I'll fly out there for half the time. But I don't want to be on camera."

"That's cool," I said. "I'm going to call Dana right now."

She shrugged. "Okay."

I held her hand as I got the UFC president back on the phone. I moved my hand up her arm and ran my fingers through her long strawberry blond hair. Audra stood there polishing off more of those treats. "Dana, it's Matt Hughes. I'll do it."

"That's great, man, that's great. Are you sure you're not interested in fighting Rich? It would really help us out a lot, you know."

"Hey, when's the last time I said no to anything?" I asked him.

"Okay, okay."

"But I also want you to know that I'm going to go out there and be a coach. I'm not going to give you guys a soap opera. Or cuss."

"Just be yourself, man," Dana said, "we'll have everything that we need."

Subject: Hi from Vegas

To: Audra Hughes <joey██@████.com>

Date: Monday, June 27, 2005 8:17 pm

From: Matt Hughes <matthew██@███com>

You said that I'm only allowed to call you four times a day, but you didn't say anything about writing you an e-mail. Ha, ha! I called Jeremy and he's going to come out here and help with the guys. Timmy called and he said that he wants to help with the coaching, so I'm going to throw him a bone and try to get him some airtime. They've got us here in some gated corporate housing on the corner of Flamingo and Cobalt. Right by the strip. There's pools all over the place, so bring your swimsuit. We've got a good-size bed because I know how much you like your sleep!

I love you so much and I would never change anything about you!!

Love you,

Your husband

*   *   *   *

The next morning I went to the *TUF* gym. I shook hands with
Rich Franklin and patted him on the back. They called him "Ace"
because he looked like Ace Ventura. Whenever I saw him he was
smiling, and when he saw me he started laughing—with me, not
at me. But sometimes, at me.

We watched the guys get put through drills: hitting pads and
light sparring, pairing up and grappling. I saw Melvin Guillard
try to pass guard on his partner. He couldn't, so he tried to muscle his way through, jumping up and using all his force. *He's
going to hurt someone,* I thought. "That Melvin guy there's a great
wrestler," I whispered to Rich.

"Really?" he said.

"Keep an eye on him, he's got some real talent."

Later that afternoon, Dana said to us, "We've got a guy trying
to quit and walk off the show. We need to go talk to him."

"Which one?" I asked.

"Eli."

We found him in his room. The three of us stood there, trying
to talk the guy out of leaving. "How can you throw this away?" I
said. "It's not like you're going home. You're going to a sequester
house anyway. It's not like you get to go be with your family. You
can't call people. You know you signed a contract."

"Man," Eli complained, "the pressure with all these cameras . . ."

"Just don't worry about it. Forget about these cameras," I
told him. "Just have a fight and have some fun with it."

"I can't do it, man. I can't do it."

Dana and Rich continued to argue with him, and he just kept talking in circles. *This isn't going anywhere,* I thought. *The guy's walking off because he knows he's the worst heavyweight here and he doesn't want to fight. He talked his way onto the show and he's talking his way off of it.* I just stood and kept my mouth shut as Dana got louder and cussed more . . . if that were even possible. This wasn't going to affect my team selections one bit.

I went online to Sherdog that night and looked over everybody's fight history. Then I went over the lists from the trainers, about what they considered each person's skills to be. In the morning Rich and I went to an office to talk over the team picks. The walls were covered with big blown-up photographs of people we knew—and ourselves. I leaned back in a chair and made myself comfortable.

"You know, I'd really like Jorge," Rich told me.

"Well, I'd really like Mike." We had an understanding. "Okay, we've got to pick the worst guy from welterweight so they can fight to stay on the show. Who were you thinking?"

"I'm thinking . . ." Rich looked over the sheet with everyone's names by their pictures. "I'm thinking Kenny."

"See, Rich? This is why you and I get along."

"That's what you thought too?" he said, a bit surprised.

"Yeah. I mean, I know you don't know much about coaching, but it's kind of obvious."

"I also don't know anything about losing a world title," he said, laughing.

"Is that why you measure your food, Rich? So you can be sure you stay on top?"

"That crack was about as weak as your so-called abs."

The next afternoon at the *TUF* house, Kenny called out Sammy to fight. Dana flipped a coin and I got to corner Sammy. Rich couldn't get his boy Kenny to make weight and he forfeited; I was one win ahead of Rich already. Then it came time to pick teams. Rich won the coin toss and I could feel my jaw clamp right up. That meant we were effectively tied, because we had each won something. But after I got all my picks—including Rob and Tom, "the GNC brothers"—I thought my team would whip Rich's.

My guys got into a huddle. I could see that some of them looked at me like a woman looking at a huge diamond: They had seen it in pictures and now couldn't believe it was actually right in front of them. "Your life as a fighter is going to start as soon as you finish this show. Not all of you are going to win, but all of you can get better and have a competitive life after the series. I'm here for you, not for the cameras. I definitely didn't come out here to be on TV."

The first challenge was introduced by Randy Couture. "Hey, Matt!" he said.

There was a welcoming look in his eyes and I realized that the man would have made a phenomenal psychiatrist. Everything about him radiated decency—except for his actions.

"Hello," I said to him, looking away immediately.

Randy acted completely professionally, and explained the game to everyone. "Here're the rules. The four welterweights from each team have to grab that heavy bag and run it across to their end zone. The first team to do that wins and gets to pick the fight. But you have to be on your knees."

We huddled together. "Here's what we're going to do," I said. "Luke's got really strong legs. Luke, you grab someone with both your legs and your arms for just a second, and then someone take that bag and run it to the end."

My team did exactly as I said. I watched Josh grab the bag and take off on his knees like he was sprinting. I screamed at him from the sidelines, and when he crossed that line I sprinted right at him. My team all ran together and cheered. "The first of many, guys!" I told them. "The first of many."

We got back to the house. Team Hughes looked around, wondering who was going to talk first. Some of the guys had their suggestions, but I wasn't hearing them. "Guys, to be honest, I've got a game plan for this," I told them. "We've got to win challenges, and when we win challenges we get to pick the fights. That's a heck of an advantage, putting our styles against theirs. *Our game plan is to get them.* Their biggest athlete on the welterweight side is Melvin. I need him gone."

"I want him," Josh said.

I looked at Josh and thought the match through in my mind. *Josh has a slight edge on everything, and the only way Melvin's going to win is by decision.* "You got it," I told Josh. The fight ended up with him winning, but getting injured in the process. Jason Von Flue was his replacement.

I looked at Jason when he walked in, and watched him talk to the guys. He was friendly and palling around with them like they were best friends already. *This is going to be a guy I don't like,* I thought. "Hey, you don't have a shirt yet," I told him.

He did a double take. "Huh?"

"You don't have a Team Hughes shirt. These guys all went through evals. You've got to earn it. Here's what we're going to do. You've got three circuits to run. It's weights, and then tread-mill. Three times. They all did it already." He got up and nod-ded, ready to show me what he was made of. And he did.

Minutes later he was on the treadmill, panting. I felt the cameraman standing right there and tried not to notice, and tried not to scowl. When Jason gave the machine the middle finger, trying to look cool on TV, I thought, *If you're here for the cameras, then I can't be here for you.* He finished his run and chugged some water. You'd think he had run a marathon. "I told you, you've got three of these."

He shook his head. "I can't do two more circuits, Matt."

"Well, just do your best," I said, already disgusted.

A little later, Randy announced the next challenge. Mike Whitehead told our team, "We got this." I didn't say anything. I knew Mike from Bettendorf, and I knew Mike was going to win the show.

We trounced Rich's team in the challenge, but then we lost the fight. And the challenge after that. When they announced that their fight would be Marcus Davis against my Joe Stevenson, I had to stop from laughing in their faces. "That would have been something *I* would have picked," I said to Rich. "Joe was my first pick, and you're putting a good wrestler and my best submission guy against a *boxer*?"

Rich looked down. "Well, Marcus picked it."

"You're the coach," I told him. "You're trying to get these guys to the end. You could have put him against Luke or Von Flue and gotten rid of them."

He nodded. "I see what you're saying." I squinted and looked into his eyes. He didn't have the craziness that every good coach has, the need for your team to put the other team into the ground. It was like he was from another country than I was. Joe ended up beating Marcus in seconds. I didn't say anything to Rich after the fight. I didn't need to.

The next day I went to the Vegas airport. Part of me wanted to stand there looking into the ramp for Audra to deplane, but I knew if I just sat down and zoned out the time would pass that much faster. I watched the people going by and tried guessing where they were from. Some were in baseball caps and sneakers—they were probably from the Midwest. Some were in suits or flashier clothes. I signed an autograph or two.

When I saw her walking toward me with Joey I bolted right up, ran to them, and grabbed their suitcases. I lifted my son to my hip and gave Audra a kiss and then a hug. "How was your flight?" I asked her. I was beaming like a dad at graduation.

"It was fine," she said. She was smiling too, which meant she was excited but would never actually tell me that.

"I missed you, Joey," I said, kissing him on the top of his head.

"I missed you too, Dad," he said, not as excited as I was.

We walked toward the parking garage. "I think you should get Joey on TV," Audra said.

"What do you think, Joe? You wanna be on TV?" I asked him. He shrugged. "All right."

"The McElroys still flying out?" I asked Audra. They were family friends.

"Yeah, they'll be here day after next. So how's the show going?"

"It's fine. It doesn't really matter. Let's go get some food. You hungry, Joe?"

Every heavyweight challenge, all Mike had to say is, "We got this." And he was right every time. One challenge was to pull the socks off the other team, and not even one of our socks got removed. Just like in the cage, when I saw a wound I went for it to open it up and finish things faster.

"Did you guys hear the same instructions that our team did?" I asked Rich's team. "It's 'take the other team's socks off,' not 'sit around, looking like a bunch of idiots.'" I watched them clench their fists, shake their heads, and bite their lips to keep from laughing just a bit. They could handle a punch to the face better than they could handle a sharp word thrown in their direction. And I knew that emotional people make mistakes in competitions, and that this would only help out my guys.

"Don't worry about him," Rich said, trying to keep from laughing himself. "He's just trying to get under your skin." His team mumbled some things, and that made me laugh at them even harder.

Finally it was time for my top pick, Mike, to fight. I took Joey to the office so he could watch me through the window. Mike's opponent was Rashad, who I had already told off for dancing in the ring and making a spectacle of himself. When I walked Mike to the ring it reminded me of coaching back at Eastern, and I realized Pat must have felt a bit like this when he led me to the cage to take on Carlos for the belt.

I watched Mike try to turn it into a wrestling match, but Rashad controlled all the action. When Mike got Rashad down on the ground, I kept waiting for Mike to finish him. But he couldn't. I yelled advice, but Mike had a dead battery. My top pick was running on empty, and there was nothing I could do. *I've never seen anyone fold this badly,* I thought. *Don't cuss at him. Don't cuss.* I ran into the cage between rounds and stood over Mike, who was trying to catch his breath. I didn't recognize the person who was looking at me out of Mike's eyes. "Get out there and work. I'm serious!" I threw a water bottle at the wall.

Rashad got the win. They brought Mike's stuff directly to the cage. We said our goodbyes then and there. When he looked at me he looked like a kid who had got caught smoking. He knew what he had done, and he had no excuse. "Take care," I told him. I managed to bring myself to shake his hand.

I ran out of there and jumped in my car. The McElroys were flying back home, and I had to go drop them off at the airport. I picked them up from the condo's basement parking lot, got out on the strip, and headed to McCarran Airport as fast as I could to make sure they made their flight. I picked up my cell and rang up Audra. "Hey, Momma. I've got the McElroys, and we're headed to the airport right now."

"Okay, I'll see you in a little bit. Ask Joey if he's hungry."

I almost drove off the road, I almost had a stroke, I almost dropped the phone—all at the same time. "I'll be there soon. I love you, honey." I hung up the phone. I looked at the passenger seat. Then I turned around quickly and looked at the backseat. There wasn't a blond boy anywhere to be found. *Relax,* I thought. *Everyone on the show knows who he is. He's probably playing with Randy or something. He'll be fine.* I called Rich Franklin right away. The McElroys were looking at me, so I tried to keep my voice as calm as possible. "Hey, Rich, Joey's there with you, right?"

"Yeah, he's fine," Rich said. "Want me to bring him back to the condo?"

"Could you?" I said. "I'd really appreciate it." I hung up and let out a deep breath. Then I realized that I hadn't been too worried, because I knew Randy Couture was there, and he was a man that I could trust with my son. Which meant he was still a man I could trust, period.

One night after taping Audra and I went to a restaurant. She was in her little black dress and I was in a button-down shirt with some jeans. If Dana hadn't made reservations, they probably wouldn't have seated us. The host looked like he knew the thread count in their fancy tablecloths. He led us right to our table. All around us on the walls were vintage photographs of the old strip.

The waiter wheeled out a tray of steaks and introduced them. "This is rib eye, this is porterhouse, this is the chateaubriand."

Audra's eyes glistened. "They all look so good."

"That's what I love most about you," I said. "I love that my woman loves her meat."

"Will you shut up?" she said, blushing. "I'm trying to make up my mind."

"You order whatever you like."

"Gee, thanks. I was going to."

"The UFC is picking up the bill, anyway."

She acted like she didn't hear me. "I'll have the rib eye, medium well," she told the waiter.

"Same for me but medium." The waiter nodded, took our menus, and rolled the cart away. "Oh, before I forget. Me and Rich are flying out in a couple of weeks to shoot a Xyience ad. I met the guy through Dana."

"Well, you just let me know when you'll be home so I can mark it on the calendar," she said, huffing.

"Hey, when I'm there, you act like you don't want me there, and when I'm gone, you ask me when I'm coming home. Make up your mind!"

"Do you really think I wouldn't rather have you at home?" she asked, kind of loudly.

"I was just joking. And I was joking before, too, about what I love about you. That's not what I love most about you, that you like a steak," I said. I tried to hold her hands from across the table and look deep into her eyes, but Audra kept getting self-conscious and looking away.

"Oh, that's not? So what do you love most about me?"

"I love the way that you look the same in the morning as you do when you go to bed at night, because you're so naturally pretty. And that you don't realize how pretty you are. I love the fact that you like being at home. And I love that I can totally trust you—your loyalty."

"My *loyalty*?" she repeated. "Matt, you make me sound like I'm some kind of a dog."

"Now Mom, be fair. That's not what I meant and you know it."

"Well, what do you mean?"

She was letting me stroke her hand at the table. She was listening. "I meant how you only went on one date when we were broken up. You didn't want to ruin any chances of us getting back together."

She shrugged. "I didn't meet anyone I liked, is all. Besides, I'm not the one you're crazy about. You always say that you married Joey and got me, too."

Audra and I both noticed the man standing next to our table at the same time. "I'm sorry to interrupt your meal, but are you Matt Hughes?" he asked. He must have been forty years old. At the very least, he was old enough to know better.

"Yeah."

"Mr. Hughes, can I please have your autograph?" The pen and paper he stuck out weren't shaking one bit. I grabbed the pen, signed quickly, and shoved it back to him without looking up. I felt Audra glaring at him.

I shook my head when he left. "If he were so sorry, why would he do it in the first place?"

Audra waited for him to walk away. "I can't believe you signed that for him."

"You're right. I shouldn't have done that. I apologize." She made a face and drank some water. "What were we talking about?" I asked her.

"Joey," she said.

"Right. You know what Dana asked me when I dropped Joey off today? He asked me if I ever wished that Joey was my son by blood. And I didn't even have to think about. Right away, I knew the answer is no. Because Joey wouldn't be Joey. He'd be someone else."

Audra smiled. "Aw, that's sweet."

"Uh-oh, I'm getting a smile. I better get a picture to remember this moment forever!"

She yanked her hands away. "Could you be freaking serious for one night? This is our anniversary dinner at a fancy steak house."

"What, just because it's our anniversary, I can't have a good time?" But Audra was still smiling, so I knew it was okay. "Do you ever think about having another kid?"

She took a sip from her glass and put it down. She was stalling. "Do you?"

"Yeah," I said. "I do."

A couple of weeks later I flew to South Carolina to shoot my ad. When I walked into the studio, there were two hanging racks full of pants, shirts, and jackets. "I picked out some clothes that I thought you would like, so why don't you look through them and find ones that are the most 'you,'" the lady said.

I started flipping through the clothes. I pulled out one navy blue shirt and looked at the label: Eddie Bauer. I started pulling

back the collars and looking at all the brands. J. Crew. Lands'
End. The pants were Abercrombie.

"I'm not trying to be difficult," I told her, "but I wouldn't
really wear any of this stuff. It's not farm material. Just pick
something out for me and I'll be happy to put it on."

"Well, where do you get your clothes?"

"To be honest, if I'm going to wear stuff on the farm, I go to
the Salvation Army to buy clothes."

"You're tell me that what you're wearing you got from the
Salvation Army?"

I looked down. "Tapout sent me the T-shirt, and the jeans I
got at the gym."

"What? They sell jeans at your gym?"

"No, they were in the lost and found. It had been long enough
that I felt comfortable that I wasn't stealing them."

She turned around, scanned the racks, and pulled out a shirt
and then some pants. She handed them to me. "Let me know if
they don't fit."

Anthony Giordano came in and grabbed me from behind.
"Hey, Matt *Huuuuughes*! How's it going?"

"Just picking out clothes, Anthony."

"Did you bring that Armani jacket for the limo shot?"

"Wait," the lady interrupted. "*You* have an Armani jacket?"

"Yeah, the UFC bought me and Rich an outfit when we were
going to be on CNBC or MSNBC or something. That's real
high-end, right?"

She blinked. "Yes. It's high-end."

After I got dressed they led me to a small set. There was a

fake kitchen with a fridge, cabinets, and a table. On the fridge door were fake newspaper articles about me and even photos of Joey; it was all so real it was unreal. There were muffins, orange juice, fruit, and a bowl of bread on the table. It was the most food I had ever seen in my life on one table. "What's all this?" I asked Anthony.

"That's your country breakfast."

"*My* country breakfast? This would never happen in my house."

"Well, for the commercial it would."

I leaned over and picked up a muffin. "I can have one of these, right?"

"I wouldn't. They sprayed it with something to make it look fresh."

I held the muffin up close and I could see that it was sparkly. I put it back down into the bowl with the others. "So what do you need me to do?"

For a day and a half I took the milk out of the fridge, talking about how great the Xyience breakfast bars were. The sound had to be perfect. The orange juice had to be just so. Then I was on a podium answering questions. Finally, I was getting out of a limo while the crew called my name over and over.

It was a great experience, and I even got to keep the clothes!

The newest Miletich Fighting Systems headquarters was still pretty much just a room in Bettendorf. The huge mats on the ground were scraped and pounded within a week. On white-boards on the side wall, the dates of upcoming fights–UFC,

Pride, IFL—were written down, with people correcting the spellings of their names in different color markers. The walls were covered with UFC event posters, in gold-colored plastic frames. The posters were puckered along the edges from all the sweat evaporating into the air all day. Parked by the mat was a covered yellow garbage can with a slit cut into the top for people to spit their saliva, blood, and tobacco juice. If we poured that bucket into a swamp something monstrous would probably come to life within twenty-four hours.

In August 2005 I sat on one of the plastic chairs by the mat. The sweat was pouring down my face and I knew I'd be sore the next day, which meant that I was happy today. A tall kid with very dark hair sat down beside me. One of the kids from *The Ultimate Fighter.* "Hey, what's up?" He tipped his head back like I was one of his buddies.

Anyone can talk to somebody they like and be nice, I told myself. *It takes somebody special to talk to somebody you don't like.* "Hey, buddy." *What's this guy's name? Stan?*

"When's your next fight?"

"November, I think. Joe Riggs." The UFC wanted me to win after the show finale aired. They weren't about to give me a tough fight.

"Oh, yeah? Me too! We're going to be on the same card."

You're a Christian now. Say something kind. "That's great."

"It's weird. One day I'm getting my BA and the next I'm on TV and everyone recognizes me and wants my autograph, and now I'm going to be on the same card as Matt Hughes!"

It's just the nature of the business. It's not his fault he got in the

UFC for being a character on TV, not from putting in the work. "That's great," I told him again.

"Yeah, I think I'm going to be going in for my MBA soon," he said, like we'd been discussing it the week before.

"*I* think I'm going to go take a shower." I got up and walked away, then stopped a second later. *Be nice. Be nice. Be nice.* I turned around and managed to give him a smile. "Good luck!"

In early November 2005, I returned to Vegas for the *Ultimate Fighter 2* finale. Dana had set up a prewrap party in a ballroom. Rich and I were up on a platform. It was fairly dark in there, and the people watching us were UFC employees and a few reporters and fans. Everyone was glad and excited that the show was going to end the next day. "Here are watches, just like I promised you, for being coaches on the show this season," Dana said. He handed each of us a watch box.

"What is this, funny-funny ha-ha time? You gave the coaches last season Hummers and you're giving us watches?" I said. "I don't even wear a watch." I stood there holding the box in my hand, waiting to see what Rich was going to do. It was like Christmastime when I was a kid, watching Mark open his gift first because I knew I'd be getting the same thing. *This can't be,* I thought. *If Rich opens his and it's a watch, I'm not even going to open mine. I don't care. I don't care who made it, I don't care how much it's worth. This is just wrong.* Rich opened his and there was a Hummer key inside. I tore open my box so fast you'd have thought it was a race.

The two trucks appeared on the screen behind us. "These are sitting right outside!" Dana said.

Rich and I ran to where they were parked and took photos and played around with those trucks for hours. But the present I got the day of the Riggs fight two weeks later made that truck seem like it was nothing.

The next day I was backstage at the Hard Rock for the finale when I saw Randy Couture. He gave me a nod when he noticed me, and I started to think. I had heard about how his ex-wife was not really a great person to live with. I didn't know all the sides of the story, but I didn't have to support divorce to support Randy Couture. Divorce does happen, and "the other woman" was now his long-time girlfriend (and soon, wife). He kept walking, thinking I didn't want to have anything to do with him. Because for so long, I hadn't. When people go through a rough patch, they find out who their friends are. And I wasn't one of those people for Randy, and I should have been.

I stopped him and he paused. He was ready to hear me repeat the things I had been saying to Audra to his face. I swallowed my words a little, because I knew whatever I said, Randy would behave decently in return. He was in his forties in a sport dominated by twentysomethings, and he acted like it. Whether he liked it or not, he was a father figure to most of the guys, including myself. And that made what I had done worse. "Randy, I just want to say that I kind of had a problem with–"

"I know," he said.

"I just wanted to say that I'm sorry, and I hope we can be friends again."

"Yeah," he said, just like that.

I was glad that I would have my buddy backstage at the shows, and that I could look in the face of the man who I'd modeled myself after. I wouldn't have to feel judgmental—or embarrassed. "Is Kim out there?" I asked him. "Because I want to say something to her, too." She had invited me to Randy's last birthday party and I had refused to go. And if Randy had gotten the cold shoulder from me, she had gotten the cold shoulder, back, and chest.

"Yeah, she's out there," Randy said.

I found her in the stands. "Hi," I said, sitting down next to her.

"Hi," she said, startled. She was pretty but still very professional looking.

"Hey, maybe I judged you before I should have," I said. "I'm sorry for that. I hope we can be friendly, and I think you'll see a different side of me from now on."

"That would be great," she said.

CHAPTER 14

The Man in Black

A couple of weeks after the *TUF* finale, I was at weigh-ins in Vegas. *Why is he acting all surprised?* I wondered.

Joe Riggs sighed and rolled his eyes in disbelief. The camera-people and the fans in that great big room started talking among themselves. Weigh-ins were a place to see the fighters up close and personal, to discuss who looked good. It was not a time for anything to actually happen. But Joe Riggs was two pounds over, which meant that he had two hours to lose the weight or the fight became a non-title shot—and I would get 5 percent of his fight money, and so would the Athletic Commission. I shook my head as I got on the scale and made weight. Fiore had been checking me hourly, so that wasn't any news to me. The fans yelled *"Hughes!"* as I stood there for pictures.

I went back to my hotel room. Audra was lying on the bed, watching TV. "Joe didn't make weight," I told her.

"So what, you get his money?" she asked.

I lay down next to her and ran my fingers through her hair. She adjusted herself on the bed, putting her head against my chest. "I mean, the money's not going to matter. Joe still gets to fight but it's not for the title now. I'd rather have another successful title defense than the cash. Hey, honey, you know what?"

"What's that?"

"Matt Peña and the guys are going to be away for about an hour." Matt Peña was my boxing coach, and he had worked me on the pads until I couldn't move my arms. He'd watch tapes and figure out people's tendencies, too. There's a rule that boxers have about a certain thing they're not supposed to do for two weeks before a fight. It makes for weak legs, boxers say. You lose your natural aggression.

But I wasn't a boxer. I wasn't really a striker, either. That was their rule, not mine.

The next day in the octagon I grabbed Joe Riggs's arm and had it secured between my two hands. The pressure on his shoulder was immense. I could feel the point where his limit was and I kept pushing past that. I took Joe's arm and pulled it behind his back. He resisted for a bit but then he tapped. I let go right away and looked down at the kid. "Are you okay? Are you okay?" I asked.

"Yeah," he said. He hadn't made weight and now he had lost.

Matt Peña ran into the ring and picked me up on his shoulder. I smiled, thinking about what I had done before the fight. I looked around the arena and found where I thought Audra was sitting. I pointed right at her. I couldn't see her but she could see me, my head huge on all those giant screens everywhere. She got up and clapped, not having a clue that she was now pregnant.

The next time I saw Joe Riggs was months later when I was visiting Audra's brother, Tommy, out in Arizona. I had a sponsor out there in Phoenix who sponsored a lot of other fighters too. I met with the guy when I was there, and Joe and his wife were at the house.

"Hey, this is my wife, Kim," Joe said.

I shook her hand. "Sorry, but I'm the guy who beat your husband up." I started laughing. Tommy started laughing. The sponsor started laughing.

Joe did not.

No one ever gets mobbed when they walk in the door at the Miletich gym in Bettendorf. The new guys usually don't come up to the champions, gushing or trying to shake hands with them. Glances are thrown sideways but heads don't actually turn. But they turned when Brock Lesnar made his appearance at the Miletich gym in late 2005.

On television Brock looked like he could take on Godzilla. But in person he was only six foot two, about halfway in height between me and Timmy. Pat led him to me to make introductions. "Nice to meet you," he said. "I'm just starting out and I'm new to this whole thing." The guy was absolutely massive, but there weren't that many massive guys in the sport—and for good reason. All that muscle takes up a lot of oxygen, and they tend to get gassed pretty quickly.

"There's a lot to learn," I told him.

"I know, I know," he nodded.

"A lot of people watch it on TV and think it's real easy. But then, I think the same thing about golf. I mean, the ball's stationary and it's not like baseball, where the pitcher's pitching a ball a hundred miles an hour. This ball's just sitting there. It looks so simple, but I know it would take me twenty years to figure it out."

"Hey, Matt, Brock's a two-time Division I All-American," Pat explained.

"No kidding. So was I!"

"Really?" Brock said. He gave me the nod; we had walked in each other's shoes.

"Let's see what you got!" I said, getting into my stance. We rolled around and right away I could see why he thought about getting into fighting. The wrestling background let him get into pretty good position and keep it. But he still left openings that experienced fighters wouldn't. Within five minutes I had my arms wrapped around his neck in a rear naked choke.

Brock stood up and it was just like when I choked out Frank Trigg for the first time. Then he fell backward with all his strength to try to dislodge me, and the force of a man one hundred pounds heavier than I was slammed me into the mat. It didn't really hurt, but it must have looked like a horse kicking off a rider at a rodeo. I kept up the choke and Brock tapped.

"Hey, we don't do that here!" Pat yelled out to him. "You could have broken Matt's rib or something."

"You're right, you're right," Brock said quickly. "You okay?"

"I'm fine," I told him, taking his hand and getting up. "Hey, it's good when someone makes you tap. The more you tap in here, the less you'll get caught when you're in the octagon, you know?" But for whatever reason, Brock stopped coming to Bettendorf and rolling with us. The revolving door at Miletich Fighting Systems kept spinning.

A couple of months later I was visiting Tommy again in Arizona. Dana called to tell me, "Matt, I've got you your next fight."

"Oh, yeah? Who's that?"

"Royce Gracie."

"Huh. Sounds good."

"That's fucking it?"

"What did you expect?"

"I expected, 'Are you fucking serious, Dana?' I expected, '*The* Royce Gracie?' I mean, obviously you know who Royce Gracie is?"

"Yeah, I know who he is."

I once saw an interview with WWF manager Bobby "The Brain" Heenan. He said that Ultimate Fighting is fake, *obviously* fake. "How could the same brothers keep winning if it was real? Come on!" Those brothers were the Gracies. And the UFC was originally created as a commercial for the Gracies' brand of Brazilian jiu jitsu. When the UFC first started, it was to settle the question, once and for all, about what would happen if a boxer fought a wrestler, or if a sumo guy fought a karate guy. Which style was the best style in an actual fight? The answer appeared to be Brazilian jiu jitsu. Ninety-nine percent of fights go to the ground, the Gracies claimed, and if you trained with them, they'd teach you how to win if you were either on top or on bottom.

Despite being the lightest man there, Royce Gracie won the first, second, and fourth UFC tournaments. He probably would have taken the third one if he did not become injured. His only loss was due to breaking his foot during a fight that lasted an hour and a half. He literally was the Ultimate Fighting Champion.

His name is technically pronounced "Hoyce," but it's not a name that is usually pronounced at all: It's whispered. It's whispered by fighters looking over their shoulders, because somehow this thin, lanky man was able to make bruisers twice his size tap their hands so that he wouldn't hurt them anymore. No one actually knew Royce. You'd hear about him but you'd never see him.

"So you'll do it, right?" Dana asked me.

"I'm not *scared*, Dana. Yeah, that's fine."

"Aren't you excited?"

"It's *fine*, Dana."

"Matt, do you know what this is going to do for you? This is going to be huge."

"So was being on *The Ultimate Fighter*, and I wasn't too excited about that, right?"

About a month later I walked into the Miletich training room. The fighters looked at me like an inmate headed for the chair. Pat came up to me and slapped me on the back. "Don't listen to what everyone's saying," he said.

"What's everyone saying?"

"It doesn't matter, because you shouldn't be listening to them. You can do this," Pat said.

"I know I can. I don't think the guy's evolved, and he's near forty. That's almost as old as you and, you know, the old gray mare, she ain't what she used to be. Ain't what she used to be. Ain't what she used to be."

A few of the younger guys, sitting on the mats in pools of sweat, looked over my shoulder. They were expecting Royce to come follow me in and, probably, take me out right then and there.

"We need to get ready for this," Pat said. He went around the room; when his eyes caught one of the fighters, he could see all their stats in his head just like the Terminator. Pat rounded up a bunch of taller guys and got them ready for me. "I want you guys to work with Matt. We're going to be doing distance and long jabs."

I traded with one guy after another, people whose names I didn't know but who, for a few minutes, were almost literally in Royce Gracie's shoes. Matt Peña stood behind me and to the left. "Hands high!" he yelled at me. "He likes to throw those long kicks. Keep your hands high, Matt. Nice. Let's try parrying."

When the guys threw punches, I blocked and then countered. For hours and days I was a living montage, as Matt Peña and Pat Miletich choreographed my striking movements. My skills got sharpened . . . just like the pain in my back.

A few days later I was back in my apartment in Bettendorf. I picked up the phone and called the UFC president. "Dana, I've got a problem and I was wondering if you could help me."

"What's wrong?" he asked.

"It's my back; it's acting up."

"How bad? You're not fucking with me, right?" Was that a prayer I heard from Dana's lips? I had seen how heavily the UFC had been promoting the fight. Everywhere, my face was side-by-side with Royce's.

"No, I'm not messing with you. I can't stand straight, and sometimes I can't even walk straight. It's bad." The truth was scarier than any prank I could have thought of.

"I'm going to fly you out here, you're going to come see our specialist, and we're going to get you taken care of."

Two days later I flew out to Vegas and got an MRI done at the hospital there. The nurse had to help me get off the bed, it was so bad at that point. Then I met with the specialist, the man that we called the Witch Doctor. He had a big protruding belly but was otherwise thin. He took me into his house, where the furniture was like something out of a magazine, with all smart neutral tones. The ceilings were high like most Vegas houses, and the back windows looked out onto a golf course. It didn't look like the house of a man who was in his late fifties. When you looked in his face, you could see that this man had lived many lives, that he had probably been a troublemaker, then a rebel, then a pupil, and now a guru. When he talked to you, you felt comforted.

"I went to a couple of chiropractors, and they just couldn't get me straight," I told him. "They could fix me but they couldn't keep me fixed."

He nodded politely, having heard it all hundreds of times. "They weren't addressing the cause, the chiropractors. They were looking at it as an anatomical problem, a structural problem in the back, and it isn't. It's an energetic problem. You have to understand, the internal system of energy actually determines how well the body functions." He laid me down in his living room on a massage table. The Witch Doctor began poking at me and pinching me. "I'm looking for pressure points and seeing what's tender," he explained. "That'll help me figure out where the problem is, okay?"

"You do what you've got to do," I told him.

He moved his hands all over me, pressing and massaging. "The kidney meridian is the master meridian," he said, pressing down. "Now I've equalized the energy on both sides of your body." He began massaging the bottom of my foot until he found a spot that was tender. "Okay, that means that your second energy center is not working. That second center is with emotion and relationships. The only reason it closes down is that we are trying to avoid the pain of the conflict and the results that it has upon our body." He kept on massaging and, just like that, the pressure on my back was gone.

The Witch Doctor helped me off the table. "It's like there was never any pain," I said, stretching my arms out.

"They call me the Witch Doctor because what I do is so effective and so fast, but the reason is because in between where we think and what we feel and where we make decisions is a whole system of energy that connects us to our body. And if you get that system working, the body will correct itself very, very quickly."

"Some of my buddies think that Royce did some voodoo on me or something."

The Witch Doctor chuckled. "Well, if he did, it sure didn't work."

On May 26, 2006, I was in LA at weigh-ins when I saw Royce for the first time. He wasn't appearing out of the shadows or throwing clouds of smoke. We were both just men on a stage. His skin wasn't taut, and every muscle looked like it had quite a bit of give to it. All he had on was a black Speedo. He was a Brazilian through and through. *This guy looks like a toothpick,* I thought, *and I'm going to snap him.*

I leaned over to him while the photos were being taken. "Are those your kids?" I said.

"Yes, that's Khonry and Khor and Kheydon." Everything he said was friendly, but it was like I was talking to someone who was hypnotized. It was hard to tell who—or what—was behind those eyes. *I'd rather fight this guy than play poker with him,* I thought.

Backstage before the fight, I got to talking with Anthony Giordano. "Matt, this guy's been a big pain in the ass," he blurted out right away.

"Who?" I asked. "Royce?"

"Yeah, Royce. He was saying all this stuff about the UFC in the interviews, and when we had to correct him, he started getting all pissed off. Then when I started asking him questions based on my interview with you—"

"Wait, you interviewed me first this time?" I said.

"Yeah, because it's impossible to get these Gracies to commit to a time or anything! And then he's showing up late or canceling, you know. Anyway, I started asking him things, and I said that I wanted to read from the transcript of the things you said and get his answers. You remember when you said, 'If my father was setting up the fights I'd be undefeated as well'?"

I chuckled. "Yeah, I do. I remember."

"He went *crazy*. 'That's not true! If he were setting up the fights, then I'd be in the first round. I always had the last fights, so I had the least amount of rest before the next match that day!' Then when I told him that you were going to put an end to all this talk about Gracie jiu jitsu, he was just beside himself. 'If Matt would beat me with a Brazilian jiu jitsu move, that would just be a testament to what we shared with the world.' So I was like, 'Well, you didn't share it for *free*. You guys made a business out of it.' So it was continuous questions based on what you said, and at some point he just refused to answer. I started laughing because he just said, 'No comment.' I never met a fighter that wasn't going to talk about what he was going to do in the cage, you know? So I was like, 'I need some answer, it doesn't have to be lengthy.' And he just snapped. 'Well, it's obvious that you've decided who you think is going to win already!' I said to him, 'Like I told you before, this is a transcript of a Matt Hughes interview. I'm simply reading what Matt's saying and asking for your comments.'

"So then we had to shoot him for a *UFC Countdown* show, and the Gracies don't allow their workouts to be taped. What they'll do is stage a workout for you, and let you tape that. My point was, I really needed a hard workout. He and his people kept stalling and stalling and stalling, so finally I said I was going to call Dana."

"Your ace in the hole, huh?" I laughed. "Your Dana phone call?"

"You're laughing, but I'm serious. I told them, 'This is what Dana wants. You want me to call him and get him to talk to you? If after he talks to you and he tells me that you don't have to do it, then fine, you don't have to do it. So do you want me to call Dana White or not?' I had to. I told Dana what was going on, and time was running out. Dana calls them, and he calls me back to say that Royce thought my interview questions were 'annoying and rude.' The Gracies said we could go ahead and shoot, but I couldn't be present. And you know Dana loves this shit. He couldn't wait to tell me that, to bust my balls. I told him, 'I don't give a shit if I get to see Royce Gracie train. Who the fuck does he think he is, Princess Di?' We went and got the footage and they even asked my guys at the door if they were me! Matt, I'm telling you all this for a reason. When you choke out Royce tonight, I want you to whisper in his ear, *'This is for Anthony.'*"

"I'll do my best, buddy!" I promised him. I gave him a nod and headed to my locker room. We sat and joked until it was time to get ready. "Hey guys, we're going to pray now. Anyone is welcome on bended knee," I announced to the room. Robbie, Pat, Matt Peña, Fiore, Jeremy, Mark, Brian, Timmy, and I joined hands and kneeled in a circle. I closed my eyes and lowered my head with the others as the Witch Doctor led us in prayer.

"Dear God," he began, "we ask You for protection. Not only for Matthew, but for Royce as well. We ask for strength—not just physical strength, but for the wisdom to know what to do and when to do it. We thank You for what You have given us, and for the purpose You have granted all of us in life. Because we know that You are there with us, and that You strengthen us as we go." As his words flowed like poetry he had spent hours writing, I felt myself spiritually in another place. *I'm not worthy,* I thought. *I'm not worthy of all God's blessings that He's given to me.* I started to shake—first my legs, and then my arms. *I don't deserve to have such a great family. I don't deserve to never have to worry about putting food on the table and clothes on my kids' backs. I don't deserve to have such total support from my family and friends. I don't deserve to be able to do what I love, all the time. I don't deserve all these things, God. Why have You chosen me? Why have I been so blessed?* My life flashed in front of me, and everything I saw was for the good, and from the Good. The tears ran down my face and I started gasping a bit for air. I cried uncontrollably, and it was like I was alone in my bed, crying until I was ready to fall asleep from exhaustion.

When I was done crying, I looked up and everyone in the circle was happy for me, and proud. They gave me quiet nods and squeezes to the shoulder, to show that they understood. I let out a deep breath and regained my composure.

"Five minutes, Matt," one of the UFC guys told me. "You're coming out after Royce."

"I wouldn't have it any other way." Hank Williams Jr. started to play as I walked out to the octagon. The fans, hysterical, stuck their hands out for me to slap as I walked down the corridor. I slapped a few, but only a few. Royce Gracie was in my house, and you don't tell me what to do in my house. At cageside I hugged my cornermen, making sure to hug my brother last and Pat right before him.

Across the octagon was Royce, the ninja, but without any ninja gear. He didn't have a mask with eyeholes; he didn't have a gi, or any nunchucks or throwing stars. He was just a soft, older-looking man with thinning hair, an emotionless face, and shorts with sponsors all over them. "Jeremy, do you see all the sponsors he's got? On his shorts?"

Jeremy turned his head and squinted through the cage wall. "Yeah, I see that now."

One, two, three . . . "Jeremy, he's got ten sponsors on his shorts! And there could be one on the back!"

"Man, that's a lot," Jeremy agreed.

"Look, there's Rain-X. He's got more ads than I do! I've got seven and he's got ten. He looks like a NASCAR vehicle. Cyto-Sport gives me product, and I use it, and there's the Muscle Milk logo on his leg! Are they giving him stuff? You can't be on both teams, you know?" Jeremy flared his eyes and motioned with his head. I turned and saw the lady from the Athletic Commission standing there. She was looking at me like I was crazy. "Do you find this weird?" I asked her.

"Yeah!" she laughed. "You guys shouldn't be talking about *this.*"

"What, should I be slapping myself in the face to get ready? I fight better relaxed. But I mean, look at all those sponsors. That's not normal, right?"

When we started to fight, he kept me at bay with his long kicks, but they didn't really connect. I got a good punch in and then took him and slammed him against the fence. *Man, he feels weak,* I thought. *I can probably do pretty much anything. I'm going to take him down.* I grabbed Royce and took it to the ground. I got on top of him, in full control of the situation.

And then I waited.

Now comes this magical Gracie move that I have never seen before, and will never see again. He's going to wave his hands, he's going to do some jive, and then boom! *I'm done.* I waited and waited. Royce didn't throw a cloud of smoke. I didn't turn into a leprechaun.

Then I started to work. Every move has a counter, and every counter has a counter. But he didn't push on my hips to try and keep me in guard at all. Whatever I did, Royce didn't take advantage of any opportunity to stay in good position. *Why isn't he bringing his leg through to try to get me back in guard? Shoot, he's setting me up for something.* But the more I worked, the less resistance I got. I slapped on an armbar and I was ready to break his arm. I had him with my legs and my hips, and I felt him writhing underneath me with all his strength. Every one of his muscles was doing what it could, panicking, to get his body out of the danger it was in. But he didn't budge me one bit.

I pushed as hard as I could, but he wouldn't tap. And the look on his face still hadn't changed. *He's not going to tap,* I realized. *These Gracies are like that. He'd rather get his arm broken than tap, but I can't get enough pressure to snap it. You know what? I'm going to get him in something else.*

I released the armbar and Royce started to flail around a little bit. Then I got his back. I took him down and flattened him on his stomach. I threw my hips down and he was locked in.

There was no room for him to scramble. I've hit a lot of people before in that situation. But when I hit Royce, that pressure went through my glove, through the tape, and I felt it on my knuckles. I had never felt that before. One, two, three . . . I kept punching him over and over. He brought his right hand out and, very lightly, Royce Gracie tapped. American wrestling had beaten Brazilian jiu jitsu.

Backstage, it was like there were champagne corks popping for half an hour. When I walked into the locker room, everyone was almost giddy. No one had doubted me, but they were still ecstatic to see that I had done it. Dana and Lorenzo Fertitta came by and congratulated me, thrilled that I had defended the new UFC against the old traditions.

Anthony Giordano came huffing into the locker room. "That was awesome, man, that was awesome. I can't believe you did that."

"Anthony, I bet any of the top five welterweights in the UFC would have beat him too. BJ would have beaten him; Georges would have beaten him. No doubt about it. It's not that big of a deal."

"Well, congrats again. I just wanted you to know: I'm going to hell, Matt," he told me.

"You're going to hell?"

"Going to hell," he said, laughing. "I was directing the live broadcast. After the fight when Royce was lying there on the ground, I saw that I had shots of his dad all upset in the audience, and his kids practically crying. I'm a dad, and my loyalties are usually to the Dads' Club. At first I didn't want to show anything, but then I remembered all the shit that he had pulled. What goes around, comes around. So I was in the booth yelling, 'Take camera four! Show Hélio Gracie! Take camera six! Let's see those upset kids! Take three! Show Royce lying on the ground beat up! Back to the wife! Back to the dad!'"

"Well, Anthony, I don't–"

But I didn't finish my thought, and Anthony forgot all about Royce as well.

A tall, gorgeous woman with long brown hair and a beauty mark came up to me and wanted my attention. "I lost a bet and I was wondering if you would sign my breast."

"I don't usually sign skin," I told her, "but since my wife is in the room I think I can make an exception." She gave me a Sharpie and I signed her chest.

"Thanks," she said, smiling a million-dollar smile. "Great fight." She took the marker, shook my hand, and left.

"Anthony, was that . . . ?"

"Yeah," he said. "That was Cindy Crawford."

If you were looking down at Disneyland the day after the Royce Gracie fight, at first you'd see exactly what you'd expect to see. You'd see huge rides shooting into the air, and people walking in so many directions it would look like they didn't have a purpose, because there was so much for them to see there, and you'd hear lots of music and kids screaming, and you'd see balloons and food.

If you looked really closely, you'd notice a redheaded guy with big shoulders and cauliflower ears. His wife at his side would be pregnant, but only barely showing in her stomach, so it wouldn't be that noticeable at first. Their son, a little boy of six, would be mellow but excited, seeing all the cartoon characters come to life. We were just three people in a crowd.

But you wouldn't have to look too closely to notice the man who was with us. He wore Affliction T-shirts before anyone else had heard of them; he was like *Vogue* for the UFC, wearing clothes today that MMA fans would be wearing in two years. With his hair shaved into a mohawk, tattoos on his skull, and a walk like Frankenstein, Chuck Liddell definitely looked like a man who beat people up in a cage. His face belonged on pictures hung up in a post office, underneath letters that warned that this man was WANTED.

"Oh my God, that's Chuck Liddell!" I heard behind me. College guys in polos and flip-flops ran over. "Hey, Chuck? Can I have your autograph!"

"Sure, got a pen?"

They always had a pen. I waited one or two seconds before I heard, "Hey, are you Matt Hughes?"

"Yep."

"Man, that Gracie fight was awesome. Can I get a picture?"

"Sure." Chuck and I posed with the guys and shook their hands. I turned back and Audra was standing there, staring. "Momma, I'm sorry. Don't be mad." I put my arms around her from behind and kissed her on her cheek.

"Joey wants to go get some candy," she said. "Let's just go."

"Matt! Matt!"

I turned around. A middle-aged woman was standing there

waving at me. I thought I recognized her as the cashier at the IGA supermarket in Hillsboro. *Shoot, I forgot her name.* I walked over to her. "Hey, how's it going?"

"Matt, my husband is your biggest fan. He just went to the bathroom. Can you wait a second? He'll kill me if I let you get away."

"Where are you guys from?" I asked.

"Kentucky."

"Oh." I looked back at Chuck, Audra, and Joey. Audra was listening to the Iceman but her attention was on me, even though she wasn't looking in my direction. I waited a minute for the guy to come back, then I shook his hand and took a picture. Then I jogged back to Audra. "I'm sorry," I told her.

"Well, you don't have to freaking go up to them when they call your name!"

"I thought I knew her," I said.

"Audra, I've had people come up to me in bars and try to show me a front guard," Chuck told her. "It's like, 'Buddy, this is a wrestling move I learned years ago. And there's a time and a place. I don't need you grabbing up on my head if I'm out having a good time with my buddies. If I'm at the playground with my kids, same thing.'"

Audra rolled her eyes. "Can't these people see that you're here with your family?"

"You're right," I said. "But what am I supposed to do?"

CHAPTER 15

Matt Hughes vs. Pain

I didn't recognize the number but I picked it up anyway.

"Hey Matt, it's Andrea. From *The Ultimate Fighter?*"

"Hey there, Andrea. How're things?"

"Good, good. Listen, I was wondering if you'd like to come out to Vegas for a couple of days to coach this season?"

"Sure, I'll do it."

When I got to the training center in Vegas, it was like I was looking at a pool table. On one side of the table was Marc Laimon, the grappling coach. He hated the Gracies, hated their arrogance, hated their big talk. On the other side was Matt Serra, the first American black belt under Royce's brother Renzo Gracie. *I could get these guys to get into it,* I thought. *This should be fun. I haven't seen Marc since I beat Royce. He's bound to congratulate me, and that's going to drive Matt nuts.* I walked over and sat down next to Marc. He bit harder than a rabid pit bull.

"Hey, Matt, that was a great fight!" he said.

"Yeah, it was a pretty good job. Hey Matt, what did you think about my last fight?" I asked Matt Serra.

I sat there and watched as the sparks flew. It was nitrogen meets glycerin.

"Laimon, you don't even fight! You don't know what you're talking about!" Serra yelled.

"I'm not saying I do fight," Marc responded. "I've never said that!"

I watched it build and build and build. *Oh my gosh, what have I started?* I wondered. *Maybe if I move away, they'll calm down and see that no one cares about this argument anymore. . . . Well, that didn't work.*

Whenever I walked into the room at the training center, Georges St. Pierre walked right out of it. It was just like Sakurai not wanting to be around me when we had a fight scheduled. Finally I cornered him at the sushi restaurant. "Georges, what practice do you want to come to and I'll go to the other one?" I couldn't stop thinking of the old joke about Canadian army rifles on sale: Never fired, dropped once. I thought, *I would not want this guy by my side in combat, or outnumbered by thugs. It's one thing to be tough in a cage with a ref, but it's another thing when you're in a street fight in an alley.*

It was April of 2006, and Audra and I were in our doctor's office for her checkup. "You know you look like you should be in college, right?" Audra told the doctor.

Dr. Sherbenou laughed. "Not quite. But thanks anyway, I think." The happy redheaded doctor made us feel comfortable, but when Audra and I sat in her office we were like Siamese twins joined at the hand. My wife's arms were still thin, her face was still thin. All that showed she was six months along was that big belly stuck in front, almost like she had just stuffed a pillow under her shirt. "You've got a heart-shaped uterus," the doctor explained. "The baby is almost entirely on the left side; her feet are coming out a bit onto the right side, but that's about it. As things stand now, we're looking at a breech birth—legs first. So, the best thing to do in these circumstances is to go in and perform a version; we turn the baby around and then a normal birth will be possible. We'd induce it right then and there."

Audra didn't squeeze my hand. It was like she was hearing the specials in a restaurant and now had to order. "What happens if it doesn't work?"

"Then the alternative is a cesarean birth."

We made an appointment for the delivery: July 21. On the way home from the doctor I picked up my cell and called my contact in Nebraska. "Hey, this is Matt Hughes," I told the guy. "Listen, I know we had planned for me to go out there and make a personal appearance at your store, but I can't."

"Really? Why not?" he said.

"We're having a child that day!"

"Wow. Well, congratulations!"

A few hours later he called back, considerably less congratulatory. "Hey Matt, it's me. Listen, I've had time to think about it. I've dumped about $10,000 in advertising and we've made these plans months ago. I'm expecting a big day. Is there any way you can move your appointment forward or backward for me? I'm going to lose a lot of money here."

I looked over at Audra, reading a newspaper at the kitchen counter and eating some cookies. I slowly made my way down the hall to the bedroom, but not so slowly that she would notice that I was trying to be slow. "Well, let me see what I can do," I said to him.

I walked back to the kitchen. I shouldn't have been whistling; it gave me away. "Who was that?" Audra demanded.

"Nobody."

"You were talking to nobody on the phone? I could hear him, Matt. Was it that guy from the health food store?"

"Yeah," I confessed.

"Well, what did he want?" she said.

"Nothing." She sat there staring at me until I gave her a full answer. "He wanted us to change the delivery date, so I could still make his appearance."

"Are you fucking kidding me? *Tell* me you're fucking kidding me."

"Mom, you don't have to say anything. I told him no."

She folded her arms and her eyebrows shot up. "You're not going out there. I don't care if he changes it to the week after or a month after. Who the hell does this guy think he is?"

"Don't worry," I said. "It's under control." I went back to the bedroom and lay on the bed, thinking. There was one person I could always count on to help me out of a jam. But I couldn't get a hold of Pat, so I called Timmy. "What are you doing on July 21?" I asked him.

"Let me check my calendar," he said. "Why?"

"I've got to make an in-store appearance and I can't do it. It's a good-paying gig, too."

"Yeah, I'll do it. No worries, man."

I smiled and called the guy back. "Listen, I've got you the heavyweight champion, Tim Sylvia. As you probably know, the heavyweight title is the most coveted title in the UFC, just like in boxing. That's much better than just the welterweight champ; they're the big hitters, the guys everyone wants to see."

He bit. "That's great. Thanks Matt, I really do appreciate this."

On Friday morning, July 21, Audra and I went to the hospital. During the procedure, I couldn't do anything to help her, unless you count suffering quietly to be a form of help. They couldn't give my wife any pain medication. Her face tightened up and a sweat covered her in seconds. The tears were pouring out, and when I made eye contact with her, I could see that she wanted me to make it stop, somehow.

"Are you up for trying a fourth time?" the doctor asked Audra.

"I don't know . . . ," my wife answered. "I don't think so."

"Maybe we should just go ahead with the C-section," I said. "She's needing this to end." They looked at Audra and she nodded at them. I got a tissue and wiped her face. They wheeled her downstairs to get her ready for the surgery. I went to go get sterilized. I put on the blue scrubs, the gloves, and the face mask.

Then they led me into the hospital room where my wife was getting ready to have our little baby girl.

Audra's head and upper body were exposed, but there
was a curtain right above her stomach which kept both of us
from seeing what was going on. They had her arms tied to the
table, splayed out, so she couldn't move them. I noticed her
stomach had wrinkles on it, and then I realized that they had
put tape over it. The wide, clear tape was on her skin around
where they were going to make the incision, to keep the skin
taut.

I sat down on a chair right by my wife's head, behind her
shoulder. With my left hand I grabbed her left hand and held
it. With my right hand, I combed her hair with my fingers.
Her hair was smooth, and it reminded me of when we used
to go on road trips, and she would sleep with her head in my
lap.

"How are you doing, honey?" I asked her.

"I'm all right," she said. By which she really meant excited,
and nervous, and a hundred other things.

Becky, the nurse anesthetist—who had also been my high
school girlfriend—stood there on Audra's other side. It was com-
forting to see her familiar face and curly black hair. Becky had
looked like a professional even in high school, and I used to
tease her about being too serious then. Now I was glad that she
could be so calm and walk us through the procedure she'd seen
dozens of times.

"Becky, what's going on now?" Audra asked.

"They've got a foot out," she told us. "Matt, you need to see this."

"No, me and Audra had a deal," I explained to her. "We see the baby at the same time."

Becky turned her head and watched. Audra tensed a bit. "Matt, they've got two feet out now," Becky told me. "You need to see this!"

"No, I'm not doing it."

"You need to look," Audra said weakly.

"She's just about all the way out, Matt. If you're going to do this, you need to see this now," Becky said.

I stood up and looked at what was happening. "All of her left arm is still in, and all of her head is still in," I told Audra. But the rest of her was visible, and she was clearly a baby, covered in glistening liquid and blood. "She's just about out." Then the doctor gave her another pull, and there she was. The baby didn't make a sound. They never asked me if I wanted to cut the cord, but I wouldn't have left Audra even for a second. They turned around with her, so I sat right back down. "I think we've got a healthy little girl," I told my wife.

"Everything's going good," Becky added. "Everything's normal."

Audra let out a breath and smiled.

They measured Hanna and began to sew my wife. Then they wrapped the baby in a blanket and gave her to me to hold. I had never held a baby even close to that small before in my life. I felt overwhelmed, like I was a completely different man than I was just minutes before. *This is my purpose,* I thought. *I'm here to take care of her, and to protect her.* I showed her to Audra, and then the doctors took Hanna.

"Matt, go tell everyone that she's okay," Audra said.

"Are you sure? Are you going to be all right?" I asked her. I looked at Becky to tell me what to do.

"She'll be fine," Becky said.

"Matt, go!" Audra told me.

I let go of her hand and walked quickly to the door. Our families were in the waiting room, and when they saw me coming they all got excited. "She's here. Hanna's fine," I let them all know. "They're finishing sewing Audra up right about now."

That night the hospital room was like *Matt Hughes: This Is Your Life.* My brother came; my mother came; my dad came with his girlfriend; both of Audra's sets of parents came; Brian came. Fiore left his twin daughters' second birthday party to see how we were all doing.

A nurse came in even later that night. "We think that when we pulled Hanna out, she sucked in some amniotic fluid. This is pretty common with a C-section because they don't have the compression to force the fluid out like they would with a natural birth. We'd like to take her upstairs for observation and run some tests in child intensive care."

Don't worry, I thought to myself. *It makes perfect sense that a baby would open up its mouth and swallow some liquid. Everything is going to be fine,* I reasoned.

I slid into that small bed next to Audra and touched her foot with mine, her hand with mine, her cheeks with mine; I wanted to be a full-contact husband, too. When I pressed against her, she would press back against me, just a little, and we lay there talking or watching TV or sleeping.

"You know what?" I whispered to her. "I'm going to go up and see Hanna again, to check in on her." Half-asleep, Audra nodded. I sprang up a flight of stairs to find my girl.

I was stopped by one of the nurses. "Excuse me, but are you Matt Hughes?" she asked.

"Yeah, I'm Matt Hughes."

"My boyfriend is a big fan of yours," she gushed. "I'll have to tell him I ran into you."

"Well, why don't you get me a piece of paper and I'll sign him an autograph?" *Maybe she'll cut me some slack with the hospital rules,* I thought.

"Thanks so much," she said, as the pen and paper appeared from nowhere. "You know, I'm going to feed her in twenty minutes. If you want to stick around."

"That sounds like a pretty good deal." I waited and then held my baby girl just right, and watched her carefully while I gave her her bottle.

"Here in about ten minutes I'm going to change her," the nurse said.

"Yeah, I'd like to change her for the first time."

After we changed her diaper, the nurse thought of something else. "I've got to change her clothes in about fifteen minutes."

"That's great! I want to interact with my child as much as possible." I changed her tiny clothes, put her in the covered crib, and walked back down to see my wife.

"There you are," Audra said.

"Was I gone long?" I asked.

"Yeah, an hour and a half. I just called up there wondering where you were."

I eased myself next to her on the bed. "Hey, I'm sorry. It's all right, Mom," I said, in my best sweet voice. "I was just feeding her and changing her and putting some new clothes on our girl. Don't get jealous. You'll have your turn. The nurse showed me how to feed her and burp her. And I know I've changed Joey's diapers, but that's when he was a year and a half. And it's different when it's a little girl not even a day old."

Then, scattered all over Illinois, the entire Hughes family went to sleep.

Subject: Tim Sylvia Appearance

From: ██████████████████@yahoo.com>

Date: Saturday, July 22, 2006 11:15 am

To: Matt Hughes <matthew██@██████.com>

Hey Matt–

Tim's appearance was a huge success and it went really well. Thanks for making it happen and congratulations on your new arrival!

Best,

██████████████

Subject: re: Tim Sylvia Appearance

To: ███████████████@yahoo.com>

Date: Wednesday, July 26, 2006 9:01 pm

From: Matt Hughes <matthew██@████.com>

I'm glad everything worked out for you.

Matt

Subject: RE: re: Tim Sylvia Appearance

To: Matt Hughes <matthew██@████.com>

Date: Wednesday, July 26, 2006 11:27 pm

From: ███████████████@yahoo.com>

I'd still like to get you to come out here. I'm looking at September. Do you have time?

Subject: re: RE: re: Tim Sylvia Appearance

To: ███████████████@yahoo.com>

Date: Thursday, July 27, 2006 1:13 pm

From: Matt Hughes <matthew██@████com>

Let me check with my wife.

Matt

* * * *

It was 5:45 in the morning when I heard Audra gasping. I got up out of bed and knocked on the bathroom door. "Mom, are you all right?" She didn't answer. I swung the door open and saw Audra sitting on the toilet. Her face was completely flushed, and all her features were tightened up. The only other time I had seen her make that face was when surgery was involved, and this was much worse. I had never seen anyone in as much pain, even given what I did for a living. "Stay right there," I said, as if she had a choice. "We're going to the hospital."

I called Audra's mom, Kathy, first thing. "Kathy, I know it's early and Hanna's only nine days old, but I need you to come here and take care of her and Joey. I'm taking Audra to the hospital."

"Oh my gosh, Matt, what's wrong?"

"I don't know. Just come over here quick." I packed a few things in a bag and waited by the living room window. I lowered my head and prayed, and with every sound I heard outside I stopped my prayer and looked up, wondering if it was Kathy. We almost knocked her over on our way out the door.

I drove to the hospital the same way I fight in the octagon. Even though I took Audra's little Honda, I drove it like I was in my Hummer: pure aggression. I pulled into the parking lot, jumped out of the driver's side, and ran over to Audra. I lifted her out of the car and helped her walk into the emergency room.

The doctors got her into a wheelchair and took her away to do a few tests. I sat in the waiting room, exhausted and half–passed out. *Let's be calm and think this through,* I told myself. *We got her to the hospital, so she's going to be fine. This can't have something to do with Hanna or we would have caught it before. Maybe it's a stone or something like that because she was hurting in the bathroom. She's going to be all right.*

They let me back by her side a bit later. The emergency room was big, with a counter running all along one of the walls and two beds in the middle. At Audra's side was the same man who, more than thirty years ago, my father had mistaken for a janitor. Dr. McFarlin, the doctor who had delivered Mark and me, had come in to make sure Audra would be taken care of. He had sandy blond Beach Boys hair, but an intense demeanor that was pure business. One of the nurses shook her head. "We can't get the catheter in," she told Dr. McFarlin. "This is the third time we've tried."

I was bent over and I kept rubbing Audra's hair to make her feel better. It wasn't like when she gave birth to Hanna, when we knew what was going on. This time, Audra was scared. And there was nothing I could do to reassure her. "It'll be fine. It'll be fine," I kept telling her.

"It hurts. It hurts," she repeated, tearful and shaking from the pain.

I turned away from Audra and put my hands on the counter. *Something's not right with me,* I thought. I fell onto my wife and she pushed me off of her. Then I fell backward and heard a crash as I slammed into the rolling table with all the tools. I felt Dr. McFarlin pull me up off the ground, but as I looked at him I had no idea who he was or what was happening. He led me to the spare bed and laid me down.

I'm not the patient here, I thought after a second. I got up and sat down on a little chair next to Audra this time.

"What's going on? What's wrong with you?" she asked, sucking in air.

"Don't worry about it. I'm fine. I'm Superman, right?"

They kept us in the hospital only to tell us that, yes, it was kidney stones and that she would pass them eventually. I stayed there that night with her, and fell asleep in that tiny bed, and because of that hospital bill we had ourselves the most expensive date of our lives.

CHAPTER 16

The Long Goodbye

Pat's office at the gym has plaster paneling, like in someone's basement. By the door there're a bunch of small lockers, with masking tape labels marking them off as belonging to "The Maine-iac" or "Matt Hughes." The desk is the simplest that could possibly be made—particle board and screws with no style to it whatsoever. The chairs are there to hold your butt, not to make you feel comfortable. That's why I sat in them; I wasn't feeling too comfortable at all.

"You sure?" Pat asked me.

"I just talked to Dana," I said. "Georges is injured, so I'm going to fight BJ instead. I've got to tell you, Grandpa, I'm a little scared to fight BJ again. You saw how flexible he is. Royce has nothing on him."

"Come on, Georges beat him."

"Yeah, because he didn't train too hard for Georges. And Georges barely won. BJ *killed* Georges the first round and

Georges barely won the last two. BJ's been on a heck of a roll. For this fight—a title fight—he's really going to be in shape."

Pat stared me down in the way that he does, half drill instructor and half guidance counselor. "You've been on a heck of a roll too, Matt. And you didn't exactly train right for BJ the first time either, you know. So don't give me this crap about being scared."

"Maybe scared's not the word. Let's just say I'm not excited and leave it at that. Remember after the first fight, when he went around running his mouth saying that I was weak? That my wrestling was terrible?"

"Who gives a shit what he said? This is a fight, not a fucking debate team. Here's what we're going to do. We'll get Peña to look over tapes, and you know he'll figure out some of the stuff that BJ does when he's striking. And then we go to work."

I imagined Matt Peña sitting two inches away from the TV, holding a jeweler's eyepiece up to the screen to analyze the tapes. Hitting rewind and then pause, and not shaving for days, as he cracked the codes of my opponent.

A few weeks before the fight, I got the full report from him. We were by the pads in the gym. "BJ likes to throw a left hook as a counterpunch," Matt explained, demonstrating a combination in slow motion. "Now I want you to try moving to the left—your left—away from my hook hand when I counter."

I threw a jab and immediately shifted left. Matt's fist landed where my head had been. We worked for hours over many days, because I knew that BJ would be hard at work running on beautiful Hawaiian beaches and climbing tall palm trees. But what I thought I knew, I didn't really know.

It was September 2006 when I saw BJ across the octagon in Anaheim. It was two and a half years after our last fight, and I was amazed. *He looks out of shape. That silver spoon's been putting a lot of food in his mouth. He looks plain fat,* I thought. *Maybe he's like Timmy or some of those Japanese guys, where they look out of shape but they're not.*

We tapped gloves and we came out striking—and I was outstriking him. He was expecting me to try to take him down, and from his expression, I could see that he was a bit surprised. I threw combinations and moved to my left. His hook came right past me almost in slow motion, again and again, just like Matt Peña had anticipated. I could feel the breeze as it went by; I could almost smell the leather of his glove. As he missed with his hook, I kept countering right off of that. It was like we had planned it, BJ and I. From outside the ring, Tito Ortiz started yelling encouragement to his friend. "Armbar! Armbar!"

My brother turned to Tito, ready to thrown down. "You better shut up," he said.

BJ got me in the eye, forcing the ref to pause the fight. I kept trying to take BJ down, and I just couldn't. I started to get pissed. *It's that crazy flexibility of his. I wish his hips would turn like a normal person's. I've never wrestled someone like this. But I can do this. I can do all things through Christ who strengthens me.* It was almost as if the fight itself became secondary. It was now a takedown war. I was going to take him down, no matter what it took, or even if it took me the whole twenty-five minutes. He wasn't going to win this one.

I went for an elbow, and BJ caught me. I could feel the pressure on my throat, and I couldn't even hear the crowd anymore.

This is serious. He's got me pretty good. For the first time in my life, I prayed in the middle of a fight. *God, get me to the next round. God, get me to the next round.* I felt BJ loosen up a little bit, and he wasn't using his hips. I raised my own hips and he slid below me. Just when I got up on top of him, the horn blew. The round was over.

"This fight's about over. Your boy's not doing well," Mark yelled at Tito.

I went back to my corner and sat down. The first thing I heard was Pat saying, all excited, "Hey, he can barely get off the ground!" It brought me right back to the second time I fought Carlos Newton, when Pat was yelling in my ear, "They're putting him back together!" *This is good,* I thought. *I made him work. But I can't believe he's gassing already. I guess he's not like Timmy after all.* I saw him sitting on his chair, and his people had his legs up, trying to get the blood flowing or something.

When the next round came, I threw jabs and combos and made a punching bag out of him. He never even really got me once. Then he shot and tried to take me down. I defended and put him on his back. "Stand up!" Pat yelled from my corner. "Stand up with him!"

I ignored my mentor. *I'm going to use my weight and I'm going to wear him out even more, make him use a lot of energy.* I kept getting good position with BJ, and he was gassing. *I'm going to inch forward, not make any mistakes or give him an opening, and win this thing.* Eventually I had him with his arms spread out beneath me, and I began to hit him. I kept hitting him, and kept hitting him, not even that hard. But he obviously wasn't defending himself at all. I looked up to Big John. "When are you going to stop this?" I asked the ref. I went back to throwing punches and elbows. Finally, Big John called the match.

"You're a freaking idiot," my brother told Tito. "Who are you? You're nobody. Why were you even here? You're not the cornerman."

Georges St. Pierre came strolling into the ring, probably at production's cue. He looked me right in the face after my victory and said into the mike, "I was not impressed by your performance." He was not joking. He was serious.

Wow, this is amazing, I thought. *Whenever they've asked me to go into the octagon after a fight, I've always said no. I wasn't going to try and take somebody's glory, even if it was someone I didn't like—and especially if it was someone I respected.* I waited for Georges to hand back the mike, and I went right up to him. "You just showed me who you really are," I said. "You came in here after not fighting tonight, and grabbed that microphone and just said what you think. You just showed me who you are." I turned around and walked away.

The Witch Doctor, at my side, started screaming at GSP. "Georges, I'm going to tell you right now, I'm through with you. What you did was wrong here. This was not good, okay?" He walked with me and my cornermen backstage. The man who usually spoke like a fortune cookie was now fuming like an angry drunk. "Can you believe him? There is a time and a place. I mean, if he didn't like what you did, that's fine. That's his opinion. But to come up to you and say it to your face in front of everyone? And for no real reason? I thought Georges really had

his head on straight, I really did. Man, I am so sorry for that,"
he said.

"It wasn't your fault."

"Yeah, but I'm sorry you had to go through that. That's just
not right and there's no reason for it. He should be ashamed of
himself."

"You know what?" I said. "The UFC could have put him up
to that, they really could have. That's pretty severe, for you to
say you're not going to work on him anymore. I would rethink
that. He's a young guy and whatever, and maybe he didn't know
what he was doing." But more important to me was the fact that
GSP was in a seeking phase of his life, and I knew that the Witch
Doctor–a former pastor–had been introducing him to the path
of the Lord. And I didn't want to have anything to do with taking
that from Georges, no matter what he said to me.

Ten minutes later, after handshaking and pats on the back
and pictures with people and their families and friends, Georges
came into the locker room. No one could believe it. It was almost
like when the bad guy rides into town in a Western; all conversation stopped. "Matt," he said in his French accent, "I want you to
know that I didn't understand what you said, and they told me
you were saying bad things about me. I'm sorry."

"Hey, no big deal. I figured that they had done something;
it's not a problem. Apology accepted."

If I had a choice, I might not have filmed *UFC: All Access*. The fighters selected only get paid in two ways: exposure, and a loss on our
records. I didn't know about the *All Access* curse, how most of the

fighters who are profiled get defeated in their following matches.

There was a certain look in Anthony Giordano's eyes when they filmed me picking up my brand new 2007 Polaris 800 four-wheeler. We brought it back to the farm and they got ready to film Rachelle Leah and me shelling corn for the show. I waited until Anthony was practically drooling. "Hey, you want to take it out for a spin?" I asked him.

"Yeah!" he said, reaching out for the keys.

"I bet you do!" The entire crew burst out laughing at him. He kicked at the dirt and rolled his eyes. He knew me well enough by this point to expect *something.* "Hey, I'm serious," I told him. "Here, take the keys."

"Ha, ha. Very funny."

"No, truthfully, you can take it for a spin."

He reached for the keys and kept an eye on me at the same time. "I can really drive this thing around?" he asked me.

"Yep. Pretty much anywhere you can see right now is our property." Anthony took a look around at the fields, at the paths that led between tall, thin trees, and at the garage, like a bunker where we kept our tractors. He got on the four-wheeler and started it up. Then he took off downhill behind the house, to drive down the paths Mark and I explored decades ago.

Half an hour later I was in the auger wagon and I pulled up to the tractor. My dad and a crew member were pulling my dad's truck around. "What's going on here?" I asked.

"Anthony got into an accident with the four-wheeler," Dad said.

"Ha, ha. Is he getting me back for teasing him or something?"

"No Matt, I'm serious. I'm going to go pull it out of the ditch with my truck."

"No, you're not going to do anything," I said. "You're the type of guy who'd hook a cable onto it and just pull away. It's my new four-wheeler. I'll take care of getting it out."

We went down to where my new toy was in a ditch. "I'm sorry," Anthony said. "I'm really sorry."

The vehicle had gone headfirst into the ditch, and I was surprised it hadn't taken his head off. "Are you okay?"

"I'm fine, just a few bruises. I popped out of there like an airplane ejector seat. I'm really sorry, Matt." He couldn't stop shaking his head. "I'll pay for the damages."

I called the shop right there. "Hey, this is Matt Hughes. Listen, some city boy who doesn't know how to drive took that four-wheeler into a ditch."

"Ha, ha, ha! Are you kidding?" the guy said.

"No, I'm not."

"Well, how bad's the damage?

"The left brake assembly is all torn up."

"That's not a big deal. We've got those parts right here."

"In that case," I told him, "come out and fix it, and charge whatever you think is fair. Make sure you make that bill out to Anthony Giordano. G-i-o-r-d-a-n-o."

I helped Rachelle Leah get into the combine and she sat there, firing questions about the farm while I did my usual work. She had that warm friendliness about her that beautiful women do, that friendliness that makes men think they care about us more than they do. "What are we doing now?" she wanted to know.

"We're taking a load of grain up to the elevator," I explained.

She reached around the window to grab the door handle. "Ow!" she yelled, pulling her arm back. "I just burned myself or something." There was a red mark on her forearm, changing colors right in front of us.

"Shoot, you must have reached too far and brushed up against the muffler. We'll get back to the house and put some ointment on it." She nodded, waving her arm and blowing on it to lessen the pain. We drove back to the house, and even though she was wincing, she didn't cry or whine.

The next day she took out the four-wheeler, too. I watched her take a jump and then, as she landed, I saw her leg slip and brush against the muffler. "Ah!" she screamed. I winced myself, because I've done the same thing a lot. An egg-shaped burn started growing on her leg. "Matt, this really hurts," she said, sucking in air. "We need to go back to the house right now, okay?"

I took her back to the house and helped her treat her wound and wrap her leg.

"Matt, this is the most fun *All Access* I've ever done. But I think we've got enough footage for here, so I'm going to get the guys and head back to the hotel," she said.

"Well, I hope you mean that, and I do hope you feel better."

She gave me a hug and I said my goodbyes to the crew. Now it was time for the *All Access* curse to descend upon me.

There were no hard feelings when I got ready to fight GSP less than two months after BJ. It was UFC 65 in Sacramento, and there were over ten thousand people at the ARCO Arena. We traded punches the first round, and I could feel his strikes through the adrenaline this time. I kept it on our feet even though my strength is on the ground, taking people down and pounding them.

Then GSP kicked me in the groin. It stung, but I regained my breath and continued. Then he got me again. I felt my legs get a bit numb. I walked over to the cage wall and leaned down. I was very fortunate; the ref was Big John. He called for a time-out. "Are you all right?" he asked me.

"John, it's not my groin. My legs feel like they're asleep."

"Well, the way I see it, I think he hit you in the leg and it slid up."

It sure didn't feel that way.

Georges kept kicking me with those low kicks, and I dropped my hands to block. Then he kicked high, faking me out, and caught me. I fell and he was on me immediately, throwing down fists and elbows. I felt nothing, not a thing. I wasn't out, but I wasn't exactly firing on all eight cylinders.

And I wasn't exactly the welterweight champion anymore.

No one knew what to say to me backstage. I sat there on one of the folding chairs, leaning forward and looking into the carpet. "Hey, Matt. I almost got in a fight out there because of you," Robbie Lawler said.

"Oh, yeah?" I asked.

As he talked he punched his right fist into his left palm over and over. "This guy in the crowd was like, 'Matt Hughes, you suck! GSP, you just beat that guy's ass!' I turned around and was like, 'Yo, you better shut the hell up!' So he goes, 'What are you going to do about it? Matt Hughes sucks! Country boys *can't* survive.' I thought I was going to have to fight him, I was like, 'Let's go! Let's go!' I couldn't just stand there and let him run his mouth, you know? Security had to take him away.'" The look on Robbie's face was like Mark, maybe even worse, with that switch that turns on and can only be turned off by violence. All I could picture was him and my brother like dogs in a fight, snapping wildly, and that mental image finally got me to smile for a second.

"That's great, Robbie," I said.

I finally got up. People were going up to Tim and shaking his hand, congratulating him quietly for his victory that night. It was like there was a wake and a birthday party in the same room, and no one knew whether to have some cake or lower their heads.

A few months later I heard about Jens being a coach on *TUF* with BJ. "Hey Jens, it's Matt," I called him to say. "Congrats on doing *The Ultimate Fighter.* If you need anything, just let me know."

"Actually, I'd like for you to come out, if that's okay. I mean, I don't want Timmy yelling at me again," Jens said, laughing hysterically.

"What do you mean?"

"He freaked out at me and Matt Peña because I'm flying Peña out here to be the boxing coach. And now he won't be able to get Tim ready for Randy. A real team player, all the way."

A month later I was on the set. The producers sat me down in the control booth at the end of BJ's practice, hoping for drama from the cameras. "BJ doesn't know you're coming," the producer explained. "We want to see what his reaction is going to be."

I watched the monitors in the control room for practice to end. I was surprised how many shots they had. *I didn't even realize where half these cameras were when I was on the show,* I thought. Eventually practice was done and the fighters were just lying around on the mats. I walked through the door and nabbed one of the assistant coaches. "Are you about done?"

"Yep," he said.

I sat down by the door that BJ would have to walk out of. "Hey," he said as he passed, as if he didn't know me.

MY CELL CALLS DURING A TYPICAL WEEKEND AT BETTENDORF				
FRI	02/23/2007	4:48PM	HILLSBORO IL	217-532-
FRI	02/23/2007	4:54PM	GRINNELL IA	641-821-
FRI	02/23/2007	4:56PM	INCOMING CL	641-821-
FRI	02/23/2007	4:58PM	GRINNELL IA	641-821-
FRI	02/23/2007	5:19PM	INCOMING CL	641-821-
FRI	02/23/2007	5:55PM	ELYRIA OH	440-610-
FRI	02/23/2007	5:56PM	IRVINE CA	949-351-
FRI	02/23/2007	6:42PM	INCOMING CL	440-610-
FRI	02/23/2007	9:07PM	LITCHFIEL IL	217-556-
FRI	02/23/2007	9:19PM	LITCHFIEL IL	217-710-
SAT	02/24/2007	9:09AM	GIRARD IL	217-627-
SAT	02/24/2007	9:30AM	MATTOON IL	217-254-
SAT	02/24/2007	9:38AM	INCOMING CL	217-532-
SAT	02/24/2007	9:40AM	MATTOON IL	217-254-
SAT	02/24/2007	9:46AM	LITCHFIEL IL	217-556-
SAT	02/24/2007	10:03AM	RAYMOND IL	217-229-
SAT	02/24/2007	10:05AM	LITCHFIEL IL	217-556-
SAT	02/24/2007	10:06AM	HILLSBORO IL	217-532-
SAT	02/24/2007	10:07AM	HILLSBORO IL	217-532-
SAT	02/24/2007	10:09AM	INCOMING CL	217-532-
SAT	02/24/2007	10:24AM	INCOMING CL	217-556-
SAT	02/24/2007	10:32AM	HILLSBORO IL	217-532-
SAT	02/24/2007	11:16AM	INCOMING CL	217-313-
SAT	02/24/2007	11:40AM	HILLSBORO IL	217-532-
SAT	02/24/2007	11:44AM	INCOMING CL	217-556-
SAT	02/24/2007	12:02PM	INCOMING CL	217-556-
SAT	02/24/2007	3:56PM	VMAIL CL	217-710-
SAT	02/24/2007	3:59PM	MATTOON IL	217-246-
SAT	02/24/2007	4:01PM	HILLSBORO IL	217-532-
SAT	02/24/2007	4:38PM	INCOMING CL	217-313-
SAT	02/24/2007	5:41PM	HILLSBORO IL	217-532-
SAT	02/24/2007	6:53PM	HILLSBORO IL	217-532-
SAT	02/24/2007	7:08PM	INCOMING CL	217-622-
SAT	02/24/2007	7:23PM	HILLSBORO IL	217-532-
SAT	02/24/2007	7:44PM	HILLSBORO IL	217-532-
SAT	02/24/2007	8:02PM	HILLSBORO IL	217-532-
SAT	02/24/2007	8:43PM	INCOMING CL	217-532-
SAT	02/24/2007	8:48PM	HILLSBORO IL	217-532-
SAT	02/24/2007	8:56PM	INCOMING CL	217-556-
SAT	02/24/2007	9:31PM	HILLSBORO IL	217-532-
SAT	02/24/2007	10:28PM	HILLSBORO IL	217-532-
SUN	02/25/2007	10:51AM	LITCHFIEL IL	217-556-
SUN	02/25/2007	10:51AM	HILLSBORO IL	217-532-
SUN	02/25/2007	12:44PM	INCOMING CL	217-532-
SUN	02/25/2007	1:00PM	LITCHFIEL IL	217-556-
SUN	02/25/2007	1:01PM	LITCHFIEL IL	217-710-
SUN	02/25/2007	1:15PM	RAYMOND IL	217-229-
SUN	02/25/2007	3:45PM	HILLSBORO IL	217-532-
SUN	02/25/2007	3:46PM	ALAMOGORD NM	505-491-
SUN	02/25/2007	4:07PM	LITCHFIEL IL	217-556-
SUN	02/25/2007	4:08PM	LITCHFIEL IL	217-710-
SUN	02/25/2007	5:52PM	RAYMOND IL	217-229-
SUN	02/25/2007	6:35PM	INCOMING CL	505-491-

"Hey, how are things?" I asked him, killing him with kindness. A few of his boys came over, fighters but still fans. I looked over and knew that BJ could hear every word they were saying. After they left I washed the mats and waited there for Jens's group to come in. When Jens came in, I gave him a hug. "You wouldn't believe what BJ's guys were doing!" I told him. "He had half the guys outside, climbing these palm trees. The other half he had inside, showing them how to gouge somebody in the eye without the ref seeing it."

"Are you serious?" Jens sputtered. "That's what they were doing?"

"No!" The guys all started to crack up.

It reminded me of an interview I had done years ago, where the reporter asked me what I was going to take most away from the sport. "That's a good question," I told him. "Let's get back to that one." As we went on with the interview and all the typical fight talk, the answer came to me. "You know how you asked me what I'm going to miss most about the sport? It sounds corny but it's true. I'm going to miss all the times I had with my friends, laughing and just having fun."

In March of 2007 we were in Columbus, Ohio, for UFC 68. Chris Lytle had been one of the guys in the Best of the Best tournament, over seven years ago. I knew Chris was tough, but I also knew that I would win against him. When he came out, he swung at me like he was trying to take my head off. *He's not going to score a knockout punch on me,* I thought. I didn't even try with my punches when I saw him swinging for the fences; I went straight for takedowns. For three rounds we basically had a wrestling match, and I took the decision.

Backstage, Tim was shadowboxing with Matt Peña and getting ready to go out to fight Randy Couture. He had a big grin on his face, remembering how he got booed during weigh-ins. It was his opportunity to shut his critics up, once and for all.

"Tim," I said, "Randy's a respected fighter. After you beat this old man, you remember that no matter what. You give him the compliments and credit he deserves."

"Don't you remember what he said about me fighting Monson? That I should have been more aggressive and not gone for the decision? What was that?" Tim asked.

"Timmy," I said, like I was talking to Joey, "it's going to be a little embarrassing for him, so don't trash talk. He's too good for that, and you're too good for that."

Tim kept smiling, but now he nodded. "Yeah, you're right. I know Randy's a good guy, I know that. I'll be cool, you'll see."

But it wasn't cool for Tim. I watched Randy knock him down seconds into the fight, and I never saw Tim come together with a game plan. Randy pushed Tim around like Jens had, totally dominating and doing all the damage in the fight.

Tim sat down between rounds, his eye swelling shut. "What round is it?" he asked Pat.

"It's going to be the fifth round."

"I thought it was the third round."

"No, it's the fifth round."

"Well, what happened?" Tim wanted to know.

"Don't worry about it. We've got to win this fight this round," Pat said. But we didn't.

Backstage, the Witch Doctor was on the floor on one knee, leaning into Tim and talking him through his tears. Tim couldn't lift his head from his hands, from the pain and the shame and the disappointment. But then he turned to the Witch Doctor and told him, "Hey, Randy's probably hurt too. Can you make sure that Randy's all right?" In that moment, Tim was finally the big man he was always meant to be.

On April 7, 2007, I was in Houston, Texas, for UFC 69. I was sitting in the front row by the production people. I wondered what it would be like to watch Georges St. Pierre become the first person other than Pat and me to defend the welterweight title. The result of the match was a given, because the accomplished fighter was taking on the winner of a reality show. My buddy Steven was at my side, and we were talking about upcoming events. I didn't expect the fight to be very exciting at all. Suddenly, I heard the crowd go nuts and then I looked into the cage.

Matt Serra threw a mean punch, and Georges started running around a little bit. *He's hurt!* I thought immediately. *Wait a minute. He can't be hurt. He's fighting Matt Serra. What happened in the last twenty seconds when I wasn't watching? He's hurt. He's hurt.* Matt Serra hit him again and knocked Georges down. This wasn't supposed to happen. As soon as Matt clipped him, I got up out of my seat and ran five feet. I grabbed Dana on the shoulder and pulled him back. He looked up at me, jaw wide open, completely dumbfounded at what was going on. It was like he had just come out of a lobotomy or something. "That's my fight!" I said, calling dibs and pointing at Serra. *"That's my fight!"* Dana didn't know what was happening.

I went back to my seat and stood there and watched the rest of the match. Sean Sherk slapped me on the back and I turned around. We looked at each other in complete shock. The fight was over. Matt Serra had beaten GSP. We couldn't stop laughing at the ridiculousness of the situation, that Serra got that one lucky punch in and tagged Georges with it. Georges had beaten both Sean and me; I would have bet the house on him (as would have 90 percent of the audience.) And if they fought again, I still would bet the house on Georges.

I was ecstatic. GSP wasn't going anywhere, and our rematch would happen no matter what. But Matt Serra had been running his mouth about me for months. If he hadn't beaten Georges, I would never have a chance to take him on. I thought Georges would crush him, and then the next person Serra fought would beat him, and he'd continue losing—or winning just enough to keep his career afloat.

Two weeks later I was at home, and not exactly thinking about the UFC. Dana called me and insisted, "You've got to do it, man. Do me a favor and help me sell this fight with you and Serra. Let's have you guys be the coaches on the show and then have the two coaches fight at the end. Come on."

"You know how much I'm going to miss my wife. I've got a seven-year-old boy who wants his dad around for the summer, and a baby girl who wants to know who her dad is."

"Dude, just fucking fly everybody out here. I don't care. We'll find room."

"It's not that simple. The last time I was there I'd get in from the show and be exhausted and wouldn't want to do anything. They're not going out there for six weeks to do nothing. Last time I got them to come for half the time, so it wouldn't be so bad."

"So you'll come?" Dana said, louder.

"There're a couple of things I need from you. I've got to have two condos, each with two bedrooms. I want to fly out Fiore, Matt Peña, and Robbie Lawler. And I'm going to need a spare rental car, too."

"Dude, that's fine. We'll totally hook you up."

"One more thing," I told him. "Last, and most importantly, as my prize I want a John Deere tractor instead of any other vehicle."

"Done. That's a great idea."

"Well, it was my wife's. I'll talk to you soon, buddy."

I hung up the phone with the UFC president and tossed the cell on the table. Then I went outside into the clean Hillsboro air to see my family and enjoy the life that matters the most in this world—the one we live at home.

Acknowledgments

I would like to thank God, as I do every single day, for blessing me with such great friends and family.

Thank you to Audra for being such a great wife and mother. I love you *so much*. Thanks to Joey and Hanna for reminding me every day why I still do this. Thanks to my family, especially Mark, for helping me keep my head on straight. Thanks to Marc Fiore and Tommy Moore for showing how friends can become family. Thank you to Kathy, Alan, Big Jim, and Barbara for treating me like a son and a friend.

I want to thank Brian Patton for all your hard work; don't sell yourself short. Thank you to Matt Ferguson for your leadership. Thanks to Michael Malice for helping me tell my story. This book was the brainchild of my editor, Jeremie Ruby-Strauss; I hope you like it. I also want to thank my webmaster, Nathan Rosario, and all my fans at www.matt-hughes.com.

Thanks to everyone at Bettendorf, especially Pat Miletich,

Jens Pulver, Monte Cox, Jeremy Horn, Tim Sylvia, Robbie Lawler, Matt Pena, and Rory Markham. Thanks to the guys at the UFC who make this great, including Dana White, Lorenzo and Frank Fertitta, Anthony Giordano, Randy Couture, Chuck Liddell, and Rich Franklin.

—Matt Hughes

First and foremost I want to thank Matt, Audra, Joey, and the Munchkin for treating me like family. The warmth of everyone in Hillsburrah whom Matt mentioned above made me doubt New York (for a second). Thanks particularly to Brian Patton for being a doer.

I very much want to thank Jeremie Ruby-Strauss, who believed in me. Thank you to Harvey Pekar for the validation and friendship. Thanks to Jud Laghi for getting the ball rolling, and to Rachel Kramer Bussel for being the matchmaker.

I would like to thank my allies who humored me when I came back from a town they'd never heard of with stories about a guy they didn't care about: Stephie Russell, Harjit Jaiswal, Michelle Levy, Flora Stepansky, Todd Seavey, (the) Jessica Cutler, Eric Dixon, Andrea Jamison, John Girgus, Heidi Schmid, Julie McGuire, Scott Nybakken, Corynne Steindler, Jake Dobkin, Lefty Leibowitz, LB Deyo, Ed Berlen, and the Westerdales. Also James Wilson, for being the one who cared. Thanks to Bob Holmes and Trish Milliken for anticipating, a little bit, Matt and Audra.

Finally I want to thank Byleth, whose story remains untold.

—Michael Malice

Printed in the United States
By Bookmasters